THE CHANGING IMAGE OF THE MAGISTRACY

Sir Thomas Skyrme

Second Edition

MACMILLAN PRESS
LONDON

First edition 1979
Second edition 1983

Published by
THE MACMILLAN PRESS LTD
London and Basingstoke
Companies and representatives
throughout the world

ISBN 0 333 36279 9 (hardcover)
ISBN 0 333 36280 2 (paperback)

Typeset by
Wessex Typesetters Limited,
Frome, Somerset

Printed in Great Britain at
The Pitman Press, Bath

Contents

Preface to the Second Edition

In the first edition I set out to record and explain the extensive reforms and developments which had occurred in the magisterial system (both lay and stipendiary) during the crucial thirty years following the Second World War, a period during which I occupied the office of Secretary of Commissions to the Lord Chancellor. I also included some background to explain how the changes fitted into the historical pattern. The new edition is wider in scope. I have brought the picture up-to-date by recounting the advances which have occurred during the ensuing five years, but I have also included some additional material to illustrate the extent to which the present is based upon the past and likewise the importance, for the purpose of understanding the current situation, of recognising it as part of a long-continuing process.

This edition, like its predecessor, is intended principally for the general reader, but it also aims to provide a source of information, which may not otherwise be available, for the research worker. In order to maintain it as a worthwhile work of reference I have updated previous statistics and in some places have added further relevant material.

During the last five years there has been no dramatic change of course, nor any fundamental variation of policy. The overall pattern is largely a projection of the post-war period covered by the first edition, but with particular emphasis on three outstanding features: the continuing rise in crime, the worsening state of the prisons and mounting delays. Previous trends have continued, though in some cases movement has accelerated. Crime, especially violent crime, escalates remorselessly, bringing further demands for effective cures, with emphasis on non-custodial treatment. Deteriorating conditions in the prisons have led to almost panic measures for the reduction of the prison population, which has tended to be regarded as an end in itself without consideration of the need for imprisonment in certain circumstances. This was particularly evident during the prison officers' dispute in 1980 and the passing of the Imprisonment (Temporary Powers) Act in that year.

Some of the most important reforms seen for many years in the criminal justice field were effected by the Criminal Justice Act 1982, which produced substantial changes in the sentencing and treatment of both young and adult offenders. These included: the replacement of Borstal training by a new sentence of youth custody, changes in detention sentences and in the law relating to compensation, and new powers to impose 'curfew' and residential care orders and to make financial orders on parents. Day training centres were replaced by locally financed day centres.

The Act also mirrored the prevailing disquiet over the prison situation by abolishing imprisonment for certain minor offences and by giving the Secretary of State power to order early release.

A number of the reforms contained in the Act had been canvassed by the Magistrates' Association, some of whose proposals were accepted by the Government against outspoken opposition from other quarters. As was to be expected, the Act met with a more enthusiastic reception from the magistrates than had been seen for some time. This reflected the rapport and co-operation between the Association and government departments which had been developing for a number of years.

The Act is, however, a notable example of the tendency of Parliament to specify complex procedural steps and impose restrictions on the exercise of statutory powers by magistrates. It becomes increasingly difficult for magistrates, both lay and stipendiary, and their professional clerks, to be conversant with all the procedural requirements; but a small fault may invalidate the proceedings.

In 1981 the Royal Comission on Criminal Procedure recommended important changes which are still under consideration. These included the abolition of committal proceedings and the establishment of Crown Prosecutors as independent prosecuting agencies.

A significant development has been the reform of magistrates' domestic jurisdiction, following the Domestic Proceedings and Magistrates' Courts Act 1978, which brought it into line with that of the High Court and County Courts. This presented fertile scope for the future, but so far it has not brought as much work to the magistrates' courts as was expected.

In contrast, road traffic offences continue to provide the courts with escalating case-loads. Interesting new developments in traffic law and procedure were contained in three successive Transport Acts, of which the second, passed in 1981, contained new provisions on drink and driving, increased the maximum penalty for certain offences to £1,000, created the new offence of failing to wear a seat belt and replaced the 'totting-up' procedure with a 'penalty points' system. A year later the third Act brought an extension of fixed penalties.

Increasing delays in the disposal of business have continued and have occupied the attention of the Magistrates' Association, the Justices' Clerks' Society and of the Lord Chancellor and the Home Secretary. The problem has led to further proposals to improve the efficiency of the present mechanism and also to relieve pressure on the courts by administrative reforms, by the appointment of more stipendiary magistrates and by such devices as extending the fixed penalty system and removing some of the existing offences from the ambit of the criminal law by a process of decriminalisation.

There have been two new consolidation measures. The Justices of the Peace Act 1979 embraced the role of magistrates and all aspects of their courts and administration, while the Magistrates' Courts Act 1980 repealed and re-enacted the Magistrates' Courts Acts 1952 and 1957 and partially repealed and amended over 130 other enactments.

A new dimension has been introduced by the United Kingdom's entry into the European Economic Community, as a result of which British courts have become subject to the influence of Community Law as interpreted by the European Court in Luxembourg.

Judicial training, which was a pejorative expression until fairly recently, has at last moved beyond the sphere of the lay justices and now also includes the whole of the professional judiciary through the Judicial Studies Board which was set up in 1979.

More sophisticated training and the continuing efforts of the Lord Chancellor to secure a high standard among those chosen to be Justices of the Peace has led to an enhanced reputation that was reflected in the Contempt of Court Act 1981 which, for the first time, enabled magistrates to commit for contempt of their courts. Yet public opinion of the magistracy is still influenced by prejudiced thought, fostered by a substantial section of the media. There is a greater need than ever for magistrates to recognise that there is no room for complacency. The most acute problem facing them, and all levels of the judiciary, is the need to meet and adjust to the rapidly changing society which they have to serve. Nevertheless, it must be recognised that the Justice of the Peace, like the jury – that other instance of involvement of the layman in the administration of justice – is far too deeply ensconced in British tradition to be in serious danger of eclipse. Not many institutions can trace their origins back for 800 years. This in itself is regarded by some as good reason for the total abolition of the office, but there is every indication that, even in this transient age, if justices can continue to maintain a positive and enlightened approach to the challenge of their task, they are likely to survive for a long time to come.

Preface to the First Edition

This book is about the magistracy during the thirty years or so following the Second World War. It relates, for the most part, to England and Wales, the mother lands of that ancient and unique institution the Justice of the Peace, but it also touches upon other parts of the United Kingdom and the Commonwealth with which I have had some concern during this period.

The book deals with both Stipendiary Magistrates and lay justices but the latter receive more attention because they have undergone a far more radical transformation than their professional colleagues and the past thirty years have been among the most interesting in their long and varied history. This has been an era of vast social, political and economic change which would, in any event, have imposed a severe strain on those responsible for administering justice, but it also brought with it a revolt against established authority, coupled with denigration of the spirit of voluntary public service and a general condemnation of the old order with which the justices were identified. The fact that they have survived is a matter for some surprise and the book seeks to explain how this has come about; but it also shows that further survival is contingent upon the justices moving with the times and retaining the confidence of the public.

'Magistrate bashing', at least in the figurative sense, has long been a popular pastime. This was amply justified in the days of Shakespeare and Dickens, but the twentieth century brought with it extensive reforms and improvements in the office of magistrate which have been most pronounced since 1949, when the far-reaching proposals of the Royal Commission on Justices of the Peace of 1948 were implemented. Today, although magistrates – both lay and professional – and their courts are by no means perfect, they play a much more valuable role in the life of the community than is generally recognised, and a reassessment of their worth and potential contribution to the welfare of the country is overdue. The Justices of the Peace, however, are still seen by the public in the image of what they were 100 or even fifty years ago. Seldom, if ever, does one hear about the new face of the magistracy. Good news is no news. The satisfactory functioning of a public office is not a matter that generates interest. Newspapers find a more ready sale for reports of magistrates' shortcomings than of their achievements and, when short of news, they have little difficulty in discovering some happenings in a magistrates' court which can be worked into a good story depicting the justices in a disparaging light. Disparagement of what is seen as the Establishment arouses widespread approval. Consequently the extent to which the magistracy has shaken off its atavistic characteristics is not generally known.

There is still ample room for improvement but, while indicating the weaknesses of the present system, the following pages attempt to identify its latent merits and to show the extent to which the magistrates have adapted to the changing world in which they must carry out their important duties. Limited space has compelled me to be selective but my approach has been eclectic and I have endeavoured to give a fair exposition of the diverse philosophies which have influenced the architecture of the magistracy during the period.

A further reason why I have chosen this period for the subject of this study is because, from 1947 to 1977, I was by chance responsible under the Lord Chancellor for the appointment and conditions of service of magistrates in England and Wales and, for a time, in Scotland and Northern Ireland. I was asked quite fortuitously to undertake this work when my distinguished predecessor, Sir Rupert Howarth, became ill. Had it not been for his chronic breakdown in health it is unlikely that I should ever have become the Lord Chancellor's Secretary of Commissions.

The circumstances in which I came initially to join the Lord Chancellor's Office were peculiar and serve to illustrate how the tide of human affairs may be diverted into channels that are both unexpected and undesired. After taking a law degree at Oxford I was called to the Bar in 1935 and was slowly building a general Common Law practice when the war began and I joined the army in September 1939. In August 1943 I was wounded during the attack on Catania in Sicily. I seem to have been somewhat accident-prone during my military career for I had previously been shot and later blown up on a mine during the North African campaign. These events persuaded the authorities that I was likely to be of little further use to the army and, after some months in hospital in Algiers, I was shipped back to England for discharge.

One day, in June 1944, while awaiting demobilisation, I was lunching with friends in the House of Commons and sat next to Ernest Bevin, who was then Minister of Labour. On hearing my story he urged me to join one of the Government Departments, who at that time were in desperate need of legal assistance. My chosen future lay in a career at the Bar, and I had just received certain tempting proposals from another quarter which could have been pursued in conjunction with the Temple. I therefore had no intention of complying with his request but I promised to consider it, hoping that I should hear no more of the matter. The next morning Bevin's private secretary telephoned and gave me a list of Departments in urgent need of legal advisers. Suspecting that the Minister had some influence over my demobilisation papers I thought it wise to show willing by visiting one or two of the Departments while taking care not to be trapped into joining them.

I was slightly attracted by the Foreign Office but I called first at the Lord Chancellor's Office because the House of Lords was the first place I came to. I never got any further. I was received enthusiastically by the Permanent Secretary, Claude Schuster, who was not usually given to rapturous welcomes. Schuster was about to retire (like his predecessor, Muir Mackenzie, but unlike any of his successors, he had just received a peerage) and his imminent departure placed the office, which was already under-staffed, in immediate need of help. He gave me a generous lunch in the Peers' dining room and I left, assuring him that I would give the matter the most careful consideration. The idea of a post in the Civil Service even on a temporary basis did not appeal to me in the least and I was confident that I should find some way of opting out with honour.

That night my chambers in Temple Gardens were destroyed by a flying-bomb. Fate had made her intentions fairly clear, so I rang Schuster the following morning and agreed to help him out temporarily, but I insisted that I should have to leave as soon as I could find alternative chambers, and that in any event there could be no question of my staying for more than two or three months. I remained for thirty-three years.

1 The Office of Magistrate

The roots of the magistracy in England and Wales can be traced to the early Middle Ages where the origins of the present Justices of the Peace are to be found. The office of Stipendiary Magistrate is a comparatively modern institution dating from the eighteenth century and will be described in Chapter 13.

Justices of the Peace are a peculiarly English institution and for some 700 years they have been deeply rooted in the way of life of the English people. Invented by the Plantagenets, justices were introduced into Wales by Henry VIII in 1536 and into Scotland by James VI in 1609. They subsequently arrived in the wake of colonisation in many British territories overseas.

The two centuries following the Norman Conquest marked a struggle between the King and the feudal barons, and the Crown was constantly striving to gain control over local affairs. An experiment in extending the Crown's influence was made in 1195 when Richard I's Justiciar and Archbishop of Canterbury, William Walter, issued a proclamation for the preservation of the peace whereby four knights in every hundred were to take an oath from all men over fifteen years of age to aid in keeping the peace. This may be regarded as the origin of the Justices of the Peace, though the term Custodes Pacis was introduced seventy years later, in 1264, when Simon de Montfort appointed Keepers of the Peace in every county. In 1327 a crisis arose when Queen Isabella secured the abdication of her husband, Edward II, and the proclamation of her son as King Edward III. Steps had to be taken to ensure that supporters of the old King did not raise rebellion or cause disturbances in local areas and, with this in view, the Statute I Edward III, 52.C16 required the appointment in every county of good and lawful men to keep the peace. The keepers were answerable direct to the new King. They constituted a police force rather than a branch of the justiciary, but two further developments soon resulted in their also acquiring judicial and administrative functions.

The Black Death, which first came to Britain in 1348, reduced the population from about 4 million to 2½ million in under two years, with unprecedented economic consequences. The value of labour was doubled and the work force sought to take advantage of the situation by demanding higher pay and by moving to where the best wages could be obtained, with the result that half the land was left untilled. The Statutes of Labourers, of which the first was passed in 1349, gave the keepers power to determine the place of work, the rates of wages and the prices of commodities. They were therefore the precursors of the Industrial Tribunals and Prices and Incomes Boards of modern times, but with far more drastic powers.

Another feature of this period was the lawlessness caused by the large numbers of soldiers returning from the wars in France, who became predators in their own land. There was a need to deal with the criminals rapidly on the spot without waiting for the periodical visits from the Justices of Assize. The keepers were therefore given power to hear cases of felony and so they acquired judicial as well as police and local government functions. A point which deserves notice is that this wide extension of the royal power to officers in local areas was in marked contrast to the policy of centralisation adopted by most medieval monarchs and it was probably a contributing factor to the divergent paths taken by the English and the Continental countries in constitutional development.

In 1361 the term 'Justice of the Peace' appears for the first time in a Statute which ordained that three or four of the most worthy in each county should be assigned to keep the peace and arrest and punish offenders. The office of Justice of the Peace is thus the first of our public institutions to have a statutory origin, although the Commissions of the Peace, under which the justices and the earlier keepers were appointed, were issued by the Crown under the royal prerogative without statutory backing. From the fifteenth century the Crown also began to grant royal charters to certain boroughs in return for favours rendered. These usually authorised the mayor and certain other office holders to administer justice within the borough to the exclusion of the county justices.

In 1362 justices were required to meet four times a year, from which the term Quarter Sessions is derived, and from then onwards their duties were constantly augmented.

By 1485 the volume of work was such that Chief Justice Husey asked: 'How many Justices think you now may suffice, without breaking their backs, to bear so many, not loads but stacks of Statutes that have since that time been laid upon them?' Much of this burden was accounted for by the multifarious administrative functions which justices were required to perform and which came to include such diverse matters as the maintenance of highways, prisons and bridges, dealing with vagabonds and beggars, administering the poor law, fixing prices and recruiting for the militia. One of the most remarkable features of our history, and one which is not often appreciated, is that for centuries the whole of local government in the counties of England and Wales was in the hands of the Justices of the Peace, who were also the only body of people to whom central government could look as an instrument for implementing its general policy or securing its local and particular requirements.

In Tudor and Stuart times the justices were the most influential class of men in the country. As a group they represented 'the gentry'. They were wealthy,[1] well educated and generally in reasonable accord with national policy, but they were also ambitious and often prejudiced. Though appointed by the Crown and, up to the time of the Commonwealth, subject to disciplinary measures by the Privy Council, they were far more than mere creatures of royal administration, for they were in fact the leaders of their counties. Moreover, most of the principal figures in public life were on the Commissions of the Peace and many of those who met to try offenders and to administer their counties at Quarter Sessions also sat at Westminster as Members of Parliament. Justices formed half of the Elizabethan House of Commons. The increased authority of the democratic legislature in England in the seventeenth century was without parallel in the rest of Europe, and the close association between Parliament and local administration through the justices was unique.

Many of the justices who did not sit in Parliament performed even more important, and certainly more spectacular, exploits elsewhere; Drake and Hawkins, for example, were justices on the Devon Commission, though their maritime exploits cannot have allowed them much time for their magisterial duties. Small wonder that there was sometimes a shortage of justices at Quarter Sessions. One finds numerous items of expenditure of the Clerks of the Peace for messengers sent on horseback to justice after justice in an endeavour to collect just two to form a court. In 1693 there was a complaint to the Privy Council of justices 'who come and take the King's wages and, before half the business is done, betake them to the tavern'. Doctor Burn, a distinguished chairman of Quarter Sessions, writing in 1776, recalls Quarter Sessions where the justices seem to have arrived at the tavern first for they never reached the court at all. But generally the work was done and the system operated reasonably successfully. If the justices are judged against the background of the times in which they lived they will be found to have discharged their duties effectively; the one exception being in London, where corruption and inefficiency among the magistrates reached a point in the late eighteenth century where the government was obliged to take drastic measures and to appoint Stipendiary Magistrates. Subsequently, as explained later, stipendiaries were also appointed in a few other centres, but never on a large scale, and the vast bulk of magisterial work continued to be discharged by the lay justices to the present day.

The justices might have succumbed to the great surge of reforming zeal of the nineteenth century which began with the Reform Bill of 1832, but in fact they survived, though bereft of most of their administrative functions. Their police duties were taken over by the modern police forces (though these duties survived in the representation of justices on the Standing Joint Committees and Watch Committees and on the police authorities which succeeded them) and their local government functions were transferred to the new County Councils created by the Local Government Act 1888; but it is remarkable that the reasons advanced at the time for relieving the justices of this burden were not that they were doing the job badly, but rather that they represented an outdated institution which must therefore give way to the new bodies based on a more democratic system of popular election. F. W. Maitland, mourning the change which was about to take place, said of the justice: 'As a governor he is doomed, but there has been no accusation. He is cheap, he is pure, he is capable, but he is doomed; he is sacrificed to a theory on the altar of the spirit of the age'.[2]

Maitland and many other contemporaries also thought that, having been divested of their local government work, the justices would lose interest in what was left and that the system would gradually lapse and become extinct. He therefore went on to say:

The outlook is certainly gloomy. If the justices are deprived of their governmental work, will they care to be justices any longer? This is a momentous question; on the answer to it depends a great deal of the future history of England.

These gloomy forebodings proved to be ill-founded. 1888 was indeed a climacteric, but far from marking the onset of twilight it became the dawn of a new era in which the justices turned wholeheartedly from administrative to judicial functions which were constantly expanded and strengthened in a fresh outburst of activity that has continued to the present day.

Long before 1888, in addition to sitting at Quarter Sessions, justices had been exercising an extensive jurisdiction sitting without a jury out of sessions. This practice had begun largely as a matter of necessity when, during times of great crisis such as the Wars of the Roses and the Civil War, it was not practicable to assemble the justices at Quarter Sessions, and they therefore sat in ones and twos, sometimes in their own houses. At first this was done without authority, but by the end of the sixteenth century powers of summary jurisdiction were being conferred on these meetings, which came to be called Petty Sessions. They were finally recognised as courts by the Petty Sessions Act of 1849. In 1889, Petty Sessions were statutorily defined as: 'A court of summary jurisdiction consisting of two or more justices sitting in a petty sessional courthouse'. Thereafter an enormous expansion of summary jurisdiction occurred, which resulted in magistrates disposing of the overwhelming majority of criminal cases. At the same time their civil work was also extended and their present matrimonial jurisdiction dates from the Matrimonial Causes Act 1878. Separate courts for juveniles, manned by justices, were first set up under the Children Act 1908, resulting in virtually all offences by young delinquents being tried summarily. The full vindication of the justices came in 1925 when a large number of cases which were previously triable only by a judge and jury were brought within the jurisdiction of justices at Petty Sessions.

We shall see in the following chapter how the process has continued with fluctuations to the present day, when the magistrates at Petty Sessions dispose of nearly 98 per cent of all criminal cases, as well as exercising a substantial civil jurisdiction which includes the disposal of matrimonial cases many times greater in number than those dealt with by the High Court. They handle almost the whole range of criminal and many of the civil matters which bring the average citizen into a court of law. In the words of Lord Merrivale: 'The justice which matters most in the homes of the people is the justice administered by the magistrates in their midst.'

The great bulk of this work is performed by the part-time, unpaid lay justices. In London and in eleven other places in England and Wales there are also Stipendiary Magistrates in addition to the justices, but elsewhere the justices handle the whole of the work alone. They undertake these duties at some inconvenience to themselves and with no expectation of material reward. Nor is there any expression of appreciation from a grateful public; on the contrary, they are more likely to be criticised for their pains.

It is a constant source of surprise to foreign observers that so large a part of our criminal jurisdiction is wholly in the hands of part-time laymen who, without any legal training, are required to decide questions of law as well as fact and who combine the roles of judge and jury by deciding both guilt and sentence; even a High Court judge cannot deprive a person of his liberty (save in very exceptional circumstances) unless a jury first convicts, but two lay justices or a single stipendiary may alone convict a fellow citizen and sentence him to imprisonment.

At first sight the system seems not only anomalous but indefensible and, having regard to their powers and vast field of responsibility, it is astonishing that the justices have not only survived but have flourished in an age when established institutions have been subject to ever-increasing denigration, when the amateur has been steadily replaced by the professional and when voluntary service is anachronistic in the prevailing climate of totalitarianism. The Justice of the Peace is the kind of historical legacy that one would have expected to be the first to founder in the revolutionary flood of the post-war years. It could not have survived had it not been acceptable to successive Governments and to the public at large. The explanation of its acceptability, despite certain latent defects, is probably threefold: first, the depth of the roots of the lay magistracy in the British social system and the inclination of the people to honour tradition and to preserve ancient institutions; second, the ability of the justices, as evidenced in their previous history, to adjust to changing conditions; and third, the intrinsic merits of the system itself which, if exploited and developed, give it a peculiar attraction not shared by any other form of judicial machinery.

The principal defects usually attributed to lay justices are that they are too ready to accept police evidence and that they rely too much on the advice of their clerk. In some degree both criticisms are still valid, though far less so than they were thirty years and more ago, and neither defect is altogether incurable. As against these disadvantages the justices have certain unique qualities on the credit side. From the point of view of the government they have two advantages; they are cheap and they are flexible. As they receive no pay they are more cost-effective than a salaried stipendiary, though the difference is not as great as is sometimes assumed because justices work more slowly than stipendiaries and if they have to sit in two or more courts to dispose of the same amount of work there will be the additional cost of extra staff and accommodation; in addition, although not remunerated, justices are entitled to allowances which can amount to a not inconsiderable sum when several of them are sitting. Nevertheless, justices are on the whole cheaper than any other effective method of administering justice that has so far been devised. In 1965, Lord Gardiner caused enquiries to be made in twenty countries to find out in each case the numbers of whole-time judges and the cost of judicial administration. The cost (excluding police and prisons) expressed as a percentage of the annual national budget ranged from 1·46 at the top of the scale to 0·16 in the case of England, Scotland and Wales, who were at the bottom. As regards the number of judges, several countries had more than 200 per million of population while Scotland with 15 and England and Wales with 8 were again at the bottom. As was to be expected, most Common Law countries were in the lowest bracket because of their single-judge systems; thus the United States had 34 judges per million population, Australia 29 and New Zealand 24. These figures should be treated with reserve as some were based on estimates, but the position of England and Wales at the bottom of the league was generally attributed to the much larger proportion of court work disposed of by their unpaid, part-time lay magistrates compared with other countries.

Justices also appeal to the government because their system is flexible; sudden fluctuations in the volume of work can be handled by calling upon justices to sit more or less often in more or fewer courts as the need arises, whereas a whole-time judge or stipendiary has little scope to expand his output if work increases, and if it diminishes he may be left partially unemployed at public expense.

These are not the only inherent merits of a properly constituted lay justice system. Two, or preferably three, heads are better than one and they are better still if they combine intimate knowledge, experience and understanding of the problems facing different sections of the local community, which can often enable them to deal with cases more justly and efficaciously than the professional courts. The collective views of a cross-section of the population, representing different shades of opinion, can be more effective in dispensing justice acceptable to the public than the decision of a single individual necessarily drawn from a fairly narrow social class and whose experience of local problems may be limited. Justices also act as a check on one another and provide a balanced conclusion, whereas there is nothing to curb a general idiosyncrasy or the spasmodic whim or irritability of a single magistrate. Furthermore, as justices attend court at intervals they approach their task with a freshness and objectivity that is lacking in a professional judge who is wholly engaged in adjudicating day after day.

The system of lay justices reflects, through citizen participation, the traditional English involvement of the layman in the administration of justice. It enables the citizen to see that the law is his law, administered by men and women like himself, and that it is not the esoteric preserve of the lawyers. Lord Hailsham, in a speech made when he was Lord Chancellor, stressed the value of the lay magistracy as a unifying factor in society as a whole, and he described their potential influence, not only on the bench but also out of court, as 'one of the characteristic institutions holding our society together'.

The identification of the ordinary citizen with the administration of justice should therefore have a popular appeal, yet when it comes to the test the average citizen seems to prefer to be tried by a professional magistrate. This is most noticeable where there is a clear choice of tribunal, as in family and adoption proceedings, and where preference is normally shown for the professionalism of the County Court rather than the lay justices' court. This may be due at least in part to the erroneous view which much of the population hold of the justices today: that they are prejudiced, prosecution-minded, middle-class bigots, motivated by lust for power and totally lacking in any feeling for those who appear before them. This description might not have been far wrong a century ago, when it could have been directed with equal justification at other institutions, but the vast changes that have occurred since then are not generally realised. The detritus of the past has been washed away and the justices of today are able to exhibit some of the latent advantages of the system which were not revealed under their predecessors. A lay justice cannot equal the professional skill of a stipendiary, but the function of magistrates is largely to decide questions of fact and for this purpose to exercise common sense and sound judgment against a background of knowledge and experience of the world at large. By this criterion the quality of the average lay justice is no less than that of the professional stipendiary.

Provided that justices are carefully chosen in the light of their ability, integrity and understanding, and can be seen to be well qualified for their work, and provided also that they are given adequate training and opportunities to enable them to become and remain proficient in the performance of their duties, then it is possible for the layman, who combines experience as a magistrate with experience in other walks of life, to offer advantages which are not to be found in the professional systems; not least of these advantages being the ability to exercise a stabilising influence within the community in which he lives to an extent not open to the professional judge. It is to this end that the reforms of the past forty years have been largely directed.

2 The Magistracy Since the Second World War

In the three decades following the Second World War the magistracy had to adjust to a period of steady national decline coupled with fundamental changes in the social, economic and political structure of British society.

At the end of a long and bitter war, when there had been drastic disruption of the mode of living to which the people had been accustomed for a generation, the country was full of high hopes and enthusiasm for the future but, in spite of the general euphoria, the majority of the population remembered the hungry 1930s and were not prepared to revert to the social conditions of the prewar years. They brought into office the Labour Government of 1945 which launched a programme of social change that was implemented with unprecedented velocity. Experience in the field of science and technology was accompanied by a spectacular build-up of social services, beginning with the National Health, National Insurance and Industrial Injuries Acts of 1946. There were great advances in the well-being of children, who were better fed, better clothed, better educated and in better health. But other less agreeable phenomena began to materialise. Traditional moral values were diluted. A decline in the practice of the Christian religion was accompanied by a weakening belief in the sanctity of marriage and a steady easing of the divorce laws, which in turn led to disastrous weakening of family influence on the young. A stable society needs stable marriage. The beneficial influence of family ties was also unwittingly undermined by the Welfare State; the young no longer had to rely on their families for their care and welfare and, with rising wages and employment, they could often make as much money as their parents. They also became more promiscuous, for the decline in moral values led to sex becoming a national preoccupation. Necessary though sex may be, it was now flaunted to the extent of perversion and, as

Lord Chancellor Elwyn-Jones observed when Attorney-General, 'the media ensure that sex is not only done but is manifestly seen to be done'.

The assumption that crime is a product of poverty was soon disproved. The affluent society brought with it an abrupt upsurge in the rate of crime, particularly crimes of violence and dishonesty. The greatest incidence of violence occurred among the young and many of the young offenders came from well-to-do families. Each year with but few exceptions, such as 1948 when there was an inexplicable lull, the criminal statistics showed a remorseless advance in criminal activity, often without a rational motive except greed or violence for violence sake. Indictable crimes known to the police numbered 498,576 in 1947. They dropped by some 40,000 in the next two years but during the following two decades they more than doubled to 1·2 million in 1967. The next ten years brought an even greater acceleration and the total reached 2·64 million in 1977[1] and 3 million in 1981.

Faced with this enigma, society did not at first react to the new climate of lawlessness in the traditional manner. Instead of harsh and drastic retribution a far more paternalistic approach was adopted. Penology during these years was dominated by a philosophy of reforming the criminal by education instead of punitive treatment. Punishment became a pejorative word and custodial sentences could be justified only in so far as they afforded the prison authorities an opportunity to reclaim and re-educate the offender. Whereas in 1947 the business of the criminal courts was considered to be the punishment of offenders, today the emphasis is on understanding.

Unfortunately, these enlightened policies were pursued with such enthusiasm that not only were they often implemented without sufficient preparation and research, but the primary object of the criminal law, which is the protection of society, tended to be overlooked and society as a whole suffered. Crime began to pay handsomely. Numbers of hardened criminals staunchly refused to be converted, while newcomers, undeterred by fear of retribution, swelled the criminal ranks. In spite of statutory restrictions on the sentencing powers of the courts and the genuine efforts of most of the courts themselves to avoid custodial sentences, the prison population steadily increased and, having numbered 18,600 in 1947, reached an all-time record of 42,000 in 1977 and rose to a further peak of 45,500 in 1981.

Crime continued to escalate and this led to demands by some for a reversal of policy and the immediate adoption of more punitive measures, while others pursued a frantic search for effective alternatives to custodial treatment.

These problems were not peculiar to Britain. Throughout the world the rule of law was under attack and man gave every indication of becoming more greedy, more selfish and more violent. On the other hand, the situation should be seen in its proper perspective for, even in this country, there was nothing novel about a wave of lawlessness and violence, and it is a characteristic of the human race to rebel against authority. History can show worse examples than we have today. What has made the present phenomenon more noticeable, however, is that there was no trace of such problems in the United Kingdom immediately before the war and the country had come to assume that this was a spectre we had put behind us for all time. Worst of all, faced with the bleak reality, no one has so far been able to devise a viable solution. It was taken for granted that authority was so well established that no serious problem could arise in the maintenance of law and order. It was perhaps this very image of established authority which led to the postwar rejection of everything which could be seen as part of the 'Establishment'. The movement to decry the established institutions was directed first and foremost at all those connected with the maintenance of law and order, particularly the courts and the police, both of whom suffered a diminution of public respect which, in the case of the police, served to undermine the relationship between them and the public and contributed to a manifest decline in police morale.

The law and legal institutions received their share of attention from the critics but, bearing in mind the revolutionary social innovations which were introduced from 1945 onwards, there were remarkably few major developments in the legal sphere until fairly recently. Apart from the Royal Commission on Justices of the Peace of 1948, referred to later, the only outstanding event in the immediate postwar period was the introduction of legal aid as part of the Welfare State by the Legal Aid and Advice Act 1949. Legal Aid as provided under the new system was applied first to the civil courts and was not extended to criminal proceedings in magistrates' courts until 1968. Its effect on the administration of justice was profound. It enabled all parties to be properly represented but it added enormously to the time taken to dispose of work in the courts. During the years that followed, there was strong resistance to any proposals for the drastic overhaul of the legal system itself and, although there were numerous reforms, these were largely of a patching-up nature, as illustrated by the establishment of Crown Courts in Liverpool and Manchester in 1956 and the extension of the system of whole-time courts of Quarter Sessions in London in 1964. There was little long-term planning. The onset of delays and increasing cost in bringing cases before the courts led to the steady growth in popularity of administrative tribunals, which became an established part of the machinery of justice.

Reform on a large scale when it finally came was mainly induced by sheer necessity brought about by the accumulation of unacceptable arrears in both civil and criminal work. The long-established system of Assizes and Quarter Sessions operating on a part-time basis was effective enough in the days of the stage coach but it could not cope with the flood of proceedings brought about by a variety of contributing causes, including the motor car, easier divorce, more sophisticated crime, legal aid and a general expansion of lawlessness. There were far more cases to handle than ever before and they took longer to try. A notable phenomenon in the work of the higher judiciary was the number of judges who in the past would have been principally occupied in trying murders and other offences of a similar nature lasting a day or two but who by 1977 were spending several months on long cases of fraud. Added to this was an unprecedented call on the judiciary to chair tribunals and conduct enquiries.

The need for a thorough overhaul of the machinery of justice had become unavoidable by the mid-1960s and this coincided with a more inquisitorial attitude towards even the most entrenched areas of the legal structure which was kindled by the reforming zeal of Lord Gardiner who became Lord Chancellor in 1964. The following year marked the beginning of an era of major change in the legal world. Within a year of taking office Lord Gardiner had established the Law Commission, with the duty of securing reform of the law and consolidating and revising Statutes. 1966 saw the appointment of the Royal Commission on Assizes and Quarter Sessions whose recommendations, largely implemented by the Courts Act 1971, effected the most drastic changes in the organisation and administration of the higher courts since the reign of Henry II. In 1969 much of the responsibility for young transgressors was shifted from the juvenile courts to the local authorities by the Children and Young Persons Act, which proved to be one of the most controversial Statutes since the war. In 1971 the Divisions of the High Court were reorganised and the Probate, Divorce and Admiralty Division was abolished and its divorce side taken over by the Family Division; and in the same year the Industrial Relations Act (a manifestation of rising industrial conflict) increased the jurisdiction of the Industrial Tribunals and created the short-lived Industrial Court on a level with the High Court.

The legal profession, though subject to frequent sniping, was spared any profound scrutiny until the appointment, in 1977, of the Royal Commission on Legal Services. As in the case of the Beeching Royal Commission on the higher courts,[2] care was taken to see that the enquiry was not dominated by lawyers, and the post of chairman fell upon one who had had no previous experience of the courts or the administration of justice. During the previous thirty years a feature of the legal profession had been a substantial increase in the numerical strength of the Bar, coupled with an improvement in financial returns, at least for the less successful counsel, since the lean years and fierce competition of the postwar period. A barrister was certainly helped by legal aid (when I began practice in 1935 my first briefs were Poor Persons' Divorces, for which I received no fee, and Poor Prisoners' Defence, which might bring five guineas for several days' work). The last few decades have also been marked by a rise in status of the solicitors' branch of the profession which is illustrated by their eligibility for judicial office. Solicitors became eligible for appointment as Stipendiary Magistrates in 1949 and the way to the Circuit bench was opened to them in 1971.

When one comes to consider the vicissitudes of the magistrates during this revolutionary era one finds that, as on many previous occasions, they have managed to adapt to the situation in their own peculiar way. At the end of the war there was no complacency about the magistracy as there was about other branches of the machinery of justice. There had been criticism in the 1930s and this had not been dispelled by the magistrates' considerable contributions to the war effort and by their administration of the Defence Regulations. Public respect for the magistrates and confidence in the summary courts in England and Wales were on the decline and this was attributed in no small measure to the presence on benches throughout the country of many lay justices who, by age, infirmity or unsuitability, were incapable of effectively administering justice. Information also came to the Lord Chancellor which suggested that graft and corruption existed in certain areas. My own researches convinced me that such malpractices as existed were on a very small scale, but that the lay magistracy did suffer from having far too many aged and incompetent individuals on the benches. It was also true to say that certain classes of the community did not get their fair share of appointments.

One of the first acts of the Labour Government which took office in 1945 was to decide upon a study in depth of all aspects of the magisterial system. The Home Secretary, Mr Chuter Ede, wanted an inquiry of limited scope. He feared that root and branch investigation would take an intolerable time and might in the end prove fruitless. Lord Jowitt, the Lord Chancellor, on the other hand felt that no worthwhile result would emerge from a narrow enquiry and that in any event the time had come for a thorough reappraisal of the administration of summary jurisdiction. A compromise solution was agreed and, in 1946, a Royal Commission was appointed with terms of reference embracing the appointment and removal of justices and their conditions of service, but the Commission had to work on the assumption that the existing system of lay justices was to be maintained.

The Royal Commission reported in 1948 and almost all its majority recommendations were accepted. Those requiring legislation were implemented in the Justices of the Peace Act 1949,[3] but the Act went much further and embraced many of the proposals of the Departmental Committee on Justices Clerks of 1944 (the Roche Committee), with the result that 1949 was not only a turning point in the office of magistrate, but also brought revolutionary changes in the finance, administration and procedure of the summary courts.

It may be noted in passing that the Act also tried to lay to rest the last surviving relic of the former police functions of magistrates by substituting the term 'Magistrates' Courts' for 'Police Courts', but the ghost still haunts us. The Act also contained the only statutory definition of 'Magistrates' which embraces both stipendiaries and those justices who are not on the Supplemental List.[4] Those who are transferred to the Supplemental List remain 'justices' but are no longer 'magistrates'. When Quarter Sessions were abolished in 1971 the position of justices in the higher courts was confirmed by the Courts Act which expressly described them as 'judges' of the new Crown Court.

For the lay justices the last thirty years have been among the most intriguing epochs in their long history. Beginning at a time when Britain was one of the world's greatest powers and the centre of a vast empire, when the established order was still held in respect, the justices, who were an integral part of that order, suffered more acutely than almost any other group in the community the subsequent shock of national decline, deterioration in accepted standards and erosion of law and order. They suffered on the whole with patience and determination and they survived. Their survival was at least partly due to outside measures rather than to their own conscious efforts, for there were many on the benches who had been appointed before the war and who were unable to adjust to the changing scene. There was a tendency, in common with the older generation in general, to which the majority of the justices belonged, to abrogate their responsibility in the face of growing social pressures; but more up-to-date methods in choosing and appointing justices, combined with greater scrutiny of their work and a progressive training policy, began to provide the benches with magistrates who, though working under mounting pressure and in the face of much unjustified criticism, kept abreast of the times and managed on the whole to compete effectively with the vast increase in the volume and complexity of their duties. Tainted at the outset with the image of ultra-conservatism and reaction the magistracy came to include significant numbers of justices from the socialist and wage-earning sections of the population, to which it offered an opportunity to dispense justice at ground level.

The number of justices has fluctuated considerably during the past forty years. In 1947 there were approximately 16,800 on the Active List in England and Wales. Many benches, however, especially in the rural areas, were overstaffed and a policy of drastic pruning was initiated in 1948. By removing some of the ineffectives and persuading them to transfer to the Supplemental List (the introduction of a compulsory retiring age of seventy-five in 1949 assisted this operation by immediately clipping 1900 off the Active List) and by not replacing much of the natural wastage, the numbers had been reduced by 1951 to 14,100. From then on there was a slow expansion to meet increasing work and by 1969 the level had returned to 16,000. A high rate of increase began in 1970 to anticipate the likely requirements of the Crown Court and to meet other demands and by December 1977 the total had risen to 23,483, an increase of nearly 6700 above 1947. The numbers on the Supplemental List had also risen from 1980 at the end of 1947 to 5920 (there was an exceptional rise after 1968 when the retiring age was reduced from seventy-five to seventy). By January 1983 the number of justices on the Active List in England and Wales, including 3648 in the Duchy of Lancaster, had risen by a further 10 per cent in five years to 25,934. Those on the Supplemental List had reached 9624.

A point of interest is that much of the rise in the number of justices since 1947 was accounted for by the larger proportion of women on the Commissions of the Peace. In 1947 the 16,800 justices were composed of about 13,100 men and 3700 women. On 31st December 1977 the numbers were 14,633 men and 8850 women. In January 1983 there were 15,606 men and 10,328 women. The larger number of women magistrates reflected the policy of the Lord Chancellor's Office to increase the proportion of women on every bench and to ensure that there were sufficient women to staff all the juvenile and domestic courts.

Efforts to reduce the average age of benches were less successful because the demands upon the time of those with young families gave them little opportunity to undertake public work. In spite of this there was an appreciable enlargement of the proportion of justices in the younger age groups. In 1947 about 25 per cent of all justices serving in the courts were over the age of 70 and 14 of these were over 90. Today no one can sit in a court of summary jurisdiction after reaching 70. At the other end of the scale, only 12 per cent of justices on the Active List in 1947 were under 50, and 1·3 per cent under 40; in 1977 43·2 per cent were under 50 and 8·9 per cent under 40.

The pattern for Stipendiary Magistrates was slightly different. The number of stipendiaries in London increased from 26 to 41 between 1947 and 1977, but in the rest of England and Wales it dropped from 18 to 11 (by 1983 the number in London had risen to 46 and in the provinces to 12). The average age of stipendiaries in 1947 was 64; in June 1977 it was 55 where it has remained. The first woman stipendiary was appointed in 1945 and 6 others were appointed later, all in London.

In an era of falling productivity the magistrates achieved a notable increase in output. Some improvement would not have been difficult as many of the lay justices in 1947 never attended their courts at all, but credit is due for the very substantial growth in the disposal of business which occurred from the early 1950s onwards. The volume of work may be illustrated by figures for the number of persons dealt with in the summary courts. In 1947 there was a total of 589,534 and in 1977 2,438,212. These figures, however, do not give an accurate impression of the actual increase in the work load because cases today take longer to try than they did thirty years ago. The magistrates' increased output can be better gauged by the number of days on which they sat in court. In 1947 the average number of magistrates' courts held per week in England and Wales, including London, was about 870; by 1982 the figure was approximately 9000. Moreover, nearly 70 per cent of the courts in 1947 sat only in the mornings whereas in 1977 some 65 per cent continued sitting in the afternoon, sometimes until after five o'clock. It should also be noted that these figures do not include sittings of the Crown Court when justices were present nor do they take account of the numerous out-of-court activities, which increased to an even greater extent than the court sittings.

Since I wrote the first edition of this book there has been an interesting growth in the influence of the Magistrates' Association; a phenomenon which had been evolving for a number of years. Later chapters will show that the Association's views have had a marked impact on much of the recent legislation affecting the criminal law. Founded in 1920, the Association's early efforts were directed mainly towards training its members. By 1930 it was interesting itself in other aspects of the magistracy but its influence was not significant. It was still normal practice at the end of the war for government departments who wished to test the reaction of magistrates to some proposed innovation to consult the Chief Metropolitan Magistrate and to dismiss any views volunteered by the Association with the comment 'that lot of amateurs'. After 1950, however, its standing increased rapidly due partly to the general improvement in the lay justice system and partly to the efforts of two outstanding chairmen of its Council, Lord Templewood and particularly Lord Merthyr. Lord Merthyr had been a member of the 1948 Royal Commission where he had urged the gradual replacement of lay justices by stipendiaries; but soon he revised his opinion, joined the Association and was elected Chairman of the Council in 1952. For the next eighteen years he directed an ambitious programme of administrative reforms with an enlightened policy on the Association's aims and activities. He secured the adoption of a new constitution under which the Council (which had hitherto been largely self-selecting and self-perpetuating) became a representative body with its members drawn on a proportional basis from local branches[5] (of which the first, for North East England, was formed in 1950). Lord Merthyr did more than anyone to establish the Association on a sound basis and to raise it to a position of influence.

Another important factor was that by 1960 some of the Stipendiary Magistrates were, for the first time, taking an active interest in the Association's work. A few became members and later chairmen of committees. This encroachment has been resented by some of the lay justices who feared that the Association would be dominated by lawyers. In fact, the stipendiaries are far too few in number to stage a takeover even if they wanted to do so, but on the other hand, their contributions, especially in the preparation of memoranda on legal topics, have raised the Association's reputation to an extent that would not have been possible without them.

All but about 4 per cent of justices belong to the Association. Most of those who do not take the view that, as they do their magisterial work without remuneration, they ought not to be asked to subscribe out of their own pockets. Since 1970 the Association has received a grant from the Government which is currently based on half the annual amount expended by the Association on training. There have been occasions when the Government seemed prepared to consider defraying all their costs, but the majority of members have always preferred to subscribe from their own resources rather than risk losing their independence, on the principle that he who pays the piper calls the tune.

It is said that the views expressed by the Association do not always reflect those of the ordinary members. This is a hazard which faces most large organisations, especially where management at all levels has to be undertaken by volunteers with unlimited energy and dedication and the necessary time. It is a risk of which the Association's officers are well aware and do their best to surmount.

There is still much aggressive hostility towards the Association from many quarters. Much of this is due to resentment of its undoubted influence and lobbying power which have increased significantly during the past twenty years. While I was chairman of the Council I was impressed by the extent of the interest taken by the Government in the Association's views and the importance attached to them. I found a genuine readiness among Ministers to listen to and indeed to seek our opinions, and on a number of occasions I and my successor were invited to frank, informal and private meetings with Ministers. This was confirmed by a statement made in Parliament by Mr Patrick Mayhew, Minister of State at the Home Office, during the committee stage of the Police Bill. He said: 'I always pay great attention to the Magistrates' Association as it considers these matters very carefully. It was of much assistance in improving the Criminal Justice Bill.' Parliament itself seems to have been of the same mind. The House of Commons Home Affairs Committee, in its report in 1981, said that the Magistrates' Association 'has long had the advantage of advice from a number of standing committees which it has established to deal with various aspects of magisterial work. The fruits of this effort can be seen in part in the high quality of evidence submitted to this and other Parliamentary Committees. It appears to us that among magistrates there exists the mechanism whereby a lead in policy can be given, disseminated and reinforced.'

The chapters that follow describe in more detail the principal changes and developments that have occurred during the period and attempt to identify the attributes and the deficiencies of the present system.

3 The Lord Chancellor and His Office

With but few exceptions, responsibility for choosing all members of the judiciary in England and Wales, including the magistrates, rests with one man: the Lord High Chancellor of Great Britain.

In this respect judicial patronage in this country differs from that in other parts of the world; but that is not the only peculiar feature of the ancient office of Lord Chancellor, which dates from Augmundus, who became Chancellor in 605, and which was the principal office under the Crown until the fall of Cardinal Wolsey. Modern Lord Chancellors like to tell their audiences that among their predecessors they number no less than three saints, though there were many others who clearly were not saints.

The Lord Chancellor combines in one individual the three branches of government: executive, legislative and judicial. He is always a senior member of the Government and its chief adviser on legal matters, and as such is subject to the convention of collective responsibility; he is a member of the Upper House of the legislature, over which he presides (but unlike the Speaker of the Commons he also takes an active part in debates); and he is head of the judiciary. Students of Montesquieu and of the American constitution regard the Lord Chancellor as an incarnate contradiction of the doctrine of separation of powers, and any defence of the anomaly is usually based on the claim that, like many British anachronisms, it seems to work within the British form of democracy. In fact, there is no need for any defence because the anomaly does not really exist. Today, the Lord Chancellor, far from being a negation of the separation of powers, is actually a confirmation of the validity of the doctrine, for one of his most important constitutional functions is to ensure that the lines of demarcation are maintained and in particular that political influences are not allowed to encroach upon the judicial sphere.

It is remarkable that the Lord Chancellor, who has no junior minister to assist him, is able to discharge so diverse an assortment of responsibilities, for his duties, like Mr Sam Weller's knowledge of London, are indeed extensive and peculiar. They include, *inter alia*, such widely divergent matters as the administration of the courts, appointments to most judicial offices and the appointment of clergy to their livings, the administration of legal aid and responsibility for the Public Trustee, the Land Registry, the Council on Tribunals, the Judge Advocate General and the Official Solicitor; and all this is in addition to sitting judicially, playing a leading role in the legislative business of the House of Lords and attending meetings of the Cabinet.

Much of this responsibility already rested with the Lord Chancellor at the end of the war and one would have thought that he had more than enough on his shoulders and might well have been relieved of some of his burden. In fact, his obligations have been extended still further.

In 1945 the office of Lord Chancellor differed little from what it had been during the second half of the nineteenth century. The administrative duties were not extensive and were principally concerned with the County Courts and the general supervision of subordinate departments. After 1945 the picture changed and the Lord Chancellor's area of administration expanded steadily from the advent of legal aid[1] in 1949 to the establishment in 1971 of a unified court service for all but the magistrates' courts. This was accompanied by a widening of the Lord Chancellor's judicial patronage, particularly in the field of administrative tribunals, and a great increase in legislation involving the Lord Chancellor and his Department.

The only quarter in which the Lord Chancellor's commitments have been reduced is in sitting judicially. This was not by design but resulted from the innovation introduced during the war whereby the House of Lords sat concurrently in two places to dispose of legislative and judicial business, instead of consecutively as previously. The Lord Chancellor, unable to be in more than one place at a time, was obliged to opt for the legislative sittings and could only attend the Appellate Committee of the Lords or the Judicial Committee of the Privy Council for three or four weeks a year when Parliament was not sitting. The time thus saved, however, has been more than taken up by the expansion of his other duties.

Broadly speaking it may be said that the role of the Lord

Chancellor's Office at the present time is threefold: advising on judicial appointments, promoting the reform of the civil law in conjunction with the Law Commission, and administering the courts (other than the magistrates' courts) and taking the necessary steps to ensure that civil and criminal cases are promptly brought to trial.

It is generally agreed that the Lord Chancellor's most important area of responsibility lies in his judicial patronage and in his duty to preserve the independence of the judiciary. It is with this aspect of his work that we are principally concerned in this book. The fact that the Lord Chancellor is head of the judiciary is of special significance in the context of judicial appointments. In other Departments of State the Minister relies upon the expertise of his officials, whereas the Lord Chancellor bases his decisions to a large extent upon his own knowledge, experience and legal training, and when selecting members of the higher judiciary he is assisted by his personal knowledge of practitioners which he has gained in the course of his own practice and which is augmented by his observations when sitting judicially and by his contacts with the profession as a Bencher of his Inn. When he needs to seek advice he is well qualified to know where best to find it. The Lord Chancellor's legal and judicial training is also of the utmost importance when he is faced with the question of terminating an appointment, for on these occasions he must, by constitutional usage, act in a judicial manner, whether the case under review relates to a member of the professional judiciary or to a Justice of the Peace.

As the Lord Chancellor's area of responsibility widened he was obliged to rely to a greater extent than before upon the advice of his officials, especially in the filling of vacancies in the lower echelons of the judiciary and in administrative posts. It must be emphasised, however, that in spite of the increased burden, no Lord Chancellor during the past thirty years has failed to take a close personal interest in the magistracy and particularly in the Justices of the Peace, and he has always given intimate attention to both appointments and removals. It is a curious phenomenon that even those Lord Chancellors who had had little or no previous experience of magistrates, and had no reason to be particularly interested in them and their duties, developed a fascination, which in lesser men could have amounted to an obsession, for the office of Justice of the Peace. This was partly due to political influences. The Lord Chancellor was constantly under pressure from members of his own or other political parties, or from his colleagues in the Government, to take action, one way or another, regarding justices. Not a week went by without the arrival of letters from Members of Parliament or constituency secretaries pressing the claims of individual candidates for appointment or claiming that a particular bench did not include a sufficient number of party members. Much of the Lord Chancellor's postbag also consisted of complaints from the general public that justices had done that which they ought not to have done or had failed to do that which they ought to have done. Similar criticism came from Members of Parliament, who objected to the behaviour of justices in general or of individual benches and justices in particular, and they not infrequently came down the Lords' library corridor to press their point in person. The Lord Chancellor's colleagues were equally active, not only in championing some cause on behalf of their constituencies, but in urging that magistrates should be made to take a course desired by the Minister's Department; usually that they should impose heavier penalties for offences in which the Department had an interest. The magistracy is of great interest to the whole population. It is an important form of public service which is open to everyone and appointment as a justice is widely sought after; but more important still, the work of the magistrate affects the entire community; not only does it involve the numerous individuals who have occasion to attend court in civil or criminal proceedings but questions of universal interest, such as the prevalence of certain types of crime in a locality, are influenced by the magistrates' policy in handling cases coming before them. The composition of magistrates' courts and the way in which they discharge their duties can have an appreciable vote-catching significance.

It is no wonder that successive Lord Chancellors, who were responsible not only for the appointment of justices but also for their conduct, training and conditions of service, devoted what might be regarded as a disproportionate amount of their time to these duties, especially if, as was usually the case, they were closely interested in politics, not merely party politics but public affairs in the widest sense. This applied particularly to a keen sociologist like Lord Gardiner, whereas the Lord Chancellor who devoted least time to justices was Lord Simonds, who was the only

Lord Chancellor since the war who had not been active in politics before going to the Woolsack. Yet even Lord Simonds came in the end to comment, like each of the other seven Lord Chancellors under whom I served, that his functions in respect of magistrates were among his most important duties.

The Lord Chancellor's programme of engagements illustrates the interest taken in this work. A large proportion of his speeches outside Parliament are delivered on occasions involving magistrates. Invitations to address audiences of magistrates began in 1950 and every Lord Chancellor, with the exception of Lord Simonds, has been anxious to accept them. A position was reached in the late 1950s when Lord Kilmuir was averaging one magisterial speech every fortnight and travelling the length and breadth of England and Wales to do so. As Secretary of Commissions I was responsible for drafting these speeches and at the same time I was also addressing magistrates myself with almost the same frequency. It was impossible to maintain this momentum and it became necessary to impose a rationing system on the Chancellor's speaking engagements to magistrates, but it was no easy task to persuade Lord Kilmuir or any of his successors to decline an invitation. Most Lord Chancellors were particularly receptive to these invitations because the occasion provided them with an opportunity to obtain some publicity for themselves and their policies which was otherwise denied them. A Lord Chancellor differs from his colleagues in the Government in that he is limited in the extent to which he can make political speeches. He has no constituency and the nature of his office precludes him from entering the rough and tumble of the political arena. Those Lord Chancellors who have served in the House of Commons before being translated to the Woolsack, which is the usual pattern, find this particularly frustrating. A Lord Chancellor has opportunities to address legal audiences – the Law Society, judges, the Bar and law students – but these occasions are not frequent and the catchment area is confined to the profession. In contrast, addresses to magistrates are invariably made to large audiences representative of all sections of the population. The magistrates themselves reflect most shades of opinion and come from many different social backgrounds, and the audience usually includes many non-magistrates: members of local authorities, justices' clerks, probation officers, social workers and the police, in addition to some legal practitioners and judges. Furthermore, the address receives extensive publicity, both locally and in the national press. It therefore affords the Lord Chancellor an opportunity to project his views and his personality to an extent and in a manner not otherwise open to him.

The expansion of the Lord Chancellor's duties since the war has been paralleled by a transmogrification of his Department. When I joined the office in 1944 it was composed of five lawyers and a small supporting staff. We all worked in the House of Lords and enjoyed a close personal relationship with the Lord Chancellor of the day. By 1960, the senior staff numbered thirteen, still all lawyers and all with offices in the House of Lords. In the early 1970s a great population explosion occurred, brought about by the implementation of the recommendations of the Beeching Royal Commission. The lawyers' stronghold was breached and the senior staff who are not legally qualified now outnumber those who are. Only a few remain in the House of Lords; others, forming the headquarters office, are housed in various buildings in London while the great majority of those working for the Lord Chancellor's Department, which is responsible for the administration of the courts, are scattered in centres throughout England and Wales and number some 10,000. The Lord Chancellor's Department has changed from a small staff of personal assistants and advisers into a medium-sized government department fulfilling many of the functions of a Ministry of Justice.

The principal officer who assists the Lord Chancellor in the discharge of his duties relating to magistrates is the Secretary of Commissions. The office of Secretary of Commissions dates from the eighteenth century when the Lord Chancellor had three secretaries: the Principal Secretary, the Secretary of Commissions and the Secretary of Presentations, the latter dealing with ecclesiastical patronage. These three were personal appointments by the Lord Chancellor and when he went out of office they too relinquished their posts, destroying at the same time any papers and files which might have disclosed embarrassing secrets to their successors. The Principal Secretary has now become the Permanent Secretary, who also invariably holds the entirely distinct office of Clerk of the Crown in Chancery. The Secretaries of Commissions and Presentations remain, but whereas the latter's duties are much the same as they were 100 years ago, that of Secretary of Commissions has changed fundamentally.

As the Royal Commission of 1948 pointed out:

The usual structure of a government department is that of a hierarchy working up through the Permanent Secretary to the Minister. The Lord Chancellor's Department has this peculiarity, that, while there is a general staff working through the Permanent Secretary . . . the Secretary of Commissions is the officer concerned with justices, and he works directly under the Lord Chancellor.

Until I was appointed acting Secretary of Commissions in 1947 the office had usually been held by some distinguished individual with experience of magistrates' courts who was appointed from outside the Lord Chancellor's Office. My immediate predecessor, Sir Rupert Howarth, had been Deputy Secretary to the Cabinet, and his predecessor, Sir Leo Page, was a well-known author of works on magistrates but had had no previous experience of government service. Both were Justices of the Peace of long-standing. In 1947 the decision was taken that all future Secretaries of Commissions, although continuing to hold that office on personal appointment by the Lord Chancellor, must be permanent, legal members of the Lord Chancellor's staff and must be prepared not only to handle magisterial work, but also to assist when required with any of the Lord Chancellor's duties. I was the first to be appointed under these new arrangements. One result of this new hybrid appointment was that although the Secretary to Commissions continued to work direct to the Lord Chancellor on magisterial business he came into closer contact with the Permanent Secretary through his other commitments. Some of his work raised questions of policy affecting the whole of the Lord Chancellor's staff and this entailed a relationship with the Permanent Secretary which was unknown before 1947. Nevertheless, communication between the Secretary of Commissions and the Permanent Secretary was never on a large scale and even at its peak, during the late 1960s and early 1970s, a week or two might pass without there being any contact between them, whereas it was rare for a day to go by without papers passing between the Lord Chancellor and myself or my deputy and more often than not we also saw him personally.

Until the end of the war the work of the Secretary of Commissions involved little more than the vetting of lists of recommendations for new justices submitted by Lords Lieutenant and chairman of borough Advisory Committees and the rare appointment of a legal chairman of Quarter Sessions. In 1948, however, the Royal Commission observed in their Report that their proposals would add considerably to the work of the Secretary of Commissions and they recommended that there should be a substantial increase in the size and status of the office. For many years little was done to implement this recommendation and it was not until the Secretary of Commissions was required to embark upon further projects which could not be undertaken without additional assistance that his staff was increased.[2]

The first extension of his area of responsibility beyond Justices of the Peace occurred in 1950 with the implementation of the Royal Commission's recommendation that the appointment of metropolitan and provincial Stipendiary Magistrates and Recorders, which had previously been the concern of the Home Secretary, should be transferred to the Lord Chancellor. There was no further major development until the Franks Committee on Administrative Tribunals and Enquiries, which had been appointed by the Lord Chancellor in 1955, recommended in its Report,[3] published in 1957, that responsibility for appointments to the growing host of tribunals should be transferred from the Ministers concerned to the Lord Chancellor. This was largely a matter of window-dressing for there was no evidence that Ministers had tried to influence tribunals' decisions, and the Lord Chancellor vigorously resisted the proposal, but to no avail. On the principle that he who does not seek a job must be best qualified to have it, almost all tribunals appointments were given to the Chancellor by the Tribunals and Inquiries Act 1958. As far as the Secretary of Commissions was concerned, I had produced what I thought was convincing evidence that I and my office were totally unfitted to deal with tribunal appointments. Within a few months nearly 12,000 such appointments had been added to my jurisdiction. The great majority of these were General Commissioners of Income Tax, who then numbered nearly 10,000 (later reduced by diligent pruning to about half that number), but the appointments also included a varied assortment of chairmen of other bodies, such as Rent, National Insurance and National Assistance tribunals. The result of the acquisition of these appointments was that, when added to Justices of the Peace (including those on the Supplemental List) and to chairmen and deputy chairmen of Quarter Sessions, Recorders, deputy and assistant Recorders and Stipendiary Magistrates, they brought the number of persons for whom the Secretary of Commissions was responsible at that time to nearly 40,000. Fortunately, they did not all require constant attention, but much work was involved in the selection of candidates for the considerable number of new appointments required each year. During 1969, which was the last year before the Lord Chancellor's Office was reorganised as described below, the number of new appointments and re-appointments for which I was responsible totalled 2287. Of these 557 were to legal posts (both whole-time and part-time) and the rest were justices, general commissioners and other lay appointments.

Sheer weight of numbers made it impossible for the Lord Chancellor to be involved personally in all these appointments and he was therefore obliged to designate categories in which it was acceptable for the process of selection and appointment to be deputed to the Secretary of Commissions, subject only to general lines of policy laid down by the Chancellor himself. The numbers involved also presented a problem to me and my office, but we were already faced with this situation in the case of Justices of the Peace, who were selected through local Advisory Committees, described later, and it was decided to handle the General Commissioners in the same manner. There are 78 Advisory Committees for general commissioners compared with 98 for Justices of the Peace. None of the other classes of appointment was sufficiently large to warrant the establishment of Advisory Committees and they were therefore processed entirely within the office. Each applicant was interviewed, usually by two senior officers, and a great deal of time was spent in these interviews and in correspondence with candidates' referees.

The general commissioners proved to be a greater burden than had been expected. The Inland Revenue persuaded us against our better judgment to embark upon the immediate reorganisation of income tax divisions throughout England and Wales. As the divisions were based on areas co-terminous with the Anglo-Saxon Hundreds it could not be denied that reorganisation was somewhat overdue, but it could have waited until more pressing commitments had been absorbed.

Pressure on the office was reduced slightly in 1955 when responsibility for justices north of the border was transferred to the Secretary of State for Scotland, but this relief was more than offset in 1974 when the Lord Chancellor became responsible for

Justices of the Peace and Resident Magistrates in Northern Ireland.

When the Crown Court replaced Assizes and Quarter Sessions in 1971, the appointment of Circuit Judges and of new-style Recorders was placed under the Deputy Secretary to the Lord Chancellor instead of the Secretary of Commissions who had previously been accountable for Quarter Sessions appointments. This arrangement was integral to the restructuring of the greatly enlarged Department brought about by the Beeching scheme, but it also intended to release the Secretary of Commissions from some of the non-magisterial pressures which had been building up during the previous four or five years, leaving him with responsibility for lay and professional magistrates, administrative tribunals and, incongruously, certain foreign and Commonwealth commitments. This process was continued after I left the office in 1977. By 1978 the Secretary of Commissions was responsible for lay justices, Stipendiary Magistrates, administrative tribunals and general commissioners and in 1982 the stipendiaries and the administrative tribunals were transferred to the Deputy Secretary to the Lord Chancellor.

One of the most noticeable changes in the work-pattern of the Secretary of Commissions after 1947 was in the amount of time he and his staff were obliged to spend away from their offices. Until 1950 it was almost unknown for anyone in the Lord Chancellor's Office to leave London on official business. For the Secretary of Commissions there were no conferences, other than the Annual General Meeting of the Magistrates' Association (always held in London) and of the Justices' Clerks Society. There were as yet no branches of the Magistrates' Association, no Magistrates' Courts Committees and no training courses for which the Lord Chancellor was responsible. It was considered unnecessary to visit Advisory Committees or to maintain any contact with magistrates except through correspondence. By contrast, in 1977 two of the Assistant Secretaries of Commissions (one of whom was Training Officer) spent more time out of London than they did in Westminster and the Secretary of Commissions himself was away for at least a day a week. There were few weekends when he was not attending a conference or training exercise or preparing speeches for himself and for the Lord Chancellor and catching up on overspill of work from the previous week. A substantial part of each day was spent in meetings with officials in other Departments and with outside organisations, while evenings were often taken up with speaking engagements at dinners and other functions. Family life was a luxury which he, like many of his colleagues, could rarely enjoy. These occupational hazards were, of course, symptomatic of modern civilisation and were to be met in many walks of life, but it is questionable whether those who are subject to these pressures, in the government service or elsewhere, are able consistently to give of their best.

It may be contended that the work now done by the Secretary of Commissions and his staff could well be absorbed into the main stream of the Lord Chancellor's Office. If all magistrates were legally qualified stipendiaries this would be the right course, but the peculiar problems presented by courts manned by part-time laymen are totally different from those dealt with in any other part of the Department. Although it is highly desirable that those who handle this section of the Lord Chancellor's work should also have experience in other areas, they need a degree of specialisation to enable them fully to comprehend the mysteries of the lay magistracy, which is impossible if they change their duties with the frequency usual in the Civil Service. It is also virtually essential, if the Secretary of Commissions and his senior officers are to discharge their duties to the best advantage, for them to serve as justices themselves and to acquire the knowledge and experience gained from regular attendance in court. They need not all be lawyers; the office would probably work just as well with fewer lawyers than at present, but at least one lawyer is necessary because points of law arise constantly in the daily run of business and in the course of legislation and, unlike other Departments, the Lord Chancellor's Office has no legal branch to which these matters may be referred. The members of the Office are their own legal advisers.

Justices of the Peace are a vast, heterogeneous host of volunteers who do not comply with the normal rules. They look for direction but not orders. They require guidance but their judicial discretion must not be impaired. The channels linking the lay magistrates with the Ministers responsible for them and their work are tenuous and delicate. The responsible officers must, through experience and training, be able to recognise all the pitfalls. They must learn to give guidance and assistance without encroaching upon the independence of the judiciary. They must be firm in implementing ministerial policy, but they must know how, without giving offence, to present and explain unpalatable government measures (which often emanate from other Departments for which the Lord Chancellor is not responsible) so that these do not deter able and conscientious magistrates from discharging their duties. Above all, they must individually have the confidence and respect of those with whom they have to work: Advisory Committees, Magistrates' Courts Committees, justices' clerks, the Magistrates' Association and the magistracy as a whole.

Before concluding this chapter, reference must be made to the interest of Ministers other than the Lord Chancellor in the work which magistrates perform or would normally be expected to perform. Until recently the only other Minister directly concerned was the Home Secretary, but from 1970 other Departments have acquired interests, notably the Department of Health and Social Security, which has assumed responsibility for the young on the principle that young people require treatment but not punishment and that they must be removed from the jurisdiction of the courts and transferred to the care of the social services. The result is that the Home Secretary, who is still the Minister responsible for law and order, can no longer plan an effective role in dealing with young delinquents; still less can the Lord Chancellor, although he is frequently criticised for failing to ensure that the magistrates' courts deal firmly with juvenile violence.

It is to be hoped that fragmentation of responsibility will go no further. In the meantime there is a need to review the overlapping spheres of responsibility of the Lord Chancellor and the Secretary of State for the Home Department, which has been a feature of government since Wolsey and Thomas Cromwell.

There seems to be a popular belief that there is no love lost between the Lord Chancellor's Office and the Home Office. If this were true a great deal of what was achieved by my office during the past thirty years would have been impossible. Without exception I enjoyed a very happy relationship with all those in the Home Office with whom I had to work, especially C Division, whose duties are principally concerned with the magistrates' courts. There were bound to be differences of view and differences of interest, but these occur even between members of the same office, and we never failed to settle our disputes with the Home Office in a cordial atmosphere, usually to our mutual advantage.

This was achieved in spite of mounting pressures which tended to weigh more heavily on the Home Office than on the Lord Chancellor's Office. The Home Office has received more than its fair share of criticism, especially during the past twelve years or so, and many were the occasions when I winced on picking up the evening paper and reading of some new attack on our overworked colleagues. Furthermore, the last three decades, which have seen a notable extension of the Lord Chancellor's territory, have also been marked by a contraction in the Home Secretary's sphere of influence. This state of affairs could hardly fail to breed jealousy, but happily goodwill prevailed and I am grateful for the help and support I received from Home Office officials on all but a very few occasions.

The fact that the present arrangement works as well as it does in spite of overlapping interests is due almost entirely to this careful co-operation between officials of the two Departments and their determination to avoid unnecessary friction. The fact is, however, that in spite of authoritative assertions to the contrary, the present situation is confusing, time-wasting and on occasions detrimental to the efficient functioning of the machinery of government.

In most areas of the administration of justice the Lord Chancellor and the Home Secretary each have certain distinct and well-defined functions. The Home Secretary is concerned with the exercise of the prerogative of mercy, the treatment of offenders, extradition, the police and the prison and probation services. The Lord Chancellor is concerned with the civil law, with civil and criminal legal aid, with costs and with the administration of the courts, both civil and criminal, other than the magistrates' courts. In the administration of criminal justice, however, the division of functions is less clearly defined. The Home Secretary is the Minister for the maintenance of law and order and as such is concerned with the substantive criminal law and with major questions of criminal procedure, whereas the Lord Chancellor carries responsibility for the appointment of all the judges and magistrates whose duty it is to interpret and apply the law. The administration of the magistrates' courts is primarily the responsibility of the local Magistrates' Courts Committees but they are subject to supervisory powers vested in the Home Secretary. The rules of procedure for the magistrates' courts, on the other hand, are made by the Lord Chancellor and so, too, are the rules governing the size, composition and chairmanship of magistrates' benches.

In the Parliamentary Session of 1962/63 the Estimates Committee made a comprehensive survey of the Civil Estimates of the Home Office and reported that some instances of the division of functions between the Home Office and the Lord Chancellor's Office were illogical and that this situation might cause difficulties in the administration and the reform of the criminal law. The Committee recommended that the Home Office and the Treasury, in consultation with the Lord Chancellor's Office, should take immediate steps to reorganise the present division of responsibility with a view to rationalising the administration of the criminal law and rendering more effective the methods of bringing it up to date.

In their reply to the Report the Home Office expressed the view that reform of the criminal law was not hampered by the present distribution of functions. There was already close co-operation between the two Departments on all matters of common concern. They went on to say, however, that the Secretary of State and the Lords Commissioners of the Treasury, in consultation with the Lord Chancellor, would take a suitable opportunity of examining any further points of detail in relation to which there might be doubt as to the precise division of responsibility between Departments. The position today remains much the same as it was then. No serious problem has arisen in the meantime largely because the harmonious relationship between the two Departments enables them to agree on most issues, or if they do not they manage to reach a satisfactory compromise, but this is not a tidy way of doing things, and it is uneconomical because it often results in two people doing the work of one. There is also the possibility of the Home Office and the Lord Chancellor's Office not seeing eye to eye on some particular matter, as has occurred on a few occasions.

The spheres of responsibility of the two Ministers need to be clearly defined and the best place to draw the line between them seems to be immediately before and after the trial, so that the whole of the administration of the criminal courts would become the concern of the Lord Chancellor, as it is already in all the civil courts and in criminal courts other than the magistrates' courts. The Home Secretary would then be accountable for bringing criminals to trial and for taking care of them after sentencing; the police and prison service would remain within his jurisdiction and so, too, would the substantive criminal law. The Lord Chancellor would have responsibility for the whole of the trial itself, including trial procedure, and for all court administration.

4 The Selection and Appointment of Justices

It is axiomatic that any system depends more upon the quality of the people who operate it than upon the quality of the system itself. In the administration of the law the most important consideration is that those appointed to judicial office should be eminently suitable to dispense justice. This applies as much to a Justice of the Peace as to a High Court judge. If the right individual is not chosen in the first place no amount of training, supervision or remedial action will produce a satisfactory result. In the case of justices this point used to be totally ignored, and even by 1947 its importance was not fully recognised. Candidates for the bench were chosen for a variety of reasons, as often as not in recognition of some service they had rendered, usually to a political party, and little care was taken to make sure that they were fit to perform the duties of a magistrate.

In 1947 there were two ways in which a person might become a justice: by having his name added to a Commission of the Peace at the direction of the Lord Chancellor[1], or by virtue of holding certain other offices.

Today there are virtually no justices *ex officio* in England and Wales, but in 1947 there were approximately 2550. They included, among others, the Lord Chancellor, Privy Councillors, all the whole-time judges, the Archbishop of York and the Bishops of Durham and Ely (but not the Archbishop of Canterbury or any other bishop) and the Vice-Chancellors of the Universities of Oxford and Cambridge; but by far the most numerous group were the mayors and ex-mayors of boroughs and the chairmen of county councils and of urban and rural district councils. It was only the local authority magistrates who created any real difficulty. Many of them were unable to adopt a judicial approach and treated the court like a council meeting. The problem was worst in the boroughs where not only were the mayor and

36

immediate past mayor magistrates *ex officio* but the mayor had the right to take the chair even if he had never been on a bench before. It was not uncommon to find the blind leading the blind and for a borough court to be composed solely of the mayor and his predecessor, neither of whom had had any real judicial experience. Nor were they invariably of impeccable character. Lord Merthyr, in his minority report as a member of the Royal Commission of 1948, recalls a mayor who had been convicted 79 times before he became mayor and had raised the score to 81 by the time his office expired (in a case like this the Lord Chancellor had power to disqualify the mayor from sitting but usually he did not become aware of his shortcomings until it was too late).

The Royal Commission recommended that the chairmen of county and district councils and the ex-mayors of boroughs should cease to be justices, but that the mayor, because of his special relationship to the borough, should continue to be a magistrate during his term of office though he should lose his right to preside. The Government were prepared to accept these recommendations which had the support of the County Councils Association, who commented in their evidence to the Royal Commission: 'The qualities which enable the chairman of a local authority to perform his duties with success are not of necessity those requisite for the office of justice of the peace.' Unfortunately, the rest of the local government lobby would have none of this and the Justices of the Peace Act 1949 did no more than remove ex-mayors from the bench and deprive mayors of the right to take the chair. An amendment to abolish all local government *ex officios* was heavily defeated in the Lords and there seemed to be no hope of ever getting rid of them in the teeth of opposition from the boroughs.

It remained for Lord Gardiner to achieve the impossible in 1968. His hand had been strengthened by the introduction of compulsory training for newly appointed justices in 1966. It was not practicable to apply this, or any effective form of training, to the *ex officios*, and consequently two classes of justice emerged: those appointed by name who had undergone training and the *ex officios* who had not. Lord Gardiner sought Government approval for the total abolition of all justices *ex officio*, and he set the example by placing the Lord Chancellor at the top of the list of those who should go. This gesture did not convince his colleagues but he had a trump card. Contrary to general belief there were many more Conservative *ex officios* than Labour and, out of a total of 1470 local authorities, only 364 were Labour-controlled. That was sufficient to persuade the Government and although the Association of Municipal Corporations remained opposed, the view which ought to have been accepted in 1949 prevailed, namely that personal suitability for the office of magistrate should be the sole criterion and that only those who have been individually selected for this purpose should serve on the bench.

The Justices of the Peace Act 1968 provided that no one might become a justice unless appointed to a commission by name. The only exceptions were Recorders, chairmen and deputy chairmen of Quarter Sessions and Stipendiary Magistrates (all of whom needed to be justices to perform their judicial duties) and two incongruous groups: the Lord Mayor and Aldermen of the City of London and the Commissioner and Assistant Commissioner of Police for the Metropolis.

Although the early justices had performed police duties, it had long been established that a serving member of the police force must not become a magistrate and the Commissioner for the Metropolis was an anachronism. Some of his administrative functions, however, depended upon his being a justice,[2] and newly appointed commissioners would appear before the Lord Chancellor in uniform to take the oaths. We tried to remove this anomaly in the 1968 Act but this would have required a fairly complex piece of legislation and we were unable to prepare it in time. It was not until 1973 that the Administration of Justice Act finally removed the Commissioner and Assistant Commissioner from magisterial office.

The City of London has always been a law unto itself. By virtue of a series of royal charters dating from 1444 the sole magistrates in the City were the Lord Mayor and the 26 Aldermen, all of whom were justices *ex officio*. From 1848 it was the rule throughout the rest of the country that courts of summary jurisdiction must consist of not less than two lay justices (save in a few circumstances) or one Stipendiary Magistrate, but until 1968 the Lord Mayor and each of the twenty-six Aldermen continued to sit singly. The 1968 Bill, when introduced in the Commons, provided for the abolition of all local government *ex officio* magistrates without exception. The City marshalled its forces in defence of its special rights. They advanced the arguments that the Royal Commission of 1948 had recommended no change, that the *status quo* had been supported by the Lord Chief Justice, the Magistrates' Association and the London solicitors, that the City courts had given general satisfaction (there had been few appeals from their decisions and most of these were unsuccessful) and that the Lord Mayor and Aldermen were exceptionally well-qualified in that suitability for judicial office was a factor taken into account in aldermanic elections and Aldermen received intensive training in the work of the bench. These arguments were not accepted by the Government, nor by the majority of the House of Commons, where Members representing other constituencies were jealous of the City's privileges. It was claimed that the Court of Aldermen was undemocratic and not representative of all classes of society and it included no women (though women were eligible for election).[3] By the time the Bill reached the Lords the City had amassed an impressive array of supporters in the upper House and, to avoid defeat, the Government were obliged to accept a compromise amendment moved by the former Lord Chancellor, Lord Dilhorne, the effect of which was to retain the Lord Mayor and Aldermen as justices *virtute officii* but to add to the City bench a number of justices appointed by name in the normal way. In future City courts would be composed of at least two justices as elsewhere but the Lord Mayor would retain the right to preside when present. When the amended Bill returned to the Commons, the Attorney-General, Sir Elwyn Jones, who later became Lord Chancellor, had the thankless task of persuading the House to accept provisions similar to those which he had induced them to reject during the earlier stages. He succeeded and the City is now the only area other than a county and the five areas of Greater London to have its own commission and the only local authority to have magistrates *ex officio*. It was a remarkable demonstration of the City's ability to preserve its ancient institutions, and its achievement was all the more impressive coming as it did at a time when the traditions for which the City stood were out of favour with a large part of the population. The victory was due to the backing which the City was able to secure, especially in the Lords, and to the able and determined staff work of the City fathers, particularly Alderman Sir Bernard Waley-Cohen who, throughout the passage of the Bill, was tireless in whipping up support and directing operations from the sidelines. The outcome was regarded as a personal defeat for the Lord Chancellor who, it was thought, was foremost among the City's antagonists. In fact he was not unduly perturbed by the turn of events; as a rationalist he found the aldermanic status objectionable but he was generally better disposed towards the City and its institutions than some of his Cabinet colleagues.

The final episode in the *ex officio* saga took place when the Courts Act of 1971 abolished Quarter Sessions and with them the old-style Recorders and chairmen of county sessions. The new type of Recorder and the Circuit Judges who came into being in 1972 did not become justices by virtue of their office, and therefore today no one except the Lord Mayor and Aldermen of London can attain the office of Justice of the Peace unless he is appointed to a commission by name or becomes a Stipendiary Magistrate.

Authority to act as a magistrate is derived from the Commission of the Peace. The commission, which is issued under the Great Seal, is a large parchment scroll bearing directions from the Sovereign to the justices in a specified area. It was addressed to justices *ex officio* by reference to their office, but until 1973 persons who were appointed individually had their names inscribed in a schedule on the authority of a fiat signed by the Lord Chancellor. This had been the practice for centuries but it received statutory force in the Crown Office Act 1877 and it was a dreadful nuisance. The commission was kept in the custody of an official in the area to which it related, but whenever a name had to be added or removed the commission, encased in a large cylinder, was sent to the Lord Chancellor's Office by post and then returned when the insertion or deletion had been made. These comings and goings, which occurred many hundreds of times a year, were inconvenient, time-consuming and costly and it was not unknown for the commission, in spite of its bulk, to be lost between town hall and House of Lords. This antiquated procedure was equalled by the archaic wording of the commission itself, which had not been revised since 1590. Fortunately, no one ever troubled to read the commission, so the fact that it was several centuries out of date did not seem to be a matter of sufficient urgency to take precedence over many other pressing problems which beset us after the end of the war. No attempt was made therefore to redraft the commissions until 1973, when it became necessary to adjust them to fit the pattern of local government established by the Local Government Act 1972. The Act replaced all the old administrative counties and municipal boroughs with metropolitan and non-metropolitan counties divided into districts. Before the Act there had been a separate commission for each administrative county and for certain cities and boroughs, but when these authorities were abolished their commissions went with them. The Administration of Justice Act 1973 accordingly provided that in future a separate commission should be issued only for counties, the five commission areas of Greater London and the City of London. This enabled us, when issuing the new commissions, to replace the otiose verbiage with a streamlined, modernised version. For technical reasons the new commission is more verbose than we would have wished, but at least it is shorter and more intelligible than its predecessor. It must be admitted that the new version does not really achieve very much because most of the justices' powers are derived from Statutes and, if these were repeated in the commission, the wording would have to be amended whenever there was new legislation. The commission is the Sovereign's authority to the justices empowering them to perform the functions of a magistrate and we therefore took what we thought was the sensible course and drafted a form of words, which the Queen was graciously pleased to accept, which really amounted to Her Majesty saying: 'All you justices go and do what you are supposed to do'.

From the administrative point of view the 1973 Act enabled us to divest ourselves of the shuttlecock system when dealing with appointments and removals and also to give effect to what had been the practice for centuries, namely that the Lord Chancellor appoints justices on behalf of the Sovereign. The Act expressly provided that justices should be appointed on behalf and in the name of Her Majesty by instrument under the hand of the Lord Chancellor. The old fiats were therefore superseded by documents, signed by the Lord Chancellor, the originals of which are kept in the Lord Chancellor's Office while copies go to the Keepers of the Rolls[4] in the counties. There is no longer a schedule to the commission and the latter remains permanently in the area to which it applies.

Until 1971 the Lord Chancellor signed every appointment fiat personally, but Lord Hailsham decided that he was not precluded from delegating this power and that in certain circumstances it was proper for him to do so. There are certain situations in which both appointment and removal are purely routine, the most common example being where a justice moves his residence to an area more than fifteen miles from the boundary of his commission.

He then becomes disqualified from acting and, unless he is likely to return in the near future, his appointment is terminated. Until 1965, such justices were not appointed to serve in their new area unless the Advisory Committee responsible for appointments in that area asked for them when vacancies occurred. The reason why there was no automatic transfer was that a bench might become overstaffed if it was obliged to accept all justices who moved in from other places. This rule seemed rather unfair on those who, having given long and useful service, were obliged to move because of their work or some other good reason, and in 1965 Lord Gardiner accepted my proposal that, in a case such as this, a justice who had served for not less than five years might transfer immediately to the commission for his new area. He would then be placed on the Supplemental List until such time as a vacancy occurred on his local bench and the Advisory Committee recommended that he should fill it. There has been a marked increase in the number of these residential moves in recent years, due to the rise in the number of justices and also to the greater propensity of the population to move about. By 1971 these events had become so frequent that Lord Hailsham, who on these occasions was obliged to sign two fiats, one of removal and the other of appointment, decided that his time ought not to be disrupted by such routine matters. He therefore delegated his authority to appoint and remove justices in these circumstances to the Secretary of Commissions and his Deputy. This was the first recorded instance for more than two centuries of anyone other than the Lord Chancellor himself being authorised to appoint or remove justices. Constitutionally the innovation was of interest because the decision to exercise the devolved power cannot always be a matter of pure routine; inevitably the Secretary must use his discretion to determine whether each set of circumstances falls within his remit. The legality of the practice was open to doubt, but it was regularised by the Administration of Justice Act, 1982 which removed the previous statutory requirement that appointments must be 'under the hand of the Lord Chancellor'.

From 1935 onwards, a candidate approved for appointment as a justice received a rather curt note from the Secretary of Commissions asking whether, in the event of his being appointed, he would give the Lord Chancellor certain assurances.[5] Having supplied these undertakings the eagerly waiting candidate received no acknowledgement or any other communication from the Lord Chancellor and, if he was appointed, the first he heard about it was usually a summons from the court to come and take the oaths. When he retired after years of devoted service the most he could hope for was a farewell letter from the Lord Lieutenant of his county. In 1950 I introduced an arrangement whereby each justice received a letter, signed by the Secretary of Commissions, notifying him of his appointment; and shortly afterwards I also arranged for a valedictory letter to be sent to every justice when he retired. The latter, expressing appreciation of the justice's services, bore the Lord Chancellor's facsimile signature. Before I took these steps there had been no open complaint about the absence of any communication from the Lord Chancellor but the appearance of my carefully thought-out letters was the signal for outraged protest, especially in regard to the notes on retirement. It was taken as an insult that a justice who had given long public service should receive a mere copy of a signature, however eminent the signatory. If the Lord Chancellor could not be bothered to sign the letters himself a senior member of his staff should have the courtesy to do so on his behalf. I amended the letters and dutifully signed each one myself, totalling about 600 a year, only to be met by even more vehement criticism. Far better, it was said, to receive a letter purporting to be signed by the Lord Chancellor himself than to have to put up with one signed by a mere official. Obviously we could not win, so we reverted to the Lord Chancellor's facsimile signature, which was quicker and easier; but in 1978, Lord Elwyn-Jones agreed to sign the valedictory letters to all justices retiring at the age of seventy. Those who retired below that age received a letter signed by the Deputy Secretary of Commissions on the Lord Chancellor's behalf. This remains the practice today.

The Lord Chancellor has exercised authority to appoint justices on behalf of the Sovereign since at least 1535 and probably much earlier. (The early keepers and justices were probably nominated by the freeholders and then confirmed by the king.) He usually did so on the nomination of various influential persons but, as political parties developed, the justices tended to be drawn exclusively from supporters of the party in office and it was not unknown, especially in Queen Anne's reign, for a new Lord Chancellor to dismiss the justices appointed by his predecessor. Gradually the right to nominate county justices fell into the hands of the Lord Lieutenant, whose own political allegiance tended to play a predominant part in the selection. Party politics continued to dominate the scene into the twentieth century, the filling of benches alternatively by Whigs and Tories being succeeded by similar tactics from the Liberals and Conservatives, but by the end of the nineteenth century the Liberals were complaining bitterly that the magistracy was always dominated by Conservative justices. This was due in part to the property qualification which required county justices to hold land to the value of £100 (£20 before 1737) thereby excluding many Liberal supporters, and partly to the fact that most Lords Lieutenant were Conservatives. When the Liberals came into office in 1905 one of their first Acts abolished the property qualification, but the Liberal Lord Chancellor, Lord Loreburn, resolutely refused to take the opportunity to pack the benches with Liberals, to the intense disgust of his own party, who then decided that the question of appointing magistrates required thorough investigation, and in 1909 a Royal Commission was appointed for this purpose.

The most important of the Royal Commission's recommendations, when it reported in 1910, was that the Lord Chancellor should continue to appoint justices but that he should be assisted by Advisory Committees which he was to set up throughout the country. In the counties the Lord Lieutenant would normally be the chairman but the boroughs were to have separate committees with chairmen chosen by the Lord Chancellor. These recommendations were accepted and the first county committees were appointed in 1912 followed by borough committees ten years later. Since then the machinery for the appointment of justices in England, Wales and Scotland has been based on the Advisory Committee system.

Until 1972 there was one Advisory Committee for each area having a separate commission, but when the commissions were changed following the local government reorganisation the committee structure was also altered to bring each committee into closer contact with the localities for which it was responsible. In the non-metropolitan counties a number of sub-committees or area panels were established whose principal duty was to discover and interview candidates and submit their findings to the main committee. There were also a few large urban areas in some of these counties which had their own main committees. In the metropolitan counties a separate committee was appointed for each district and in a few of the largest districts there was more than one committee.

It remained the normal practice for the Lord Lieutenant[6] to be chairman of the committee in a non-metropolitan county. In metropolitan counties he was given overall responsibility for co-ordinating the work of the district committees, though each of these had its own chairman. Most Lords Lieutenant are dedicated to the work and, because of their standing and independent status in the county, they are probably the best choice for the chairmanship that could be found. The Royal Commission of 1948 envisaged the possibility of the Lord Chancellor appointing someone other than the Lord Lieutenant to take the chair, though no such appointment had been made up to that time and there were many who regarded the Lieutenancy as carrying with it the chairmanship *ex officio*. To place the matter beyond doubt I introduced a new practice in 1955 whereby I wrote on the Lord Chancellor's behalf to each new Lord Lieutenant offering him the chairmanship. When he accepted, which he invariably did, the Lord Chancellor formally appointed him chairman.

The only instances of a Lord Lieutenant not chairing a county committee were in Essex (in circumstances described later) and in Greater London. In the county of London the Lord Lieutenant was always chairman until 1967, but he was not in as close contact with the magistracy, or with the population as a whole, as his colleagues elsewhere. Furthermore, the committee, which met in County Hall, was dominated by political intrigue and, although the Duke of Wellington, who was Lord Lieutenant in the years immediately following the 1948 Royal Commission, tried to break this influence, it had become too deeply rooted, particularly during the earlier chairmanship of Lord Crewe. In 1967, when Sir Gerald Templer succeeded Lord Alexander of Tunis as Lord Lieutenant, Lord Gardiner took the opportunity to move the committee from County Hall to Inner London Sessions at Newington Causeway and to appoint Lord Denning, the Master of the Rolls, as chairman. Sir Gerald took this as a personal slight, which was unfortunate as none was intended and the change was no reflection whatever upon him. Lord Denning was succeeded as chairman in 1977 by Judge West-Russell, and other Circuit judges served as chairmen of the committees for the four outer commission areas of Greater London.

Advisory Committees and sub-committees vary in size; most

committees have about twelve members and sub-committees six or eight. Members are appointed by the Lord Chancellor, usually after consulting the chairman. Until 1925 they served for an indefinite period, but since then the term of appointment has been six years, half the committee retiring every three years. The appointment, however, was usually renewed until the member reached the age of seventy, with the result that most committees were in dire need of new blood; but from the early 1960s the six-year rule was applied fairly rigidly. Today the Lord Chancellor is usually willing to re-appoint members for up to twelve years.

Members of committees are drawn from different sections of the population and, as far as practicable, from different parts of the area for which they are responsible. With a view to ensuring that appointments do not become the perquisite of any one political party each committee and sub-committee includes a number of recognised supporters of different parties, though it is a condition of appointment that they must not regard themselves as representing party interests. Every committee contains at least one Conservative and one Labour member and most also have a Liberal. In recent years, Plaid Cymru and SDP supporters have been appointed as such to some committees.

It is the Lord Chancellor's policy to include a number of politically independent members in each committee, but this is easier said than done. There are few, even among those who consider themselves to be totally devoid of political sympathies, who are not regarded by others as tarred with some political brush, and it is a common complaint by the 'political' members of Advisory Committees that the 'independents' are in fact supporters of one of the other parties.

Before appointing a political member to a committee the Lord Chancellor usually ascertains from the party headquarters that he is known to be a supporter. This practice was condemned by the 1948 Royal Commission, but it has continued to be applied by successive Lord Chancellors largely as a matter of self defence. In answer to the familiar complaint that a party is being overlooked when appointments to the bench are made in a particular area he can reply that no recommendation is accepted if it is opposed by any member of the Advisory Committee and that the committee includes a member of the party concerned. Nevertheless, the practice is not altogether satisfactory. In spite of the clearly defined conditions of appointment it leads both the party and the individual member to think that his principal function is to secure the appointment of party supporters to the bench. It also leads to situations where party headquarters, though confirming that the person the Lord Chancellor has in mind is a supporter, press him to appoint someone else who they think is likely to get better results. Recently this has been carried to the extent of the party claiming that the Lord Chancellor's candidate was not a supporter at all even though he subscribed to their funds.

The functions of Advisory Committees are not confined to choosing candidates for appointment. They also involve constant scrutiny of the effectiveness of justices after they have been appointed, the review of the magisterial position in their respective areas and drawing the Lord Chancellor's attention to any need for additional appointments when these are required. Each committee submits to the Lord Chancellor an annual report on the state of its benches and the performance of the justices, including a list of individual attendances.

The Lord Chancellor is not obliged to accept the advice he receives from a committee. Committees are not statutory bodies and they have no standing of their own. They are appointed by the Lord Chancellor to assist him in performing his duties, but responsibility for appointing and removing justices rests entirely with him. If something goes wrong it is the Lord Chancellor who is answerable to Parliament and not the committee. It is not uncommon for a Lord Chancellor to decline to accept a list of recommendations from a committee on general grounds (e.g: there are already sufficient justices in the area or the list contains a disproportionate number of candidates of the same sex or with the same social background), but it is rare for him to feel it necessary to turn down an individual candidate as being personally unsuitable.

The Lord Chancellor is equally free to appoint a justice without consulting the committee or against their advice. There have been only two cases of this kind during the past forty years and both led to confrontations with the Lord Lieutenant. Lord Jowitt appointed two individuals who were known to him personally to the commissions for Essex and West Sussex. Neither were acceptable to the respective committees and both Lords Lieutenant protested. Sir Francis Whitmore of Essex carried his protest to the extent of resigning as Lord Lieutenant and chairman of the Advisory Committee. Since then no Lord Chancellor has made an appointment on his own knowledge of the candidate without the concurrence of the Advisory Committee.

Occasionally a member of the Lord Chancellor's family is recommended for appointment. There have been three such cases since 1945; in each the Lord Chancellor took no part in initiating the proposal and was careful to stand aloof until the Advisory Committee submitted the name to him in the normal way. Married daughters of Lord Jowitt and Lord Dilhorne were appointed while their fathers were Lord Chancellor, and Lady Hailsham became a justice for the City of London while her husband was in office.

It is generally thought that the whole process of appointment is shrouded in sinister mystery. This is quite untrue. The proceedings of Advisory Committees are strictly confidential but that is because personal matters which may be embarrassing to a candidate are often disclosed. It is also true that the names of members of committees are usually not published, though this is left to the discretion of the committee itself. Most committees prefer anonymity because it protects their members from being lobbied. There have been occasions when members whose identity had become known were subjected to such undue influence and persistent importuning that they felt obliged to resign. Experience also showed that disclosure of the composition of a committee led to dissatisfaction among sections of the local population, who complained that they were not represented; yet if members of every section were included the committee would become unmanageable.

There is really no need for anyone outside the Lord Chancellor's Office to know who are the members of a committee. The Lord Chancellor and not the committee is answerable for the way in which appointments are made, and the usual motive for wishing to have the names is to be able to bring pressure to bear upon them or to criticise them publicly. Any person or organisation who wishes to recommend a candidate for the bench may do so through the secretary of the committee, whose name and address are published or may be obtained from the courts or the local authority.

Steps are constantly taken by the Lord Chancellor's Office and by Committees to dispel the myth of secrecy. Arrangements are made for television and radio programmes to be presented and for articles to appear in the press explaining the procedure and pointing out that anyone may recommend a candidate. Usually this publicity, if it makes any impression at all, is soon forgotten and the press are reluctant to repeat the performance. On a number of occasions, both national and local newspapers have refused to print articles containing a factual description of the magistracy because they were 'not sufficiently sensational'. In some instances where an article did appear and aroused public interest it did more harm than good because the Advisory Committee became submerged in a spate of wholly unsuitable candidates. On one occasion the Inner London Committee published what amounted to an advertisement for recommendations and received over 800 names to fill barely a dozen vacancies. Not surprisingly, the candidates and their sponsors were incensed when told that they could not even be considered for several years. This understandable reaction occurs all too frequently, in spite of efforts by the committees to explain that many are recommended but few can be chosen. However well qualified a candidate may be, he cannot be appointed unless there is a vacancy, and even then, before deciding who should fill it, the committee must have regard to age, sex, occupation, social background and other matters which may affect the balance of the bench. A brilliant, highly educated pillar of local society who lavishes his time on good deeds and public service will not be chosen in preference to a sound, competent female factory worker if there is a paucity of women wage-earners on the bench in question.

As part of the service in publicity the Lord Chancellor's Office publishes a booklet on how justices are appointed and what they do which is issued free of charge through local authorities and Citizens' Advice Bureaux or direct from the Office; but, in spite of this, whenever there is a shortage of things to complain about there is always someone to dig up the old chestnut of the clandestine routes to the magistracy.

When our explanatory booklet was first published in 1967, we took the precaution of issuing at the same time a Welsh version for distribution in the Principality and I had it translated by the experts in the Welsh Office. The day after it was issued I received a vitriolic letter from a member of the Welsh Language Society suggesting that if we had the audacity to play about with his language we should at least get it translated by someone who knew what he was doing.

With few exceptions, everyone is eligible for appointment as a justice. There are no statutory qualifications, except that a magistrate must reside in or within fifteen miles of the boundary of his commission, and the only essential requirement is that the candidate must be personally suitable to carry out the important public work which he will have to perform. There is reason to believe that even a foreign subject may legally be appointed a magistrate. This question arose in 1962 when Princess Chula of Thailand was recommended for appointment to the Cornwall commission. The Princess was an Englishwoman and resided in Cornwall, but had become a foreign subject on marrying a Thai prince. The Lord Chancellor, Lord Kilmuir, and his advisers came to the conclusion that, notwithstanding the Act of Settlement, an alien was not disqualified from appointment. Lord Kilmuir decided, however, that as a matter of policy the subject of another country ought not to become a justice because he or she must be assumed to owe allegiance to a foreign power rather than to the United Kingdom. For this reason Princess Chula, who was otherwise well qualified, was not appointed. Citizens of some Commonwealth countries, however, have been appointed and also a few with dual nationality.

Fifty years earlier Princess Chula would have been ineligible for appointment because of her sex. It was not until 1919, under an Act with the peculiar name of the Sex Disqualification (Removal) Act, that women first became eligible to serve as magistrates and to hold other public offices. Lord Birkenhead, the Lord Chancellor, immediately set up a special Advisory Committee, with the Marchioness of Crewe as chairman, to recommend the first lady candidates for appointment. The committee began by recommending its own members, who included Mrs Lloyd George, Mrs Beatrice Webb and the Marchioness of Londonderry, and they were appointed on 1st January 1920. A further batch of 212 ladies, covering all areas of England, Scotland and Wales, was appointed on 14th July. Lady Crewe's committee, however, were not the first ladies to become magistrates. Mrs Ada Summers, the Mayor of Stalybridge, became a justice *ex officio* as soon as the Act came into force on 23rd December 1919. From 1949 strenuous efforts were made to increase the proportion of women on each bench to ensure that there should be at least one present in every juvenile (and later domestic) court. As already mentioned, the proportion of women to men on the benches has risen from 1:3·5 in 1947 to 1:1·5 in 1983. In 1981 Lady Ralphs became the first lady to be elected chairman of the Council of the Magistrates' Association. This was in marked contrast to the appointment of women to legal judicial posts. The comparatively small number of women practitioners in the legal profession was largely accountable for the absence of women among the professional judiciary until fairly recently. The first appointment of a woman as a Stipendiary Magistrate was in 1945 and as a Recorder in 1956. The first woman County Court judge was appointed in 1962 and she (Dame Elizabeth Lane) was also the first to become a High Court judge, in 1965. In 1983 four women held office as Stipendiary Magistrates, 22 as Recorders (out of a total of 453), ten as Circuit judges (out of 342) and three as High Court judges (out of 77). None were in the Court of Appeal or among the Law Lords. Altogether seven women were appointed Stipendiary Magistrates between 1945 and 1983.

In 1978, an unsuccessful lady candidate for appointment as a justice took proceedings against the Lord Chancellor before an Industrial Tribunal which ruled that the case did not fall within its jurisdiction under the Sex Discrimination Act. It is a pity that it could not have been decided on the facts because for many years the Lord Chancellor's policy had been to increase the proportion of women magistrates and the principal obstacle in the way of achieving this had been the comparatively small number of women candidates who were forthcoming. Only about one woman to every twelve men is recommended to the Advisory Committees, though there is a greater need for their presence on the benches than ever before, especially having regard to the increased number of women and girls who now appear before the criminal courts. Generally speaking, women justices give more of their time to the work both in and out of court but tend to become more emotionally involved in the cases with which they have to deal.

Except for bankruptcy, there is virtually no statutory disqualification for appointment as a justice, but the Lord Chancellor has indicated a rather varied assortment of persons whom he is not prepared to consider, including police officers, traffic wardens, members of the regular armed forces, persons whose occupation would be incompatible with the duties of a magistrate and anyone who has been convicted of a serious offence or who, by reason of defective sight or hearing or other infirmity, cannot carry out all the duties of a justice. Close relatives must not serve in the same division. The most frequent ground for disqualification is age. The Lord Chancellor normally imposes a maximum age limit of 60 for first appointment, but as far as possible only persons below 50 are chosen. The lower limit is 21, but the youngest justice appointed since the war was 23. Twenty-four were below the age of 30.

Thirty years ago there seemed to be few people who were not interested in becoming justices. Today, although there are always plenty of suitable candidates, there is no longer the overwhelming eagerness to seek appointment that there was before. The change of attitude has been due to the increasing commitments and shortage of available time of all sections of the population and to the greater demands of the bench itself. In 1947, many justices regarded their office as one of social distinction only and those who were too busy to attend court just did not turn up. Today the Advisory Committees are alert to eliminate anyone who may regard the office as a status symbol and to see that no one gains appointment as a reward for services rendered. Those who are appointed must complete a minimum of 26 court sittings a year and will be relieved of office if they fail to do so; and they are also required to do their fair share of out-of-court work. Most of those who now seek appointment do so because they are genuinely interested in the work and are not motivated by a desire to improve their social status.

The aura of the minor knighthood, as H. G. Wells called it, has gone, but its reality when I first joined the Lord Chancellor's Office was very apparent and was revealed by the lengths to which people were prepared to go, and the tactics they would adopt, to obtain appointment for themselves or their associates. There were many occasions during my first years as Secretary of Commissions when I was offered inducements, sometimes backed up with veiled threats, to secure the appointment of some individual to the bench. What was particularly irksome about these episodes was that my indignant reaction was sometimes interpreted merely as dissatisfaction with the level of the price offered. On one occasion a certain individual sent me a case of whisky in support of his application, and when this was returned with the information that his name was no longer on the list of candidates he had the temerity to call at my office with an envelope containing £200 in cash.

It did not escape me that persons such as this, who were

prepared to risk both a criminal charge and the loss of what in those days was a considerable sum, might be motivated by considerations not entirely confined to social climbing and, with the assistance of Scotland Yard, we found that there were several ways in which an unscrupulous magistrate could gain considerable advantage, especially if he were a licensing justice.

Many of these incidents had political undertones. One day there came into my possession a list, prepared by the local branch of one of the principal political parties, which set out the honours it was thought should be bestowed upon those who had given good service to the party. The list included JP and its position was immediately below CBE. It was not unusual for a promise to be made during a parliamentary or local government election that a supporter of a successful candidate would be rewarded with appointment as a magistrate, and those who made these promises found themselves in an uncomfortable position if they could not honour them. Several individuals prominent in local government came to my office to tell me that their political future would be in jeopardy if those they had nominated were not appointed. The trouble was that these people excelled at nominating candidates who were manifestly unfit to administer justice and I fear that a number of promising political careers must have come to an abrupt end.

Although the reforms of the last forty years have led to a higher standard of choice the system of selection of lay magistrates is still not ideal. Too much emphasis is laid on political considerations and further attention needs to be given to means of obtaining a wider field of choice among all sectors of the population and of enabling Advisory Committees to spot in advance those who will make good justices.

Since 1970, Advisory Committees have been required to interview those candidates who seemed *prima facie* to be suitable for appointment. This avoided some of the unfortunate errors which occurred previously when many of those recommended to the Lord Chancellor had never been seen by a committee member, but there is still no detailed guidance to committees as to the qualifications for which they are looking; indeed no one has devised an empirical test of a candidate's suitability for judicial office. This applies also to the appointment of professional judges. Britain has an advantage over many countries in that its judges are appointed after they have shown their paces during years of practice as barristers or solicitors and while serving in temporary appointments as Recorders and deputy judges (now called assistant recorders), yet there are occasions when a man who has given every indication of being excellent judicial material while in practice is sadly disappointing when elevated to the full-time bench. It is normal practice for the Lord Chancellor, where he thinks it appropriate, to consult existing members of the judiciary on the merits of candidates. Mr Justice 'A' may say that in his opinion 'B' who has appeared before him as a practitioner would make a good judge; but does Mr Justice 'A' know what he is looking for? How can Advisory Committees hope to find the right answer when choosing laymen who may never have been in a court of law in their lives?

One needs to begin by defining the qualities that one is seeking and then to devise a means of determining whether or not a candidate possesses them. In 1970, I considered whether a system of aptitude tests could be added to the interviewing procedure. Anthony Webb, who was then Deputy Secretary of Commissions, examined the techniques used by appointment agencies in business management and other fields and he and I were convinced that there was a case for pursuing the project, but we were unable to obtain financial backing. Both we and those whom we consulted were also unable at that stage to contrive an effective method of determining the most essential quality of all: a judicial mind.

A great deal of research would be needed to isolate the essential characteristics of judicial office; and having done so one would need to train assessors in systematic interviewing. Short of this there seems to be no feasible alternative to the existing method, which has not been altogether sterile.

Attempts are made from time to time to have the present system replaced by something considered to be more 'democratic', usually meaning that access to the bench should be by popular election. Other parts of the world which have adopted the elective method, notably some of the States of America, have found that this is not the ideal answer. In June 1977, Mr Bruce Grocott, Member of Parliament for Lichfield and Tamworth, was given leave to introduce a Bill 'to provide for the democratic selection of magistrates', his proposal being that in future justices should be appointed on the nomination of district councils. Mr Grocott's Bill made no further progress, and I feel sure that anyone who has had much experience of the problem will agree that his is not the right solution. If the district councils themselves decide who is to be appointed the benches will tend to be confined to persons who have become prominent in the local government sphere to the exclusion of others and, as the County Councils' Association pointed out in 1947, the qualities needed to make a successful councillor are not necessarily those requisite for the bench (this is borne out by the experience in Denmark, where lay judges are nominated by local authorities). If everyone is to have a fair chance of being chosen it will be necessary to adopt some form of selection agency in each area similar to the present Advisory Committees, and one may question the wisdom of subjecting such a committee to the supervision of a district council or other authority which is, by its nature, a political body.

Those who seem to be in a position to take a disinterested and objective view of the problem are generally agreed that the present arrangements are basically right and that future action should be directed towards improving the existing machinery rather than to introducing something entirely new. Both the Royal Commissions on Justices of the Peace, after studying the question in considerable depth, came unanimously to the conclusion that, so long as the office of Justice of the Peace remains, the best method of appointment that can be devised is the present system based on Advisory Committees answerable to the head of the judiciary who, in this context, is answerable to Parliament.

5 The Political and Social Composition of the Magistracy

The Advisory Committee system was introduced primarily to curb political influence on the appointment of justices, but during the period up to 1949 it clearly failed to achieve this object because the committees themselves were overwhelmingly political. In many places recommendations were the outcome of party bargaining and it was common practice for members of a committee to fill vacancies in an agreed proportion, each accepting the nominees of the others. The worst example of this was in the county of London where appointments were invariably the result of a political carve-up. The committees therefore exacerbated the evil they were supposed to cure.

Three members of the 1948 Royal Commission expressed the view, in a dissenting memorandum, that provided that justices were drawn from every social class no regard should be had to political affiliations in the composition of Advisory Committees and of benches. I always shared this view and it was my constant hope that a day would come when the Lord Chancellor would state categorically that political views would be totally ignored in the selection of justices, but although some Chancellors would have liked to grasp this nettle none felt able to disregard political considerations entirely. One of the most politically minded Lord Chancellors was Lord Jowitt, who came to the Woolsack in the overwhelming Labour victory of 1945. Not surprisingly he was under immediate pressure to flood the benches with Labour appointments. Soon after he assumed office an impressive deputation from the party, headed by three Ministers, came to see him to press the issue. They pointed out that the benches were predominantly Conservative and included only a small proportion of Labour supporters. Now that Labour was in power the position should be reversed and they urged, indeed demanded, the immediate appointment of large numbers of Labour justices. One would have supposed from Lord Jowitt's record that he would have yielded readily to the powerful persuasion of the party which had brought him to office. In fact, in his reply, which I noted at the time, he did not yield an inch:

> Look here, what you fellows don't seem to understand is that I am now Lord Chancellor of Great Britain and as Lord Chancellor I am responsible for the administration of justice in this country. Kindly remember that when it comes to the administration of justice I don't care a damn about politics.

A few years later Lord Jowitt felt compelled to modify his views.

The Labour Government in 1945, confronted with gross under-representation of their supporters on the benches, as the Liberals had been in 1908, reacted in the same way and appointed a Royal Commission. In 1948 the Commission stated in their Report: 'We are of the opinion that it is not in the public interest that there should be an undue preponderance of justices drawn from one political party.' Soon afterwards Lord Jowitt asked me to issue to all Advisory Committees the following directive, which has been embodied in the philosophy of every subsequent Lord Chancellor:

> The Lord Chancellor cannot emphasise too often or too emphatically that the first and much the most important consideration in the selection and appointment of justices is that the candidates should be personally suitable in point of character, integrity and understanding and should be generally recognised as such by those among whom they live and work. . . . Subject to this overriding consideration Lord Jowitt is of opinion that it is impracticable to disregard political affiliations in making appointments. Once an adequate number of suitable persons is available it is of the very greatest importance (a) that they should be drawn from all sections of the community so as to represent a microcosm or cross-section of all shades of opinion and (b) that there should be no overweighting in favour of any one section . . . In carrying out the duty entrusted to him by the Crown the Lord Chancellor finds that political af-filiations are a convenient guide to follow but this does not imply that he will only appoint persons who are known to be

adherents of a particular party. Persons of no known political affiliations or those who are known to be independent of any party will also be appointed.

It was never the policy of Lord Jowitt or his successors to maintain 'proportional representation' on the benches. This would have been impossible as it would have involved the appointment of large numbers of new justices to redress the balance every time there was a swing at an election and further appointments might have been needed from time to time to counteract changes of political colour amongst existing justices. Furthermore, it was not always possible to persuade candidates and those already appointed to disclose their political views. Advisory Committees are not concerned therefore with maintaining a political balance but rather with avoiding an imbalance and with seeing that justices are appointed from different sectors of the community. In their search for candidates, committees approach local organisations and although these bodies are mostly non-political the majority of the persons they recommend tend to support the Conservative Party, with the result that many committees have more Conservative candidates than they require but are unable to find sufficient from Labour and the Liberals. Whenever new parties emerge committees are asked to bear them in mind when selecting candidates. Following this procedure the first Plaid Cymru justices were appointed in 1972 and the first SDP in 1981. The main sources of Labour recommendations are the Party itself and the trade unions. The only effective way in which most lower-paid workers can become known is through political activity and the majority of them choose to do so in the Labour Party. The unions, on the other hand, have many members who do not vote Labour but it is only the Labour supporters who are normally included in union recommendations for the bench.

It is not possible to give accurate figures for the political composition of the lay magistracy because the information must be obtained mainly from statements made by justices at the time of appointment. It would appear, however, that even in 1983 there was still a substantial preponderance of Conservatives over the other parties, the percentages being: Conservatives 41, Labour 28, Liberals 11, SDP 1, Plaid Cymru 0·3, and 'Independent and not known' 18·7.

Inability to eliminate political considerations from the appointment of justices was due only marginally to the political background of the Lord Chancellors themselves. No appointments to the professional judiciary have been made on party political grounds since the war, although there were plenty of earlier instances, and recent Lord Chancellors would probably have been prepared to apply the same policy to the lay magistracy if they had felt that this was the right course. Where their own political experience played a decisive role was in convincing them that the public would not believe that justice could truly be done by courts that were manifestly overweighted in favour of one party. Unlike whole-time professional judges and magistrates, who must not exhibit party allegiances after appointment to the bench, justices are not expected to be political neuters and many of them are active in their respective party organisations and are known to be so by the local community. Many members of both Houses of Parliament serve as magistrates (74 members of the Commons were justices in 1977 and so too were 121 peers, many of whom took a party whip). It cannot be claimed that benches have no political complexion for it is there for all to see, and it was on this ground that the ideal of total disregard of political allegiances in the appointment of justices was abandoned. On the other hand, steps were taken after 1949 to contain the political element within reasonable bounds and these went some way towards eliminating earlier defects, but there must always be a price to pay for democratisation of the courts. In spite of precautions there are still occasions when political bargaining is found to exist; but a greater danger arises from enforcement of the policy that no bench may be allowed to become overweighted by supporters of any one party. It is not at all unusual for the Lord Chancellor to refuse to accept recommendations because a certain party is under-represented. He may point out that the party in question polled many thousands of votes at the last election and may comment: 'Don't tell me that you cannot find one or two good candidates among all that number.' It is curious how difficult it sometimes is to do just that; and even when a candidate of the required political complexion is found he is not infrequently turned down as unsuitable by members of his own party on the Advisory Committee. Sometimes committees show great ingenuity in dressing up a candidate from one party in the guise of another to satisfy the Lord Chancellor's requirement. On one occasion Lord Hailsham was asked to fill a vacancy on a bench composed exclusively of Conservatives. The candidate recommended was another supporter of the same party but the committee, with fingers crossed, described him as a Liberal Conservative. Lord Hailsham wrote in the margin: 'A Liberal Conservative is a Conservative and not a Liberal, just as a fly button is a button and not a fly.'

The principal danger of insistence upon political balance, or avoidance of imbalance, is that it can lead to debasement of the standard of the bench. Members of Advisory Committees are busy people most of whom undertake the work because they regard it as a public duty. They receive neither remuneration nor any other reward; not even the satisfaction of public approval because their identity is usually not disclosed. It is understandable that a committee, when faced with refusal to accept its recommendations which are the fruit of long and careful search, will in desperation take the easy way out and put forward a candidate who satisfies the political criterion but is not of the calibre one would hope to find on the bench. This happens all too often, with disturbing results. In Chapter 11 reference is made to those magistrates, fortunately few in number, whose conduct falls short of what is required. About three in five of these were appointed in circumstances of the kind just described.

The Lord Chancellor's contention that it ought not to be too difficult to discover just a few suitable candidates among several thousand voters is not unreasonable. Lord Elwyn-Jones gave a great deal of thought to solving this problem and he enlisted the help of the Labour Party and the TUC. Both General Secretaries, Len Murray and Ron Hayward, agreed to assist in finding suitable candidates through their respective organisations while accepting the Lord Chancellor's insistence that the choice must turn on suitability for the job and not on the candidates' service to the party or union. The results were disappointing. By the time the recruiting scheme passed to regional and local level the emphasis on judicial quality was forgotten and was replaced by the old bogey of swamping benches with leading Labour and union supporters (in total disregard of the Chancellor's warning that these tactics were bound to be detrimental to the party and union image). Some branch organisations demanded the right to nominate members of Advisory Committees and even to have their own nominees appointed to the bench without question. In many areas the Lord Chancellor's well-conceived plan was totally misconstrued and merely served to generate a militant reaction.

The redeployment of Advisory Committees with a sub-committee infrastructure went some way towards solving the problem because the sub-committees were better equipped than the committees for larger areas to acquire an intimate knowledge of each petty sessional division and of the local sources from which reliable information and recommendations could be obtained. A sub-committee may be prone to parochialism but this can be rectified by the main committee through which recommendations must be processed. This is about as far as one can hope to go towards curing the remaining shortcomings of the present system, unless the committees are expanded still further and provided with ample whole-time staff, which cannot be contemplated with the resources now available.

Conflicting opinions on the need to avoid political disparity on the commissions has been paralleled by controversy over the social-class composition of the magistracy. As long ago as 1910, the Royal Commission stated: 'It is in the public interest that persons of every social grade should be appointed Justices of the Peace', and for many years Advisory Committees have been required not only to prevent political imbalance but to ensure that each bench represents a social and occupational cross-section of the local community.

There is a general but erroneous belief that the Lord Chancellor attaches more importance to political than to social balance. Several Lord Chancellors are on record as saying that an occupational spread is by far the more important consideration. Lord Hailsham constantly urged Advisory Committees to find more wage-earners and Lord Gardiner stated more than once that if a bench was short of Labour and wage-earning justices he would rather appoint a Conservative manual worker than a business-man who was a member of the Labour Party. But it is often more difficult to find a manual worker who is able and willing to serve than a Labour supporter. If approached, many wage-earners are not prepared to let their names go forward. Some are uninterested, some fear that their jobs or promotion prospects may be adversely affected by their absence when on the bench. Some have told me that their appointment would be unpopular with their mates on the factory floor, especially if they are part of a team. Many wage-earners with whom I have spoken seemed to attach more weight to these considerations than to the possible loss of a day's pay; and this is borne out by the fact that there was no noticeable improvement in recruitment after a loss-of-earnings allowance was introduced by the Justices of the Peace Act 1968. In rural areas, where one would expect to draw freely on the agricultural workers, it is particularly difficult to find wage-earners willing to serve. In 1966, Lord Collison, the General Secretary of the National Union of Agricultural Workers, undertook at Lord Gardiner's request to find a few of his members to serve as justices. After nine months only two candidates were forthcoming in the whole of five counties.

The appointment of wage-earners to the bench has been criticised on the grounds that a magistrate needs to have knowledge and experience extending beyond his own limited occupation and social class and this cannot be expected of one who spends his life doing a routine job and who takes no prominent part in the community. How, it is asked, can such a person have sufficient breadth of outlook and know enough about the problems of the rest of the population to be able to give sound judgment in the varied and sometimes complex cases which come before the court? This is true, but I would make the point that not only are there some wage-earners who are active in other spheres but also, although the outlook of the factory-floor worker may be limited, he does know more than anyone else about the way of life of his work-mates and, although such a man may be unable to take the chair or to play a positive part in the proceedings when the court is concerned with other types of case, his contribution can be invaluable when dealing with factory workers, who constitute an appreciable part of the population.

The social class composition of benches has long been one of the greatest sources of controversy in the magisterial field. Roger Hood of Cambridge, after conducting a survey in 1965–7, concluded that, whereas in terms of sex and age, the magistracy was becoming more broadly representative of the wider community, 'there seems to be no evidence of any significant changes in the social-class backgrounds from which magistrates came in the years between 1946 and the second half of the 1960s'.[1] In 1976, John Baldwin of Birmingham University, after studying a sample of magistrates appointed between 1971 and 1972, formed the opinion that 'the extremely narrow social base from which magistrates were drawn in the immediate post-war years still remains'. If it is true that magistrates are not drawn from a wider social spectrum than they were forty years ago a great deal of time-consuming effort by seven Lord Chancellors and their staff has been totally misdirected.

The difficulty is to compare like with like. Baldwin was comparing newly appointed justices with the whole body of magistrates covered by the Royal Commission's figures in 1948. His analysis of a sample of 255 new justices, out of a total of 1527 appointed during the period, was necessarily based for the purpose of comparison on the Royal Commission's classification in 1948 and he very fairly observes that this is not easy to apply. The last two of the six classes in the classification were: '(5) salaried employees who fall outside other groups'; and '(6) wage-earners'. The two classes at the top end of the scale were: '(1) those without gainful employment' and '(2) professional people'. Baldwin's own analysis shows that the proportion of justices in his sample who were not gainfully employed dropped between 1947 and 1972 from 3·5 per cent to 0·6 per cent in the case of men and from 16·7 per cent to 3·5 per cent in the case of women. At the other end of the scale however, the wage-earners also dropped from 15 per cent to 13·1 per cent men and from 7·7 per cent to 3·5 per cent women. Baldwin comments that this 'shows clearly the total absence of any extension of the working-class representation on the bench'. This is not a fair picture because it implies that those at the bottom of the scale, who are usually assumed to be the most numerous section of the population, are under-represented on the bench, whereas it could be said that they are also represented by many of the justices falling into some of the other categories and who have increased in number since 1947. One of the difficulties arises from the definition of 'wage-earner', which is currently taken to mean a person paid on a weekly basis. The fact is that the proportion of the population who are weekly wage-earners is smaller now than it was forty years ago and a large number of people who might fairly be regarded as representative of this class are now salaried workers. It must be assumed that this trend will continue, for Britain is one of the few Western countries which still maintains the old form of wages system. Elsewhere wage packets are things of the past and every worker has an account into which a salary is paid, mostly at monthly intervals. An interesting corollary of this is that the hijacking of security vehicles is a much more popular pastime among criminals in

Britain than it is in other countries, where they are not so out of date as to carry around in vans large sums of cash for wages.

According to the Lord Chancellor's records,[2] the number of manual workers on the commission at the end of 1977 amounted to 8·2 per cent of the total but some of these were not paid by the week. On the other hand, those employed in clerical work accounted for 5·7 per cent, but not all these were paid a weekly wage and some received a salary. Going to the other end of the scale, one might assume that class (2) 'professional people' would be composed largely of the legal and medical professions and the armed forces. In fact the law accounted for only 1·4 per cent and the forces 1·1 per cent (serving members of the armed forces and of the police are disqualified from appointment as justices). The medical profession (including dentists and pharmacists) provided a sizeable element of 10 per cent, but the largest contingent in the 'professional' class (and also the largest among all occupations) was in education, which made up 12·5 per cent of the total and these included a fairly wide spectrum of university, technical college and school teachers (teachers have made a significant contribution to the magistracy, and an even larger number of justices would probably have been drawn from the profession were it not for their difficulty in getting time off to attend court and also the fact that, as local authority employees they, like councillors, are disqualified from hearing cases in which the authority is involved). Furthermore, the class (2) 'professionals' also included trade union officials. Figures are not available of trade unionists on the benches in 1947 but in 1952 whole-time officials amounted to 1·2 per cent of the total of justices, whereas in 1977 they accounted for 2·7 per cent. Although these justices are not counted as wage-earners they are obviously representative of that section of the population, and the Lord Chancellor would place them in that category when deciding whether a list of recommendations contained a sufficient proportion of wage-earner candidates.

In my own experience some of the best magistrates have been men and women with moderate political views in the trade union movement. They had wide experience and understanding of human nature and human failings and their judgment was invariably wise and sound. We need more of these justices but often people who are recommended through their union seem unable to adopt a wholly unbiased approach when sitting in judgment on their fellow creatures (as their colleagues on the Advisory Committees are the first to point out). One or two trade union justices have resigned from the bench because they found it embarrassing to adjudicate when members of their own or of other unions were before the court. One of them told me that he found it particularly difficult because he felt that the sentences imposed in these cases by his middle- and upper-class colleagues were far too lenient. They readily accepted the statement of the accused as to his means and financial commitments, which indicated that he could not afford to pay even the smallest fine. The union official knew better.

If one looks only at those in the lowest social class it cannot be denied that their share of magisterial appointments has not increased significantly since 1947 despite the efforts of the Lord Chancellor's Office. There are several reasons for this. First, there is the reluctance, already noted, of wage-earners to become magistrates. Secondly, the channels of recommendation do not work as effectively for wage-earners as for other groups; the unions, the Labour Party and other bodies, when asked to put forward candidates, seldom include rank-and-file workers. Thirdly, there is a reluctance, even among wage-earners themselves, to regard persons in this category as being wholly qualified to administer justice. If one may take account of comments made to me by wage-earners who have become involved in court cases, it would seem that they prefer to be tried by someone who is not a member of their own class. The right of every Englishman to be tried by his peers is not of overriding importance on these occasions.

There is a widespread assumption that any magistrate who is not a wage-earner must be at the other end of the spectrum and is probably a large landowner or a company director. There are certainly many such people on the commissions but they are not predominant. Company directors make up 10·5 per cent of the total and the managerial class accounts for a further 10·6 per cent. Landowners are now far fewer than in 1945 and they, combined with tenant farmers, come to only 6·5 per cent. Obviously the percentage is higher in the rural areas where the land-owning and farming justices are concentrated, but who else is able and willing to undertake the work in these places? Agricultural workers are reluctant to do so and this leaves only a few shop keepers, doctors, clergy and a sprinkling of employees of the local authority, all of whom are represented on the country benches. Thirty years ago we drew heavily on railway workers (who made excellent magistrates and were usually allowed plenty of time off to attend their courts), but the closure of the railways has dried up this source of supply and in many country districts there is not even a bus whose driver can be enlisted.

The categories of person required to complete a bench must mirror the social structure of the community it serves and they will therefore change as the principal elements in the population change. In recent years a new factor has appeared in the sudden development of large immigrant populations in some parts of the country, where they have brought with them novel and formidable problems, not least in the sphere of the law. By the early 1960s it seemed desirable to try to find a few immigrants who could serve as magistrates and thus give confidence to the others and encourage them to uphold the law. In 1961 I sent a circular to Advisory Committees in areas where these problems had arisen, asking them to consider the appointment of members of the immigrant community to the bench. Several committees had already given thought to the question and, in April 1962, the Nottingham committee submitted the name of Mr E. G. Irons, a West Indian engaged in welfare work, who became the first immigrant magistrate.[3] By the end of 1977 78 immigrants, mostly from the West Indies, India and Pakistan, had been appointed to benches throughout the country and since then there has been a steady increase in the number of non-white justices. Some were distinguished individuals, such as Lord Pitt and Professor O. R. Marshall, and in most cases the experiment proved to be highly successful. Some, however, were unable to withstand the pressures to which they were subjected. They faced problems with which the indigenous white population was not confronted. They were not only links between their own community and the administration of the law but, as magistrates, they were obliged to deal with all classes of persons who came before the courts and their knowledge and understanding of other sectors of the population was often limited. Moreover, some areas contained several different racial groups and a justice appointed from one group was not always accepted by the others. There were instances where such an appointment, far from pleasing the immigrant population as a whole, provoked demands for the immediate appointment of representatives from the other groups.

Understandably, some justices drawn from ethnic minorities found the pressure too great and resigned. Two just disappeared without trace. Three were convicted of offences requiring their removal. In all about one in ten of those appointed have left the bench but most of those who remain are doing excellent work and are an asset to the community. The first non-white stipendiary was Anura Cooray, a native of Sri Lanka, who was appointed in London in 1982. (Only a few days later the first non-white Circuit Judge, Mota Singh, QC, a Sikh, was appointed.)

The controversy over the social composition of the magistracy usually turns upon whether benches are predominantly upper-class to the exclusion of the rest of the population. The Lord Chancellor does not seek to strike a numerical balance between representatives of each social group; there seems to be no good reason why he should do so and it would be impossible to achieve this result because of the movement of individuals from one group to another. The declared policy of each Lord Chancellor since 1945 has been to make sure that each bench is a microcosm of the local community within which it operates, and this amounts to seeing that in every petty sessional division there are at least some justices from each of the principal social and political groups in the area and that the bench is not dominated by any one group. I would claim that we have gone a long way towards attaining this object.

6 Training

Until fairly recently it was generally assumed that every person appointed to judicial office was endowed by nature with the ability to dispense justice and needed no guidance or instruction in his duties. This view persisted in respect of the judges and Stipendiary Magistrates until the 1960s, and even in the case of lay justices training was not regarded as a matter of importance before 1948. Before that time law and procedure were fairly simple and easy to understand. Training became necessary when Parliament began making the magistrates' duties more complex and started introducing new sentencing options with a wealth of restrictive detail in the operation of these options.

The term 'training' when applied to any branch of the judiciary is open to objection on the ground that training provides the means of influencing or conditioning the mind of the trainee and when applied to judges could constitute a threat to judicial independence. The point has provided interesting exercises in semantics but, although in 1978 a working party under Lord Justice Bridge[1] (as he then was) suggested 'judicial studies' as an alternative, 'training' has been used generally in this context throughout the period and appears exclusively in Statutes and I have therefore adopted it in this chapter.

The first steps towards systematic and co-ordinated training were taken by the Magistrates' Association, which was founded expressly for the training of justices and whose Royal Charter, granted in 1962, states that one of the Association's objects is to 'educate and instruct magistrates in the law, the administration of justice, the treatment of offenders and the best methods of preventing crime'. The Association encouraged justices to undertake some measure of training and it provided the means in the form of meetings, conferences and literature, but it received no assistance from the government until 1970 when an annual contribution to its training expenses began to be made in a grant from the Lord Chancellor's Department.[2] The response to the

Association's efforts was disappointing and by 1949 the great majority of justices had had no training of any kind.

The Royal Commission of 1948 concluded that justices ought to receive some instruction and they recommended that every justice on appointment should give an undertaking to follow a course and not to adjudicate until he had done so. This recommendation was not accepted at that time because it was thought that some well-qualified persons might be deterred from accepting appointment if they were not certain that they would be able to honour the undertaking. It was also felt to be unnecessary. If the system of selection operated effectively one should be able to assume that those who became justices were the sort of people who would do all they could, without additional incentive, to fit themselves for the work. By and large this assumption proved to be correct, but there were exceptions that could not be ignored.

The first statutory recognition of magisterial training appeared in Section 17 of the Justices of the Peace Act 1949, which required each of the new Magistrates' Courts Committees set up under the Act to make and administer schemes of instruction in accordance with arrangements approved by the Lord Chancellor. The Section was not brought into operation until April 1953 because it was necessary first to set up the committees and to let them settle down, but in the meantime the Lord Chancellor's Office circulated a model scheme to assist committees in framing their plans. Between 1953 and 1954 almost all committees adopted the model scheme or evolved ones of their own based closely upon it. This did not mean, however, that thereafter training was undertaken by all newly appointed justices throughout the country. Although most committees discharged their duties conscientiously (some were over-enthusiastic and endeavoured to provide schemes which were unreasonably lavish and costly) there were a few who made little attempt to comply with their training obligations; and even where courses were provided, not all justices availed themselves of them, not so much because they were uninterested but because they were prevented from attending by their other commitments or by difficulties of transport.

This state of affairs was not immediately apparent to the Lord Chancellor because he had no inspectorate and no means of monitoring the schemes and assessing their effectiveness. When he did become aware of the position there was little that he could do because there were no sanctions for failure either by committees to provide adequate schemes or by individual justices to participate in them. In an effort to meet some of the deficiencies the Lord Chancellor's Office and the Magistrates' Association co-operated in preparing a postal course, and between 1955 and 1965 this was taken by over 3000 justices at their own expense. In one way or another justices in general profited from training during this period and the standard of work improved noticeably in consequence; but by 1960 it was clear that the benefits would be limited unless the system was radically improved.

At that time two courses of action seemed to me to be essential: the assumption of direct control of training by the Lord Chancellor (to which I return later) and the introduction of obligatory training, at least for newly appointed justices. By obligatory I meant an obligation not only on all new justices to undergo training (most of them were keen enough to do so anyway), but also on the Magistrates' Courts Committees to see that everyone received it.

There were still many who argued that all training was profitless and that no extension of the existing system could be justified. This was the almost unanimous opinion of the professional judges and was shared by successive Lord Chancellors from 1951 to 1964. Some members of the Magistrates' Association on the other hand took a different view and began in 1961 to canvass obligatory training for all new justices. At the Association's Annual General Meeting in 1962 a resolution was passed by a majority of 4:1 urging 'amending legislation to provide a basic form of obligatory training to be completed by newly appointed justices before taking up magisterial duties'. This was not accepted by the Lord Chancellor and when Lord Dilhorne succeeded to the Woolsack in 1963 he was more firmly convinced than his predecessors that training could serve no useful purpose. He agreed, however, to reconsider the Association's resolution and, after careful study of the supporting evidence, he was converted to the view that at least some form of training was desirable and that there was a case for replacing the voluntary basic courses with an obligatory system.

It was not altogether clear how best this new policy could be implemented. I therefore submitted proposals to the Lord Chancellor for the establishment of a national body to study the implications of the project and to advise him on the planning and implementation of the modified system. The proposals, if accepted, would entail some increase in the Lord Chancellor's staff to service the new advisory body and to conduct the additional work within the Office, and I therefore recommended the creation of a new post of Magistrates' Training Officer (not an altogether apt title) to be filled by someone of considerable standing and experience.

No one was more effective than Lord Dilhorne at getting something done once he was convinced that it ought to be done and, having accepted my proposals, he allowed no time to elapse before securing their approval by the Government. The proposals could be implemented by administrative action without legislation and, in June 1964, Lord Dilhorne announced the appointment of a National Advisory Council on the Training of Magistrates, under the chairmanship of Sir Carl Aarvold, the Recorder of London; at the same time Anthony Webb, an English barrister and former Attorney-General of Kenya, was appointed training officer and secretary to the Council. These arrangements were well received by Parliament and the public, the press taking delight in announcing that magistrates were to be sent back to school.

After exhaustive enquiries into the working of the existing system the National Advisory Council found that newly appointed justices were almost unanimously of the opinion that they needed some form of basic training and many thought that it should be compulsory. The Council accordingly prepared a syllabus for the basic training of new justices and of those newly appointed to juvenile court panels. In both cases instruction was to be carried out in two stages, the first to be completed before the justice adjudicated in court, or served on the panel, and the second within a year of appointment to the bench or the panel.

In a White Paper published in 1965 the Government indicated their intention to implement these proposals and obligatory basic and juvenile court training was introduced for all justices appointed in England and Wales from 1st January 1966. (It later became obligatory for members of domestic court panels.) Recognising the voluntary nature of a justice's service it was decided not to impose compulsory training by Statute but to require each person who was approved for appointment to give an undertaking that, if appointed, he would complete a prescribed course within a year and would tender his resignation if, for any reason, he failed to do so. It has been rare for an appointment to be terminated in these circumstances. In the few cases where a justice has not completed the course within the required period there has usually been a sound reason and he has been given an extension of time.

Since 1966 no new justice has objected to obligatory basic training, and it has been noticeable that those appointed since then have been more assiduous in attending refresher courses than those appointed earlier.

The National Advisory Council also prepared a comprehensive *Handbook* for new justices which was sent by the Lord Chancellor's Office to every justice on appointment from 1974. The *Handbook* superseded an earlier booklet, called *Notes for New Magistrates*, which had been sent to all new justices from 1953 onwards. This booklet (an adaptation of one previously published by the Magistrates' Association) was elementary and would have been replaced much earlier had my office been able to devote sufficient time to producing a more comprehensive work. Even the Advisory Council's *Handbook* was not exhaustive and, like its predecessor, it contained no guidance on the treatment of offenders. This lacuna was filled by a separate booklet entitled *The Sentence of the Court*, which was published by the Home Office in 1964 following a recommendation by the Streatfeild Committee that there should be a booklet of general information for sentencers. It was issued by the Lord Chancellor's Office to every newly appointed justice and also to judges and Stipendiary Magistrates. These publications soon became outdated and needed constant revision to keep abreast of changes in the law. It was a serious defect of the training system that sufficient resources were not available to undertake this work, and from time to time we were obliged to consider whether more harm would be done by distributing obsolete manuals than by not issuing any at all. The *Notes* and their successor, the *Handbook*, were kept reasonably up to date by addenda but by 1974 *The Sentence of the Court* had become so antiquated, following a spate of legislation on the treatment of offenders, that it was decided to cease circulation until a new edition could be written. Regrettably this was not completed until the summer of 1978 and for four years magistrates and the higher judiciary were without any book of reference on their sentencing powers.

The National Advisory Council had been set up to consider, and if thought desirable to implement, proposals for obligatory training. By 1973 it had completed its task and was disbanded; but there was no question of dispensing with an advisory body, indeed there was greater need than ever before for a standing committee, with wider terms of reference than the Council, to keep the whole concept of magisterial training under constant review. In 1974 the Lord Chancellor replaced the Council with an Advisory Committee whose duty was to advise him generally upon the training of magistrates. The Committee included representatives of the Magistrates' Association, Magistrates' Courts Committees, justices' clerks, the Home Office and members of the legal and teaching professions. Mr Justice Boreham was appointed chairman and I was vice-chairman. The Committee as a whole meets about four times a year to formulate policy and submit recommendations to the Lord Chancellor, but a great deal of work is done by sub-committees on specific projects, which have included the production of new handbooks for basic and specialist training and of manuals for the guidance of those responsible for administering the training schemes. The days of the Committee are clearly numbered and it seems probable that it will be absorbed into the Judicial Studies Board mentioned below.

A feature of all magisterial training in this country has been the emphasis placed on the importance of sentencing. Since 1952 basic training has included visits to penal institutions and, in addition, sentencing exercises for justices have been organised on an increasing scale since the mid-1950s. In May 1977, the Lord Chancellor informed the Magistrates' Courts Committees that he wished every justice to participate in an exercise at least once every two years and preferably every year. The aim of the exercises was not only to help justices to acquire sentencing expertise and an understanding of penology but, by bringing together justices from a wide area, to minimise disparity in the level of sentences imposed by different justices and different benches. With this object exercises and conferences were held nationally as well as regionally. An exercise was always included in the annual training conference of the Magistrates' Association and in 1969 the Lord Chief Justice held an exercise for the chairmen of benches throughout England and Wales at the Royal Courts of Justice.

For many years various courses were available on a voluntary basis for the more experienced justices, but in 1977 the Advisory

Committee decided by a majority to advise the Lord Chancellor to introduce obligatory refresher training. Some members of the Committee saw practical objections to this. They thought that justices would resent compulsion beyond their basic training and that some persons would be deterred from accepting appointment by the prospect of being subject to obligatory training throughout their service. It was also feared that Magistrates' Courts Committees and training officers would be unable to accept the additional burden of work involved in monitoring the system and ensuring that every justice complied with the requirements. Enforcement presented a special problem. What action should be taken if justices failed to follow the training? If they were to be dismissed the benches might lose many experienced and valuable magistrates.

The Lord Chancellor's Office had always been of the opinion that the difficulties inherent in operating compulsory refresher training outweighed the advantages, but in 1976 the two key elements in the training process, the Central Council of Magistrates' Courts Committees representing the training authorities and the Magistrates' Association on behalf of the trainees, both urged the introduction of obligatory courses at regular intervals throughout a justice's career. The Justices' Clerks Society, representing those upon whom the administration of the courses would mainly fall, remained sceptical, but by the end of 1977 they had come to accept what seemed inevitable, provided that the clerks received better financial recognition for their services. After consulting all interested bodies the Advisory Committee recommended that every justice appointed after 1st January 1979 should be required, in addition to his other assurances, to undertake to attend approved training totalling not less than twelve hours every three years.

The Lord Chancellor hesitated for some time to accept these recommendations lest they should lead to the loss of numbers of good justices. He was finally convinced by the discovery that the great majority of justices already underwent as much voluntary refresher training as could reasonably be expected of them and therefore the introduction of compulsory further training would not add to their burden, but on the other hand, about 20 per cent never attended anything beyond their court sittings after completing their basic training. To deal with this minority he finally directed that obligatory refresher training as proposed by the

Committee should be introduced for all justices appointed after 1st January 1980.

The scope of training is inevitably limited by the availability of the trainees. Justices are ordinary citizens who undertake important but onerous and unremunerated public work which makes substantial demands upon their time. It is a tribute to their dedication that all but a very few are prepared, and even keen, to accept training on top of their regular duties, but the time at their disposal is limited. Training strategy is therefore governed by the necessity to compromise between giving every justice the instruction he needs to fit him for his work and his capacity to undergo it. Sophisticated teaching projects which may be highly beneficial to the justices must be ruled out as impracticable. Useful items have had to be omitted from existing schemes and it is for this reason, for instance, that the work of the probation officer is incompletely understood by a large number of justices. Public demands for magistrates to be given more training must be rejected because additional commitments would be beyond their capacity.

In 1972 courses in the Welsh language were introduced for justices in Wales. Those who appear in the courts in Wales often speak in Welsh and, although many of the justices are also Welsh-speaking, some are not. (In 1973 an enquiry conducted by the Lord Chancellor's Office showed that out of a total of 120 petty sessional divisions in Wales 47 were in a position to provide justices and a clerk who could conduct a trial entirely in Welsh.) By 1977 more than 300 magistrates had attended the language course.

The success of any scheme must depend to a large extent upon those who operate it and, in the case of magistrates' training, this means the Magistrates' Courts Committees and, above all, the training officers. Each committee is required to appoint a training sub-committee and one or more training officers who operate with the guidance of manuals and notes issued by the Lord Chancellor's Office. A few training officers serve on a whole-time basis but most are part-time. The majority are justices' clerks. The predominance of the clerks was the inevitable consequence of the localised training established by the 1949 Act, which has been conducted mainly in the justice's own court area. A clerk is generally well fitted to discharge this duty but there are certain qualifications. The clerks' primary function is to act as clerks of the courts and for many of them this, together with their office work, leaves no time for other activities except at the expense of some of their traditional duties. Furthermore, not all clerks are endowed with the gift of teaching and most have little opportunity to acquire it. It is also claimed that it is wrong for a clerk to be in charge of the training of his own justices lest they should thereafter look to him implicitly for direction in all their duties, including the exercise of their personal discretion.

Since 1966 universities and other centres of higher education have come to play an increasing role in magisterial training. Universities have the advantages of experience in the practical organisation of courses and of ample accommodation and facilities for residential courses. They also possess a ready source of skill in the education of mature students such as magistrates. Greater use could be made of universities than has been done so far, but responsibility for training magistrates cannot be transferred to them completely. Instruction needs to be practical and empirical and some university teachers adopt a too academic approach. Those responsible for training must also be completely familiar with the objects it is designed to achieve. Universities may have varied views on what they would wish the magistracy to be like. They should assist in creating a better magistracy but should not be able to create a magistracy of their own choosing.

During the past fifty years no section of the community has taken a greater interest in the magistrates' courts than the teaching profession, particularly those engaged in higher education. A considerable number of eminent academic lawyers have served as justices; and not a few young advocates, when appearing for the first time in the magistrates' court of a university town, have misguidedly come prepared to impress the bench with their esoteric knowledge of the law only to find the Professor of Law in the chair. Many distinguished members of university faculties, like Professors Sir Carleton Allen of Oxford, Winifred Cavenagh of Birmingham, A. N. Allott of London and R. M. Jackson of Cambridge, have played an active part in magisterial affairs far beyond their own commissions. Outstanding among university contributions to magisterial training has been that of the extra-mural department of the University of Birmingham, where Dr Denis Gray, himself a justice and a member of the national Advisory Committee and Chairman of the Central Council of Magistrates' Courts Committees, organised frequent courses and seminars covering a wide field.

Dr Gray also pioneered video and sound tapes as training aids for justices. Visual instruction, particularly in court procedure, has obvious advantages and, as long ago as 1951, a training film entitled 'Four Men in Prison' was made to enable justices to appreciate the effect of different custodial sentences. There seemed to be considerable merit in this form of training technique, but the 1951 experiment had a cool reception and in view of the cost of production (£50,000 at that time) it was not repeated. Video tapes, however, are not only much cheaper than films to produce and distribute but have other advantages, including the instantaneous filming of audience participation; though they too have not come up to initial expectations. They are most effective when in the charge of an experienced tutor and they are not satisfactory when there is a large audience because it is difficult to produce the relaxed discussion that this form of exercise demands.

Training when first introduced consisted mainly of formal lectures, but the emphasis now is upon informal discussion-groups and practical exercises. The syllabus for the second stage of basic training requires that at least three of the ten sessions should be wholly devoted to some form of exercise, thus fulfilling the Chinese proverb, quoted in the Lord Chancellor's Office pamphlet *Basic Training for Juvenile Court Magistrates*: 'I hear and I forget, I see and I remember, I do and I understand'. All schemes are intended to have a heuristic value, and their objectives are to provide essential information, to promote skills, encourage a judicial and questioning approach and build up self-confidence (nothing does more to destroy public confidence than a court's obvious lack of confidence in its own ability).

In theory it may seem superfluous for mature men and women who have been carefully chosen for their experience and personal qualities to be required to undergo formal training beyond that gained by attending court. The most essential qualification for the magistracy is a judicial mind and sound common sense, which are congenital qualities; nevertheless, if present in embryo, they can be developed with training and experience. The 1948 Royal Commission observed: 'Judicial conduct is not ensured by intellectual ability or even by the possession of a suitable temperament, it is a specialised discipline or technique that has to be learned.'

Although there can be no substitute for practical experience, the work of magistrates has become so complex that no one should be expected to undertake it without some prior explanation of what it is all about. A justice who has had no basic instruction will be unable to make much useful contribution to the proceedings until he has had years of experience and, in the meantime, his ignorance may cause considerable damage. Before adjudicating a justice needs to be familiar with the mechanics of the court room, the basic rules of procedure and the functions which he and others in court are required to perform. He should acquire some knowledge of legal terminology and must know enough about the rules of evidence to avoid mistakes in the questions he asks. He must learn that criminal procedure in this country involves proving guilt and not necessarily finding the whole truth. He must also be disabused of any prejudices to which he may be subject. Usually justices are quick to grasp that the first principle of adjudication is to reach a decision on the evidence alone and not on any predisposition; but occasionally even experienced justices err in this regard. In 1974 a bench chairman stated that, other things being equal, he made it a rule to believe the police. He ought to have learned not only to give the accused the benefit of the doubt but also to keep his mouth shut.

A justice cannot become master of all the skills involved in proceedings in magistrates' courts. In particular he cannot be an expert lawyer, and he should not be encouraged to think that he can. Lord Goddard, LCJ, in his evidence to the 1948 Royal Commission, pointed out that justices are not reproved for being wrong in law but that failure to act judicially is a reason for censure. The vast majority of decisions which justices have to make turn on questions of fact; when they do meet a point of law they should seek the advice of their clerk.

An evaluation of justices' training was carried out in several studies by Dr Nigel Lemon, later collaborating with Dr Roderick Bond, between 1971 and 1982.[3] Their conclusions were that experience and training were more likely to affect a justice's knowledge of procedure and of the sentencing practices of his bench than his own views on penal philosophy and policy. Furthermore, as a result of their experience they become increasingly cynical of defendants and the prospects of their reform and more committed to the aims of deterrence and punishment. The training programme, however, cannot be held responsible for such effects and is likely to ameliorate rather than exaggerate the influence of experience.

As facilities for training are extended the defects of the present system dating from 1949 become more apparent. The 1948 Royal Commission took the view that local conditions varied so greatly that centralised administration of training would be impracticable. Localisation of control also found support on the ground that it was wrong in principle for the executive, in the form of the Lord Chancellor or the Home Secretary, to direct the teaching given to persons holding judicial office. It was this rather than the practical advantages of decentralisation which led to the 1949 Act placing responsibility for training on the Magistrates' Courts Committees financed by the local authorities. It was a mistaken view because it contemplated the Lord Chancellor solely in his executive capacity and ignored the fact that he was also head of the judiciary and already exercised direct supervision over judges and magistrates through his power of removal, a duty he traditionally exercised in a judicial manner. Had this point been taken in 1949 the shortcomings that have impeded the system up to the present time could have been avoided.

If it is accepted that justices need training it would be difficult to devise a less efficacious system for ensuring that they get it than that provided by the 1949 Act now re-enacted in the Justices of the Peace Act 1979. Responsibility rests primarily with the Magistrates' Courts Committees but there is no sanction compelling them to discharge this duty. The cost is borne by the local authorities but they have no say in the manner in which the committees spend the money. If an authority objects to a committee's expenditure they may appeal to the Home Secretary, but he is not the Minister concerned with training and is hardly in a position to know whether or not the expense is justified. In any event, the Home Secretary can only disallow a payment, he cannot compel a committee to spend money on training if it does not choose to do so. On the side-lines stands the Lord Chancellor, who has the responsibility of finding the right people to serve as magistrates and of seeing that they do their job properly after appointment, but who, although his approval is required before a committee can administer a scheme, has no means of ensuring that they administer it in the manner he thinks best, or indeed that they operate it at all.

All the early attempts to remedy the present inadequacies by giving the Lord Chancellor more effective oversight of the system met with opposition, and it was not until 1973 that the Administration of Justice Act gave him powers of direct intervention. The Act provided that if a Magistrates' Courts Committee did not administer courses of instruction to the Lord Chancellor's satisfaction he might step in and make good the default and recover the cost from the committee. The Act also enabled the Lord Chancellor to provide additional training himself and to pay for it out of central funds.

In spite of these provisions the system still falls short of what is needed to ensure that justices are trained in the most efficacious and economic manner. Responsibility is still fragmented and the weakness of the system has been particularly apparent in the last few years, when important new recommendations by the Advisory Committee on Training have coincided with a period of financial stringency. Many of the committee's proposals have met with widespread approval but attempts to implement them have in some cases been baulked by Magistrates' Courts Committees and local authorities. The Lord Chancellor might enforce the proposals by exercising his powers under the 1973 Act, but that would be an unsatisfactory way to proceed. It may well be that none of the committee's recommendations for general or specific training should be implemented in the present financial climate, but this is a question that should be decided on its own merits. Local councils naturally point to the Government's strict limits on expenditure, and any additional cost of training magistrates must be met by a corresponding cut-back on something else which the council may regard as being of more importance. Magistrates' Courts Committees may be more ready than local authorities to see the advantages of improved training, but they too are local bodies and many, though not all, have close links with their councils, whose views they tend to support. The Lord Chancellor, whose duty it is to formulate national policy, should also have scope to carry it into effect and should then be answerable for the result and be responsible for budgeting and for justifying the cost.

Expenditure on training has always been negligible. Most of the annual cost arises from the allowances paid to justices when following courses (justices who attend a training function approved by the Lord Chancellor are entitled to the same allowances as when they attent court). Very little is spent on the training machinery itself. The idea of training the judiciary may have a certain popular attraction, but it is in no way comparable to the political appeal of the social services and some other beneficiaries from the public purse. Nearly thirty years after Parliament recognised the need for justices to have training the total annual amount spent on such training in England and Wales was about £150,000, less than 0·3 per cent of the £43 million spent on running the magistrates' courts.

This chapter has been dealing with the training of lay justices. Until recently it had been assumed that forensic experience was all that was required to equip Stipendiary Magistrates and other professional judges for judicial office. All British judges and most stipendiaries are chosen from among barristers and solicitors in active practice. This is basically different from the system in Civil Law countries, where there is usually a judicial career structure. In those countries a student, after undergoing basic legal education and having passed the requisite examinations, enters a judicial service where he spends the rest of his career moving up the judicial ladder on periodical promotion. The Civil Law judge, having had no previous experience or instruction (other than academic) prior to his appointment, requires training before he is considered qualified to adjudicate. Thereafter he undergoes further training at stages throughout his working life, sometimes at a judicial college such as the École Nationale de la Magistrature in France. In the Common Law system the main qualification for appointment to the bench is extensive experience as an advocate and this alone has generally been regarded as sufficient. (This does not apply universally throughout all Common Law countries. In the United States, where there is considerable variation in the method of judicial appointment, greater interest has also been taken in the training of professional judges than has been the case in the United Kingdom until fairly recently.) In this country those who are chosen are normally selected because, as outstanding legal practitioners, they are assumed to be capable of extensive and rapid self education in legal matters without the need for guidance and assistance from any external agency. Also, an experienced barrister is familiar with the problems of presenting evidence and is aware of the difficulty of adjudicating facts. His mind is able to identify that which is legally and logically relevant and to distinguish matters that are irrelevant. Furthermore, before receiving a full-time appointment he has usually had an opportunity to gain experience and to show his paces while sitting as a part-time judge.

By 1960 doubts were being expressed as to whether practitioners who have a detailed knowledge of the law and who have demonstrated that they have acquired a formidable collection of forensic skills are sufficiently qualified to act as judges, especially as a vast increase in judicial work has coincided with a greater tendency for practitioners to specialise. In 1963 Lord Parker, the Lord Chief Justice, held a conference for senior judges on the treatment of offenders and from then onwards there has usually been an annual conference, chaired by the Lord Chief Justice. These have revealed that there is even more disparity of views on sentencing among the professional judges than is usually to be found among justices. From 1968 these conferences have been administered by the Lord Chancellor's Office who, in that same year, introduced a week's course directed mainly to criminal trials and intended for newly appointed judges, Recorders and Stipendiary Magistrates. From 1972 the course was residential and was held at the Froebel Institute in Roehampton in September, immediately before the beginning of the Michaelmas law term. The course dealt in depth with sentencing problems and included judicial administration and directions to juries, and the participants visited a number of penal institutions, probation offices and hostels. Attendance was voluntary. The course was under the supervision of a High Court judge assisted by a Circuit judge and was administered by the Lord Chancellor's training Officer, whose task was not an easy one; the Bench and Bar are sensitive to officialdom and much tact was required.

The changing approach to judicial training was reflected in a controversial report entitled *The Judiciary* published by a sub-committee of *Justice* in 1972. The report recommended that a judge should receive training for a period of three to six months after appointment and should be required to visit a variety of penal institutions. The sub-committee was also of the opinion that there was 'very considerable need for some sort of judicial staff college, training centre or judicial institute' where training courses for judges, magistrates and members of administrative tribunals could be held. This proposal had much to commend it from the point of view of the lay justices as well as of the professionals.

A climacteric was reached in 1975 when the Lord Chancellor, the Lord Chief Justice and the Home Secretary jointly appointed the working party, mentioned earlier, under the chairmanship of

Lord Justice Bridge, to study the needs of sentencers for training and information. They concluded that existing facilities were excellent within their limited scope but too restricted in scale and availability. In April 1976 the working party issued a consultative paper embodying provisional proposals which included a three- to four-week initial training course which all new judges were to be required to attend. The proposals met outspoken opposition, particularly on the ground that a course lasting three to four weeks would be too long, and there were some critics who still regarded any form of training as a waste of time and money. The working party revised their views in the light of the reactions to their proposals and presented a final report in April 1978 in which they recommended the establishment of a Judicial Studies Board, with a salaried director of studies and a secretariat provided by the Lord Chancellor's Department, which would have responsibility for all judicial study and would report to the Lord Chancellor, the Lord Chief Justice and the Home Secretary. This plan was adopted and the Board, comprising a mixed membership of judges, barristers, solicitors, academics, administrators and others with experience of the criminal courts, was appointed by the Lord Chancellor in 1979 with Mr Justice Watkins VC as its first chairman. The working party's detailed proposals for training were also largely accepted. Newly appointed full-time judges and Stipendiary Magistrates are required to attend an initial study programme which, for those with previous judicial experience, lasts one week and for others two weeks. Judges are further required to attend continuing study programmes of not more than one week (initially about two years after first appointment and thereafter every five years). Newly appointed judges are also required to undertake a week's pupillage with an experienced judge.

The working party also recommended that the Board should have an institutional base at a university. For financial reasons this has not yet been accepted and seminars continue to be held at the Froebel Institute. The proposal, however, has much merit. There is clearly a need for some sort of judicial training centre which could provide courses not only for the professional judiciary and administrative tribunals but also for lay justices and for those in charge of justices' training, many of whom have received no education in the science of training.

7 Work and Procedure

There is an essential difference between procedure in the magistrates' courts and in the higher courts in that magistrates are judges of both law and fact and have the dual functions of deciding both guilt and sentence, whereas on indictment responsibility for conviction rests with the jury while sentence is the concern of the judge. Proposals to transfer offences from the higher to the magistrates' courts have always met with the objection that they would infringe the right of the citizen to be tried by jury. In spite of this, the process of relegating offences to summary trial which began a century ago accelerated in the 1960s and 1970s. The reason for this was not only that the confidence of Parliament and the public in the lay magistracy rose with the greater reliability and competence of the justices, but because this coincided with an increasing need to relieve pressure on the higher criminal courts. The Criminal Justice Act 1961 extended the list of indictable offences triable summarily and in 1975 the James Committee[1] was set up for the express purpose of finding ways to relieve pressure on the Crown Court by extending the jurisdiction of the magistrates. The committee made a number of recommendations in this direction but only the least important were implemented (Criminal Law Act 1977), as the combined legal and civil liberties lobby secured the defeat of those proposals which would have given magistrates exclusive jurisdiction in minor cases where the personal reputation of the accused was at stake. In addition to these extensions of jurisdiction in Petty Sessions, the Courts Act 1971 increased the role of justices in the Crown Court.

Forty years ago demands made on justices were light. They were under no obligation to attend on a stipulated number of occasions; indeed, as already noted, an appreciable number sat infrequently and some not at all. Those who did attend usually had plenty of time to do so and were not normally subject to marked pressures. Much of the work was done by justices who had retired or were of independent means with ample leisure and these comprised a significant proportion of the bench. Today, the office of Justice of the Peace is a sinecure for none. It cannot be undertaken by busy men and women without some sacrifice of their personal affairs and the great majority of justices are occupied full-time in earning their living or looking after their families. They are subject to more rigid disciplines than their predecessors and find it difficult, and often impossible, to put in extra attendances or to sit longer hours than normal if there is an emergency. This loss of flexibility has coincided with a greatly enlarged work load due not only to an extension of jurisdiction and an increase in the number of cases coming before the courts, but also to the introduction of more complex procedures, to legal aid[2] and (resulting partly from legal aid) to a larger number of pleas of not guilty. The enlargement of the work load was most noticeable between 1965 and 1977 when the number of persons dealt with in the summary courts rose from 1,368,048 to 2,438,212.

The greatest volume of work arises from breaches of the road traffic laws, which rose in numbers as motor vehicles came to occupy an increasingly important position in the modern world, for industry and commerce as well as for the private individual. The pattern of offences committed on the roads varied during the period, the greatest increases being for driving while disqualified and driving under the influence of drink and drugs (especially after the Road Safety Act 1967), whereas there was a decline, beginning in the early 1960s, in dangerous driving and failing to stop after an accident; but the overall rise was substantial and by 1977 about 1 million persons were being charged with motoring offences in the magistrates' courts each year. This accounted for 59 per cent of all cases and about 75 per cent of non-indictable offences.

A better understanding of motoring cases has developed from the larger proportion of magistrates who are drivers themselves,[3] though non-motorists claim that this has made the magistrates too sympathetic towards the driver.

The greater part of traffic cases relate to minor offences, but these are disproportionately time-consuming because the defendants ignore summonses more often than in any other type of case, though the despatch of business was greatly accelerated by the Magistrates' Courts Act 1957 which enabled the accused to plead guilty by post and be dealt with in his absence. Further relief came in 1960 with the introduction of 'ticket fines' for illegal parking and some other minor offences which gave defendants the opportunity to pay a fixed penalty by post without the case coming to court at all.[4] The Transport Act, 1982 (the third such Act in three years) extended fixed penalties to some of the less serious moving traffic offences including speeding. Another proposal for relieving magistrates of routine traffic cases was to allow police to levy a fine for speeding on the spot. This has not been viewed with favour in this country because it was thought to place too much power in the hands of the police. Sentencing in traffic cases is considered further on page 147.

The establishment of special traffic courts has been considered on several occasions since 1955. The advantages to be gained by such courts have varied with the eye of the proposer. Ministers of Transport have seen them as a means of securing tougher penalties, while the motoring organisations have taken the opposite view and assume that the courts will be composed of persons well versed in traffic matters who will be more under-standing of the motorist's problems. Demands for separate traffic tribunals were also made by those who wished to remove motorists, who are normally law-abiding citizens, from the stigma of criminality which attaches to those convicted in the ordinary magistrates' courts. In 1965 the Law Society prepared a memorandum recommending that a distinction should be made between 'offences' and 'breaches' of the Road Traffic Acts; the former, which would include 'deliberate, conscious or vicious breaches of the law and reckless acts or omissions', were to continue to be dealt with in the ordinary magistrates' courts, while the remainder would go to traffic courts composed of justices drawn from a panel to which they would be elected for a three-year term. The proposal for two separate categories of offence was supported by the Magistrates' Association but they thought that specially constituted courts were unnecessary.

Reference has already been made to the sense of grievance felt by those convicted of motoring offences, who form a large and articulate part of the population, with the result that the criminal courts have lost much of the public respect which they previously enjoyed. For this reason alone the concept of separate traffic tribunals needs to be considered further. Successive governments, however, have refused to accept that breaches of road traffic laws should be treated differently from any others. The fact that the offence may be a minor one can be indicated in the level of penalty imposed. But the principal reason for not pursuing the idea of traffic courts has been inability to reach a decision as to who should man them. If it is a question of setting aside a separate sitting of the magistrates to deal exclusively with these cases this is already done in some places, but if the courts are to be composed of specialists, whether or not legally qualified, who will handle nothing but traffic cases, few if any suitable candidates are likely to agree to serve. The handling of long lists of postal pleas or cases of non-payment of fixed penalties is about the most boring occupation that the human mind has devised since the treadmill. No competent person would undertake such work without the inducement of an unrealistic rate of remuneration; or if they were to do so, it is doubtful whether they could avoid adopting a purely mechanical approach to such a monotonous duty. Under the present system magistrates are less prone to this failing because they are presented with a varied diet, yet even so it requires some effort to maintain an individual approach to each case.

A totally different branch of magistrates' work which also occupies a great deal of time but is often overlooked by observers is their civil jurisdiction. It is anomalous that these matters are allocated to courts primarily concerned with administering criminal law and it would be more logical if they were within the exclusive jurisdiction of the County Courts,[5] but they are largely relics of earlier days when Parliament relegated a variety of odd duties to justices as a cheap and easy method of dealing with fairly simple problems. Magistrates are therefore entrusted with enforcing rates and income tax and there are many Statutes which confer a right of appeal to magistrates from a determination by a local authority and, although most of these date from before the war, several Acts have added to the list within comparatively recent years.[6]

The bulk of magistrates' civil jurisdiction, however, relates to domestic matters: separation, maintenance and affiliation orders and guardianship and custody of children. This family jurisdiction is among the most important of the justices' functions and it is also the most confused as there has been much overlapping with the High Court and the County Court for which no coherent principle is apparent. Although the magistrates' matrimonial jurisdiction dates from 1878 when the switch from local government to purely judicial functions began, the origins of the family work are in the Poor Law of Elizabeth I which was under the jurisdiction of the justices and required a man to maintain his children so that they did not become a burden on the parish.

A matrimonial case can occupy far more time than any other because it may last indefinitely if the order has to be varied on successive occasions. An attempt to help the courts to enforce orders was made by the Maintenance Orders Act 1968 which provided for attachment of earnings, but this has been less effective than expected because of the ease with which a husband can switch jobs faster than he can be traced.

Proposals have been made from time to time to transfer the whole of the magistrates' family work elsewhere. In 1974 the Finer Committee on One-Parent Families[7] recommended that all family jurisdiction should be concentrated in a new system of specialist family courts, the lowest level of which should be composed of justices sitting in the County Court with a Circuit judge as chairman. This proposal was not accepted because Circuit judges already had more than enough to do, and in 1977 it was overtaken by recommendations of a Law Commission working party. These were implemented by the Domestic Proceedings and Magistrates' Courts Act 1978 which provided for the establishment of courts composed of justices drawn from a panel specially appointed to deal with domestic proceedings. The Lord Chancellor was empowered to make rules governing the size, chairmanship and composition of the domestic courts and the manner in which panel members should be elected. The Act also extended the jurisdiction which the magistrates were to exercise in these new specialist courts and assimilated the law to that administered in the High Court. A guiding principle which is enshrined in S. 26 of the Act is that, before hearing an application, a court must consider whether there is any chance of reconciliation between the parties. For a number of years prior to 1978 the matrimonial jurisdiction of magistrates had been in decline and it was thought that the Act would lead to a revival in this branch of their work. In fact, although the situation varied widely from one area to another, there continued to be a general drift of business from the magistrates to the County Court. Most solicitors favoured the County Court but the move was due in some degree to lack of initiative on the part of many magistrates to provide an effective service. The Magistrates Association and the Justices'

Clerks Society, however, recognised the Act as a challenge and in 1981 issued a joint paper to domestic court panels with a number of suggestions on how to make it work. They pointed out that a court composed of three people, selected and trained for the work and drawn from a range of social backgrounds, including both sexes and with the possibility of a spread of ages, all with wide experience of the local community, should be an ideal tribunal to handle domestic problems, especially in the role of conciliator. The family court concept, however, is by no means moribund and will undoubtedly be revived at a future date.

A curious feature of magistrates' work during the past twenty years has been a revival of interest in their administrative duties which, since 1888, had been mainly confined to liquor licensing, a duty they had performed since 1532. An important change for the good took place in 1953 when the Licensing Act required each bench to appoint a licensing committee of not more than fifteen magistrates to replace the vast crowds of justices who used to throng the annual Brewster sessions, many of them heavily biased for or against the consumption of alcohol. The idea had been gaining ground, however, that the justices' licensing work could usefully be extended into other fields. The Betting and Gaming Act 1960 gave magistrates the duty of granting licences to bookmakers, betting offices and betting agents and the Gaming Act 1968 empowered them to licence premises for gaming and bingo. From then on, a number of schemes were promoted for extending the justices' licensing powers beyond gaming and liquor to cover football grounds, transport and almost anything else that the government sought to regulate. These moves were resisted by the Lord Chancellor, for the most part successfully, on the ground that magistrates were appointed for the purpose of discharging judicial and not administrative functions and that in any event they already had more than enough to do, but it was not always easy to convince his colleagues. In 1962 the Royal Commission on the Police thought that police authorities would be greatly assisted in their tasks of 'enhancing the standing of the police force and appointing its senior officers if they were to include a proportion of justices', and they went on to say that justices 'constitute a body of public-spirited citizens whose services cannot be enlisted through the normal machinery of local government'. There are obvious advantages in drawing on the justices for innumerable local duties; they are an uncommitted group of citizens with knowledge of local conditions and reflecting diverse views and, if the system works as it should, they have a reputation for impartiality. There are therefore distinct attractions to the authorities in placing responsibility upon the justices for taking administrative decisions, especially if the decisions may be unpopular ones. On the other hand, this policy could add enormously to the justices' work and it would be incompatible with the justices' present role. This message seems at last to be getting through and recently the licensing of music, singing and dancing was transferred to the local authorities, though the justices were left with the registering of private clubs. There is a strong case for transferring all licensing functions to the local authorities. In so far as serving on police bodies is concerned, the Lord Chancellor has questioned the propriety of justices appearing to be involved in police activities and has given guidance on the extent to which they should participate in crime prevention panels and police consultative groups and as lay visitors to police stations.

A side of magistrates' work which has diminished fortuitously is document witnessing and giving advice to the public. In the 1940s most documents requiring attestation were taken to justices, who were also consulted on a variety of subjects. It seems to have been thought that there was a greater aura of respectability and confidentiality surrounding a matter if it were referred to a justice rather than to anyone else. The public no longer feel this way and, with the establishment of Citizens' Advice Bureaux and other advice centres, the habit of turning to a magistrate for advice has lapsed. At the same time, the categories of persons qualified to attest documents have been expanded, in many cases at the request of the Lord Chancellor, in order to minimise the calls on justices for document witnessing. Nevertheless, they still have plenty of out-of-court work, including prison visiting, serving on numerous committees, granting summonses, warrants for arrest and search and the taking of declarations. Requests for search warrants have increased with the illegal possession of drugs and contraband, and the gas and electricity boards apply more frequently than in the past for authority to enter premises to shut off supplies. A heavy responsibility rests on the justices who, while acting in the public interest, must not be too ready to accept assurances by police, customs or electricity boards that the entry is necessary.

One of the most ancient and highly useful powers of justices, which dates from 1361, is to bind over to keep the peace. It is of particular value as a preventive measure; an apprehended breach of the peace may be averted by requiring persons who seem likely to commit an offence to enter into recognisances to pay a specified sum which is forfeited if they fail to comply. The device is used most frequently in domestic cases or ones involving disputes between neighbours, but it has wide scope as a measure of preventive justice. On the other hand, there have been moves to abolish the power on the ground that it is wrong in principle to 'try' a person in anticipation of his committing an offence (though a similar situation may arise on an application for bail). The Magistrates' Association and the Justices' Clerks' Society have urged that the procedure be preserved and extended and that the power to make an order be mandatory at the discretion of the court (at present no order can be made without the consent of the party concerned). Lord Lane LCJ has pointed out that the law on this subject is 'in an unsatisfactory state' and it is at present under consideration by the Law Commission.

In court, the magistrates' work is governed by rules of procedure which, before 1949, were contained in various Statutes that had to be amended before any change could be achieved. The Roche Committee of 1944 and the Royal Commission of 1948 both recommended the appointment of a rule committee similar to those already existing for the higher courts and the County Courts, but the 1949 Bill, when introduced, ignored this recommendation because the Home Secretary, within whose province the adjectival criminal law was assumed to lie, preferred to have everything in a Statute. Credit is due to the Magistrates' Association for pressing the proposal through the Chairman of their Council, Lord Templewood, who successfully moved an amendment in the Lords which was incorporated in Section 15 of the Act.[8] All procedural rules in magistrates' courts are now made by the Lord Chancellor on the advice of and after consultation with a committee which he appoints under the chairmanship of the Lord Chief Justice. Under this flexible system the rules may be amended at any time without new legislation, though they must be laid before Parliament subject to negative resolution procedure.[9]

Although the rules are made by the Lord Chancellor the secretary of the committee has always been a Home Office official, but the Secretary of Commissions or his Deputy serves as a member. (I was one of the first members to be appointed, in 1950.) The committee has been criticised because, unlike the committees for the Supreme Court and County Courts, it conducts all its business by post and the members never meet. It includes certain eminent statutory members such as the Lord Chief Justice, President of the Family Division and Director of Public Prosecutions, who cannot easily attend meetings and who, moreover, have no direct interest in the running of magistrates' courts nor are they disposed to give detailed attention to the development of the rules. Review tends to fall behind the impetus of change in court machinery and there is need for a more positive and continuous system. There is advantage in the imprimatur of higher authority, but the system would benefit from the appointment of a small, active working group (as suggested by the Justices' Clerks' Society) to review the rules in detail at regular intervals and to report to the statutory committee.

Procedure was greatly improved by two important Statutes: the Criminal Justice Act 1967 provided simplified committal proceedings using written statements in place of oral evidence, and the Criminal Law Act 1977 reclassified all offences into three categories. The 1967 Act relieved magistrates of a vast amount of tedious committal work but it added unexpectedly to the burden of the higher courts because it enabled the magistrates to commit without considering the evidence and many cases went to trial which would have been thrown out by the magistrates had they been informed of the evidence as they were under the old procedure. On the other hand the Act did not entirely eliminate long committals because the shortened procedure could be followed only with the consent of the accused, and the number of occasions on which the old-style committal was chosen began to increase in the early 1970s, especially in fraud trials. The Royal Commission on Criminal Procedure which reported in 1981, recommended the abolition of committal proceedings. Cases would go straight to the Crown Court, subject to the right of the accused to make an application for discharge, in which case the magistrates would enquire, as they do now, whether there was a case to answer.

In 1981 the Contempt of Court Act empowered magistrates, for the first time, to commit for contempt. Previously, the view had been held that they could not be trusted to deal with acts of contempt of their courts. The Act, reflecting the new aura of confidence in the justices, extended contempt proceedings to magistrates' courts and provided for the offender's immediate arrest and the imposition of imprisonment up to one month or a fine of £500.

A totally new prospect was revealed when the United Kingdom joined the European Economic Community in 1972. Thereafter British courts, including those of the magistrates, became subject to community law, as interpreted by the European Court in Luxembourg. So far most magistrates have not been directly involved, though some have been affected when dealing with heavy goods vehicles and those in coastal areas are sometimes faced with fishery prosecutions to which community law applies. In 1977 a Northern Ireland farmer was charged in Armagh with moving pigs contrary to Northern Ireland regulations. The Resident Magistrate, in response to legal argument, referred the validity of the regulations to the European Court who decided that they were contrary to European law. On receiving this ruling the magistrate dismissed the case.

One noticeable change since 1947 has been in the dress worn in court. Gone are the days when a defendant was sent away and told to come back wearing a collar and tie. Clothes which would previously have been the subject of severe rebuke turn out to be the defendant's normal working attire. So long as he behaves himself with reasonable decorum no comment is made. Similarly, on the bench itself there is more tolerance and, indeed, while endeavouring to preserve the dignity of the court, a conscious attempt is made not to look too stuffy. As a young barrister I found nothing more disconcerting than a row of awe-inspiring matrons sitting in judgment, each with an almost identical pudding-bowl-like object placed squarely on her head. During the past forty years there has been no greater source of discord among justices than the question whether women magistrates should or should not wear hats. The strife ended with a strategic victory for the non-hat faction, only to be revived from time to time by some new sartorial innovation such as the trouser-suit. But the outcome by 1977 was that most benches, by their appearance as well as by their conduct, gave an impression of far less formality than their predecessors.

All Lord Chancellors for whom I have worked have regarded informality and absence of ceremony as the essence of summary procedure, and for this reason they have never favoured the wearing of distinctive costumes by members of the bench or by advocates appearing before them. There is, however, nothing to prevent magistrates from wearing some insignia or special clothing, within reason, if they wish to do so, except for the fact that they would be obliged to pay the cost out of their own pockets. This consideration or the fact that most benches prefer informality has deterred courts from adopting any form of uniform, but there is one exception in the case of the City of London, where the justices wear blue and black robes. Since time immemorial the Lord Mayor and Aldermen of the City have robed when sitting in court and when, in 1969, non-Aldermen were admitted to the bench it was decided that they should wear gowns provided at the City's expense.

Somewhat stronger views have been expressed about justices robing when they sit in the Crown Court. Why, it is asked, should they be made to appear as second-class citizens by having to wear ordinary clothes when the Circuit judge or Recorder, who is merely *primus inter pares*, wears wig and gown? Financial restraints have made the authorities reluctant to pursue this idea and they were relieved to find that the great majority of justices were content with the present arrangements. After all, the position is not altogether novel. Whole-time chairmen of Quarter Sessions used to robe and the part-time chairman of Dorset sessions wore a top hat in court.

Stipendiary Magistrates robe when they preside as Recorders or deputy judges in the Crown Court but not when sitting in Petty Sessions (except in Hull, where the stipendiary always robes). It has been suggested that all stipendiaries should robe in their own courts, but this has not been accepted by the Lord Chancellor on the ground that it would create an undesirable distinction between their courts and those of the lay justices.

Those who engage in the work of a Justice of the Peace are expected to do so without reward beyond the satisfaction of performing a valuable and interesting public service. When I became Secretary of Commissions no magistrate ever received an honour in respect of his magisterial work. This was said to be an application of the constitutional principle that the Judiciary must not look to the executive for favours. High Court judges received knighthoods but they invariably did so immediately on appointment and before they had had time to show whether they were well disposed towards the Crown. On the same basis the Chief Metropolitan Magistrate was always knighted on appointment. No Justices of the Peace, however, received any recognition. This seemed rather unfair, considering that many people were honoured in respect of work for which they were remunerated while the justices were paid nothing and many were out of pocket. In 1950 I suggested that, although justices should continue to be ineligible for recognition in respect of their work on the bench, even if they had served as chairmen of their courts with distinction for an exceptionally long period, those who had given outstanding service to the administration of justice in some other capacity, such as the chairmanship of an Advisory Committee or a Magistrates' Courts Committee, should not be barred. This proposal was accepted and thereafter it was customary for the Lord Chancellor to submit from time to time the names of justices who had given eminent service in this capacity and a number of them were honoured. Inevitably, as in other fields, numbers of deserving candidates were not recognised, and as the years passed other unexpected problems arose. An MBE might be appropriate for the chairman of a small borough committee but it would be thought derisory for chairmen in the largest cities like Birmingham. Higher honours, however, are conferred more sparingly, with the result that whereas an appreciable number of those who had performed lesser duties in smaller areas received due recognition hardly any of the chairmen of the most important committees did so. Between 1951, when recommendations were first permitted, and 1983 the CBE was conferred only three times in respect of magisterial service; two of the recipients were chairmen of branches of the Magistrates' Association and the other, A. J. Brayshaw, was the Association's secretary. There were two knighthoods (apart from those bestowed on the Chief Metropolitan Magistrates), in both cases for service as Chairman of the Council of the Magistrates' Association of England and Wales (Lord Merthyr was created KBE in 1969 and Sir William Addison a knight bachelor in 1974). The tightening of the honours system in the 1960s resulted in a reduction in the number of awards to justices and also affected the Chief Metropolitan Magistrates, who had previously been knighted immediately on appointment. Since 1963 every Chief Magistrate has had to wait for some time after taking office before receiving recognition.

There has also been a shift of attitude towards financial

compensation to justices. At one time justices were paid four shillings a day which, when introduced in 1388, was sixteen times greater than a labourer's wage. This remained the rate until 1854 when remuneration for justices was abolished, although it had fallen into disuse much earlier,[10] and for a century the idea of payment, even of expenses, was repugnant to the public and the magistrates alike. Opinion about payment for voluntary public service had begun to change by 1947 when a Local Government Act provided for the payment of expenses to members of local authorities, and the Royal Commission of 1948 recommended that justices should be entitled to recover their travelling expenses when attending court. On the other hand, the Royal Commission were firmly opposed to payment for subsistence or loss of remunerative time because, in their view, public respect for the justices was due in part to the fact that the work involved some self-sacrifice and loss and no possibility of gain. The Justices of the Peace Bill of 1949 followed the Commission's recommendations and provided for a travel allowance, and when an amendment was moved in the Commons to entitle justices to compensation for loss of earnings it secured only six votes. During the next fifteen years more and more persons in voluntary public service became eligible for allowances, including reimbursement for financial loss, but for a long time it was not extended to justices because of the views expressed by the Royal Commission, with which the majority of magistrates themselves agreed. In 1968, the Labour Government were persuaded that more wage-earners would accept appointment if they could qualify for a loss-of-earnings allowance, and provision to this effect was accordingly made in the Justices of the Peace Act of that year. As already noted, there is no evidence to show that this has made any appreciable difference to the willingness of wage-earners to serve, but there are now many in the trade union movement who feel that further steps should be taken to remunerate justices over and above any loss they may incur (and there are hidden snags, such as loss of pension rights when sitting). They take this view not only as a matter of principle, but because they think that without it many of their members will not be able to undertake the burdens which the modern office of magistrate involves. There may be some force in this, but on the other hand the payment of anything amounting to a salary could be the beginning of a slippery slope. It would soon be argued that if justices are to be paid it would be best to dispense with lay magistrates entirely and to replace them with the whole-time salaried lawyers who would dispose of the work more expeditiously.

Another sign of growing concern for the protection of justices against financial loss appeared in 1961 when the Lord Chancellor and the Home Secretary appointed a working party, under my chairmanship, to consider the liability of justices and also of justices' clerks and Clerks of the Peace for expenses, damages and costs incurred in connection with legal proceedings brought against them in the course of their duties. Before 1949 the extent of a justice's personal liability was obscure, but the Justices of the Peace Act of that year enabled a Magistrates' Courts Committee to authorise the payment out of local funds of costs and damages awarded against a justice in respect of acts done out of Quarter Sessions, while acts done in Quarter Sessions were covered, at the discretion of the Standing Joint Committee, by the Local Government Act 1888. There were no provisions for dealing with actions against justices' clerks and Clerks of the Peace. The working party recommended that all justices and clerks should be entitled to indemnification for acts done in good faith in the execution or intended execution of their duties, that no distinction should be made between judicial and administrative functions and that this protection should extend to stipendiaries, Recorders and chairmen and deputy chairmen of Quarter Sessions. The decision whether payment should be made to a justice or clerk was to rest with the Magistrates' Courts Committee subject to appeal to an authority appointed by the Lord Chancellor; in the case of proceedings for prerogative orders or acts done in Quarter Sessions indemnification was to be at the discretion of the Lord Chancellor. These recommendations were implemented in the Administration of Justice Act 1964.

These provisions of the 1964 Act have been invoked, on average, less than once a year, more often on behalf of a justice than of a clerk, and the results have not always been in the justice's favour. In 1969 Lord Lindgren, the chairman of the Welwyn bench, and two colleagues were severely criticised by the Divisional Court and ordered to pay the costs of a successful application for prerogative orders on the grounds that the accused in a case they had tried had not had a fair hearing because of constant interruptions and remarks by Lord Lindgren. The justices asked the Lord Chancellor to exercise his powers under the Act and to pay the costs amounting to £599. He did so in the case of the other two justices because they were not in a position to restrain their chairman, but he ruled that Lord Lindgren's share should be paid out of his own pocket and not from public funds.

One further landmark in the history of personal liability of justices was the decision of the Court of Appeal in Sirros v. Moore in 1974. Until then it had been assumed that magistrates did not enjoy the same protection as other judges but this case placed them on precisely the same footing as judges of courts of record, who are protected from actions brought against them in respect of judicial acts, whether within or without their jurisdiction, provided that they honestly believed that they were acting within their jurisdiction.

It is generally agreed among those concerned with magistrates' courts that the standard of their work has improved steadily since 1950, but some aspects are still open to criticism. Reference has already been made to the tendency of many justices to rely too heavily upon guidance from their clerks, while some are too ready to accept police evidence, and a few are too inclined to reject it merely because it comes from the police. There are still inconsistencies in different parts of the country with regard to sentencing, the award of costs and the criteria for granting legal aid. There is also a failure in some courts to give adequate consideration to those who attend as parties or as witnesses. Most magistrates believe that they go out of their way to consider the interests of all these persons but they do not always appreciate what it is like to come into a court of law for the first time and to be faced with legal jargon and seemingly meaningless procedure. This applies more to Stipendiary Magistrates than to lay justices as the latter have not been brought up in an atmosphere of recondite legal idioms, but after serving for a while they too acquire a degree of abstruse phraseology. Justice cannot be administered satisfactorily when it relies on evidence from parties and witnesses who are nervous, confused and too frightened to say more than seems absolutely necessary. Bewildered witnesses and parties are still to be found all too often, especially in some of the metropolitan courts, where congestion and shortage of time has become so acute that it is no easy task to avoid disposing of cases in a sausage-machine manner. Blame must lie partly with the authorities responsible for administering the courts and for the training of the magistrates, but responsibility rests primarily with the presiding magistrate, be he stipendiary or chairman of a lay bench, and to some extent with the justices' clerk, whose handling of individuals is often an immediate cause of their bewilderment. These situations are not confined to magistrates' courts and it should be emphasised that they are far less prevalent today than they were twenty years ago. The new generation of magistrates and clerks usually recognise that their aim in administering justice should be to ensure that everyone leaves the court satisfied that, whatever may have been the outcome of the case, they have had a fair trial.

In one respect, however, work in the magistrates' courts has deteriorated since 1947. Delays in the bringing of cases to trial have been increasing since the mid 1960s (and much earlier in the metropolitan courts). An advantage of the system of part-time justices is the comparative ease with which increases of work, whether long-term or short-term, can be absorbed. This has never been the case in the metropolitan magistrates' courts which, like all those staffed by the professional judiciary, are organised on the principle that it is uneconomic to have more judges than are needed to dispose of immediate work. The hypothesis that it is in the public interest for judges to be kept constantly occupied lest the public should have to pay them for doing nothing leads to far worse consequences when there are unexpected increases in court business and arrears accumulate. It also means that the public and the police waste time and money while they are sitting about waiting for cases to come on. Listing of cases with fixed times of hearing would avoid this, but until there are more courts it would increase delays. Justices' courts, on the other hand, have been able in the past to absorb an upsurge of work by sitting for longer hours or on more days a week, but in recent years their ability to do so has been limited by shortage of accommodation, any increase in the number of court rooms being inhibited by financial limits and staff recruitment problems.

With a view to making maximum use of limited court accommodation several experiments were made in the 1960s with holding courts in the evening and at night as well as in the daytime, but they were discontinued for a number of reasons: reluctance of court staff to work a shift system, opposition from the legal profession, who required time after normal court hours to attend conferences and deal with paper work, transport difficulties and the fact that after a long day's work elsewhere the magistrates were not in the best state to administer justice.

Contrary to expectation a sample enquiry also revealed that most members of the public prefer to take time off from work to attend court rather than encroach upon their leisure hours.

Apart from the rise in crime and the state of the prisons (referred to later), the most serious matter facing all courts is delay. It is a truism that 'justice delayed is justice denied', but a number of factors have contributed to the growing weight of arrears during the last thirty years. As will be seen later, this provoked dramatic changes in the structure of the higher courts in 1972, but until more recently the problem did not appear to be as acute in the magistrates' courts and therefore less drastic steps have been taken to deal with it. Not all causes of delay are susceptible to quantification and some have nothing to do with the courts themselves. The Director of Public Prosecutions and the understaffed police forces[12] take longer to prepare cases for prosecution, while firms of solicitors accept more work than they can cope with and a shortage of advocates, both barristers and solicitors, leads to delays in the defence. Once the case comes to trial the court is inhibited by a number of checks which have been imposed by Parliament during the last twenty-five years with the idea of safeguarding the defendant. In a wide category of cases magistrates must call for social enquiry reports; when contemplating a custodial sentence for the first time they must enquire into the possibility of legal representation; they must adjourn before disqualifying an absent defendant and adjournments are also required in many other types of case. The Bail Act 1976 added greatly to the time required for dealing with bail applications, and long adjournments are usually necessary when records of previous motoring convictions have to be obtained from the Swansea computer. Legal aid has led to more pleas of not guilty and to cases taking longer to try. A larger number of fines are imposed where previously a custodial penalty would have been awarded, but in nearly 40 per cent of these cases the defendant fails to pay within the time ordered, thus entailing enforcement proceedings which, in the largest courts, may involve up to 10,000 further cases a year.

A Home Office working group made a number of suggestions in 1982 for improving waiting time and these have been adopted with advantage in many courts. They have led to a clearer perception both of delay as a general problem and of the specific factors which can contribute to it. Some courts have also instituted schemes of pre-trial review which, by bringing together the prosecution and defence, together with the clerk, some four weeks before trial, have shortened the final hearing by saving lengthy oral examination of witnesses and sometimes by a change of plea to guilty.

Quite apart from delays, magistrates' work is becoming so complex and wide-ranging as to perplex even the full-time lawyer magistrate and some reduction in the existing scope of their duties is essential in the interests of efficiency. This becomes even more urgent in face of current trends to relieve pressure on the higher courts by extending the exclusive jurisdiction of the summary courts. In 1975 the James Committee recommended that magistrates' administrative duties and civil jurisdiction should be removed thus allowing them to develop to the full the skills required in their primary role of administering the criminal law. This recommendation was not implemented, partly because the civil work would have been transferred to the already fully occupied County Courts. All schemes for shifting work away from the magistrates have been baulked by inability to find an alternative tribunal. The Government have also accepted that in certain respects justices have advantages over County Courts; they can normally act more swiftly, the procedure is less expensive and in most cases they have a higher degree of local knowledge. These advantages are not likely to be found in any other type of tribunal unless it is constituted on much the same lines as the magistrates' courts.

If civil and administrative work cannot be transferred elsewhere, magistrates should at least be relieved of that part of their criminal jurisdiction which is not strictly necessary. Reference has been made earlier to extending the fixed penalty system. It can be argued that much more could be done to reduce pressure on the courts, while at the same time achieving a better end product, by a policy of 'decriminalisation'; that is to say removing some of the present offences entirely from the ambit of the criminal law. Thus, the habitual drunkard who comes before the court week after week is either sentenced to a small fine or is imprisoned because he cannot pay. This is utter waste of the court's time and totally ineffective as far as the drunkard is concerned. In 1971 a working party suggested that, in place of court proceedings, the police should be empowered to take a person drunk in public to a detoxification centre where he would be detained until he was dried out and any necessary medical and social investigation carried out. So far nothing has been done to amend the law and there are no more than two detoxification centres in the whole country. The reason is financial but, as the Magistrates' Association who strongly support the proposal point out, it would be money well spent. (The procedure would not, of course, apply where drunkenness formed part of some other offence, such as one involving driving a car, nor to those situations, which are becoming more frequent, where alcoholic intoxication has a significant influence on serious crime. 50 per cent of murders and violent offences are alcohol related.)

In 1980 *Justice*, the all-party group of lawyers, issued a report, entitled *Breaking the Rules*, which pointed out that in the modern world, Parliament has found it necessary to regulate so many everyday activities that it has become well-nigh impossible for even the honest and law-abiding citizen to get through the average year without infringing some regulation, and he finds himself prosecuted in the same court as robbers and rapists and finishes with a 'criminal record'. *Justice* recommended that there should be two classes of wrongful conduct (as already in some other countries), one called 'crimes' and the other 'contraventions'; the latter being what might be described as 'administrative transgressions'. Penalties for infringement would be imposed by the ordinary courts in the case of crimes and by some other authority in the case of contraventions (subject to a right of challenge by the contravener in the magistrates' court). A system of this kind would offer scope for more effective and imaginative penalties as well as relieving pressure on the courts. Having one's car towed away (which can already be done by the police without resort to the courts) is known to be a greater deterrent against wrongful parking than paying a fine. Under the *Justice* proposal, the Post Office, for example, would be able to impound an unlicensed television set which would probably be a greater incentive to buying a licence than the prospect of a fine, and would be more expeditious than procedure through the courts.

Looked at from virtually every angle, including reversal of the current trend towards disrespect for the law, there is a strong case for 'decriminalisation' which has the support of most magistrates and their clerks (the Justices' Clerks' Society issued a valuable paper on the subject in 1982). How far such a process should go needs careful consideration. Obviously the present system should not be changed merely for the sake of expediency, but it is difficult to find any sound reason for delaying legislation to remove at least the absolute offence from the ordinary process of the criminal law.

No mention has been made so far of the treatment of offenders or of the work of the juvenile courts or the Crown Court. In view of the importance of these subjects they are dealt with in separate chapters.

8 The Juvenile Courts

I have assigned a separate chapter to juvenile courts for two reasons. Firstly, the treatment of young offenders raises one of the most important problems confronting magistrates, and indeed all sections of the community. A nation's children are its most valuable asset and their future lives and the well-being of the rest of the population will depend on how they are treated. Secondly, during the past thirty years there have been more significant changes in the treatment of young offenders than in any other area in the administration of justice, and no other issue has aroused so much feeling among magistrates and their clerks.

Until 1847 children charged with indictable offences were tried at Assizes and Quarter Sessions in the same manner as adult offenders and they received harsh sentences: youthful pranks were often followed by imprisonment in the company of hardened adult criminals. A powerful movement for penal reform in general developed during the nineteenth century and, as part of this, children became triable in the summary courts and by the beginning of the twentieth century some English magistrates were sitting unofficially in separate courts to deal with young offenders. Basically, however, children continued to be treated in the same manner as adults until 1908, when the Children Act formally established a special system of courts in which all juveniles were to be tried. The Act also abolished imprisonment for those under seventeen, except in exceptional circumstances, and provided for treatment aimed at reforming the offender rather than punishment. The United States had pioneered juvenile courts from 1881, but after 1908 Britain made up for lost time and was among the leaders in the development of special courts for young offenders. On many occasions in the 1950s and 1960s I arranged for foreign delegations to study our juvenile courts, which were generally regarded as being among the best in the world.

At the end of the war the juvenile courts in England and Wales were governed by the Children and Young Persons Act 1933 which, though amended, has remained the principal Statute governing the composition and procedure of those courts which are responsible for 'children' (those under fourteen) and 'young persons' (over fourteen and under seventeen). The courts are required to sit in different places and at different times from the adult courts and the hearing is less formal.

Juvenile courts are composed of justices specially selected for the purposes. In London they are appointed by the Lord Chancellor,[1] on the recommendation of an Advisory Committee; in the rest of England and Wales they are elected every three years by the justices in each division from among their own number. In the early 1960s I received complaints that in some areas justices were elected on seniority rather than aptitude for juvenile court work and, after consulting interested bodies, we took the opportunity in the Justices of the Peace Act 1964 to empower the Lord Chancellor to extend the London system to other parts of the country if he thought it desirable. The offending benches saw the red light and changed their practice, with the result that the Lord Chancellor never found it necessary to exercise his new powers.

The composition of a juvenile court is governed by rules made by the Lord Chancellor under the Children and Young Persons Act 1933. The rules disqualify justices from serving on a juvenile panel after reaching the age of sixty-five. The Lord Chancellor would have liked to impose a maximum age of fifty for first appointment but this was never done for fear that there might not be sufficient justices below that age who were prepared to accept appointment to the panel. Each court must consist of three justices (or a single stipendiary)[2] and in 1947 it had to include at least one man and 'so far as practicable' one woman. The reason for this sex discrimination was that, as women did not become eligible for appointment as justices until 1919, there were not enough on the commissions to staff all juvenile courts; but by 1947 there was considerable agitation by women's organisations to correct this discrepancy and, during the next six years, Advisory Committees were required to take positive steps to increase the proportion of women justices, with the result that by 1954 the rules were able to be amended so as to place men and women on an equal footing.[3]

The jurisdiction of juvenile courts is twofold. Part is criminal, involving the trial of offenders for breaches of the criminal law, and part is civil and is concerned with care proceedings where a juvenile is in need of care or protection or is beyond control. The 1933 Act established the overriding principle that all courts when exercising their powers must have regard to the welfare of the child.

From 1945 previously accepted theories on the treatment of young offenders underwent extensive reappraisal. More and more attention was focused on the care aspect of court proceedings and upon the need to remove the young as far as possible from anything that might savour of the criminal courts. This coincided with a great expansion of the social services and, whereas formerly the juvenile courts themselves had tended to act as a kind of welfare agency, a body of opinion began to emerge in favour of transferring this side of the court's work to officers of the local authorities, who were given new powers in both welfare and education by the Children Act 1948. This movement culminated in the Children and Young Persons Act 1969 which transferred much of the responsibility for young offenders from the courts to the local authority social services.

By the early 1950s efforts were being made along new lines to keep the young out of the courts. In 1951 Liverpool adopted a Police Juvenile Liaison Scheme based on cautioning instead of prosecuting juvenile first offenders. The results were impressive and the precedent was followed by other police authorities.

Throughout the 1960s there was a spate of activity. In 1960 the Ingleby Committee[4] supported the retention of juvenile courts but also recommended a further move away from the concept of criminal jurisdiction. The Children and Young Persons Act 1963 extended the welfare powers of local authorities and required them to do preventive work on behalf of children. In 1964 the Kilbrandon Committee issued a Report[5] on children and young persons in Scotland and the Labour Party produced *Crime—a Challenge to Us All*, containing recommendations by a group headed by Lord Longford and including Lord Gardiner, the future Lord Chancellor. This had considerable influence on the Labour Government which came into office shortly afterwards and which published a White Paper, *The Child, the Family and the Young Offender*, in 1965. This proposed that juvenile courts should be abolished and that offenders under 16 should be dealt with by 'family councils' and those aged 16–21 by 'young offenders courts'. The family council was to consist of two social workers from the local authority children's department and other suitable persons. These proposals ran into heavy opposition and were dropped, but a further White Paper, *Children in Trouble*, which was published in 1968, was better received and formed the basis for the Children and Young Persons Act 1969, which can be seen as part of the continuing process that began in 1847 and was a logical extension of the underlying philosophy of the Children Act 1908. Its aim was to spare young offenders the stigma of criminality by dealing with them as far as possible outside the criminal law and to support and treat them in their families and in the community. It provided for 'intermediate treatment' which would allow a child to remain in his home but would also bring him into contact with a different environment. The Act took away the power of magistrates to send a child to an approved school or to make a fit person order and it abolished sanctions in default of payment of fines and substituted supervision orders, which carried no penal sanctions, in place of probation orders.

The Act also provided for the abolition of three important facilities for dealing with young offenders; attendance centres, detention centres and Borstal training, which are described later.[6] This part of the Act was not brought into force immediately, and the Conservative Government which came into office in 1970 had different views on the value of these disposals. By the time a Labour Government was returned in 1974 opinion generally was more favourable to their retention.

The Act proved to be an example of idealism outrunning resources. Its provisions were not given a fair chance to prove themselves effective because they were brought into operation before there had been adequate groundwork. Experienced probation officers were replaced by local authority social workers who were not specifically trained in this type of duty, and in most cases they had no secure accommodation at their disposal. Local authorities, in the aftermath of the Seebohm reorganisation of social services, failed in many cases to keep pace with the extra demands made upon them in terms of both staff and facilities.

The 1969 Act was well designed to deal with the majority of young offenders but it soon became apparent that the new system was unable to cope with the minority of hard-core persistent offenders. The activities of these youngsters, carried out with apparent impunity and with increasing contempt of authority, began to arouse considerable public criticism of the courts on the assumption that they were failing to administer the law. Not surprisingly the magistrates felt deep resentment and frustration. When dealing with a child under fourteen there was virtually nothing they could do beyond making a care order; what happened to the child thereafter depended entirely upon the local authority, and frequently he was returned to his home and immediately proceeded to commit another offence. In some cases the police took the view that it was a waste of time to bring a child before the court.

In 1976 the Lord Chancellor's attention was drawn to a boy of thirteen who had committed eighty-one burglaries and was brought before the court, who placed him in interim care pending full consideration of his case. In the space of ten days he escaped six times and committed nine further burglaries. His parents asked that he should be sent to secure accommodation but the local authority had nowhere secure and were not prepared to turn a key in a lock. They tried keeping the boy in his pyjamas but he again escaped. This was repeated a further three times, with the boy absconding on each occasion, and at last the local authority agreed to put him in a locked room. There was, however, no secure accommodation which could contain him so that remedial and educative work could begin. This kind of situation was repeated throughout the country and it became quite normal for a child appearing before a court to have been found guilty of three or four similar offences within the previous few weeks and for the magistrates to find themselves obliged to make the same order at each hearing.

In 1976 the House of Commons Expenditure Committee[7] suggested that courts should be enabled to make a 'secure care' order which would oblige the local authority to keep the child in secure accommodation, but the Government would not accept this on the ground that it limited the local authorities' discretion.

In 1972 several juvenile court justices, unable to discharge what they saw as their public duty, resigned in desperation and others followed. The magistrates were accused of exaggerating the juvenile problem and of being motivated purely by resentment at losing their former powers. This was a gross distortion of the truth. For many years previously juvenile court chairmen like Basil Henriques and John Watson had been among the leaders of the movement towards greater understanding of the problems of young people, and the work of the courts generally was conducted by justices who were genuinely concerned with these problems.

They were almost at the opposite end of the spectrum from the callous sadists which some of their detractors would have made them appear to be. Many were in the teaching profession or were involved in social work. By 1972 most had undergone special training in the duties of the juvenile courts. The great majority were wholly in sympathy with the philosophy underlying the 1969 Act. They saw that it provided a sound framework for dealing with children in trouble, but the success of an enactment does not depend upon a legislative framework but on a number of factors such as financial implications and local decisions. What they criticised was the method of implementing, or failure effectively to implement, the new policy.

The magistrates, while agreeing wholeheartedly that the care of juvenile offenders was of the utmost importance, pointed out that this could never be the sole consideration. The interest of the victims and of the public in general should be protected and therefore the problem must be recognised as one of law enforcement. The courts were responsible for the protection of society and should be given the proper tools to discharge their duties. The Magistrates' Association asked that the recommendations of the House of Commons Expenditure Committee should be implemented and that they should have power to make secure care orders. Referring to the inability of magistrates to make orders for the custody of juveniles on remand when bail was inappropriate, they pointed out that this frequently resulted in the court being obliged to resort to the wholly unsatisfactory expedient of remanding the juvenile to prison while enquiries were made pending trial. In these cases the local authority had told the court that they regarded the child as unruly and that they had no accommodation in which they could hold him.

During this period an uneasy relationship developed between the courts and the social services. There tended to be a fundamental difference of philosophy between magistrates and the social services, who resented any suggestion that the courts should assume greater powers. Many of those in responsible positions were inclined to approach the problem as if it were a battle of competing ideologies, whereas in truth there was little disagreement in principle but merely over method and priorities. The result was an undesirable atmosphere of confrontation instead of co-operation. The picture changed as the social services became experienced and gained the confidence of the courts. The former differences seem to have been largely overcome.

Magistrates were not alone in criticising the operation of the 1969 Act. In R. v. D.[8] the Court of Appeal reviewed the case of a boy of fifteen who had 'an appalling record'. The court took the view that the proper course was to send him to a community home, but they found that 'if a care order is made, very often the only effect is that the offender is returned to his home within a short time'. Lord Justice Lawton observed that the decision whether the boy would go to a community home did not rest with the court but with 'unknown social workers and psychiatrists', and, he commented, 'the bureaucratic machinery is such nowadays that the court has no control whatsoever over where the boy should go'. The court was concerned not only with the boy but with the public and they felt that it was not in the public interest that he should roam the streets as he pleased; they therefore felt obliged to confirm an order for Borstal training as the only means of keeping him in secure accommodation though in other respects they considered this to be the wrong treatment.

It was not until 1982 that a further major enactment was passed. This was the Criminal Justice Act which, *inter alia*, introduced residential care orders. Where a juvenile already the subject of a care order is found guilty of an offence punishable with imprisonment in the case of a person over 21, the court may add a condition to the order that for a period not exceeding six months the power of a local authority to allow a parent or guardian etc. charge and control shall not be exercisable.

In the 1969 Act emphasis was laid on a social welfare response to juvenile offending, but in fact welfare disposals declined (before 1969 fewer than 200 males in the 14–17 age group were sent to Borstal in a year; after 1969 the figure reached 2000 per year). The 1982 Act was intended to restore the confidence of the courts in the effectiveness of non-custodial measures. Community Service Orders were extended to offenders under 16 and juvenile courts were given new powers to impose conditions in supervision orders, including requirements to follow directions from a supervisor and to refrain from participating in specified activities on certain days and also to undergo 'night restriction' (this and other provisions of the Act, including the abolition of Borstal, are explained further in Chapter 10.

Prior to 1982 a number of other Statutes had affected the

juvenile courts. The 1969 Act had already been strengthened by the Children Act 1975 and the Criminal Law Act 1977. Under the latter the supervision order, which had lost much of its credibility, could contain conditions such as 'regular attendance at school'. The 1975 Act aimed to improve the provisions of the 1969 Act whereby local authorities are given power to restrict the liberty of a child 'to such extent as the authority thinks appropriate'. There was a strong lobby, among justices and others, for an annual judicial review of care orders and the 1975 Act authorises the making of regulations to this effect. The Child Care Act 1980 empowers local authorities to assume parental rights and duties in respect of a child in care. The Magistrates' Association believe that this power should be transferred to the juvenile courts where the parents should have the right to be heard, especially on the issue of access or of reclaiming the child. It does seem anomalous that juvenile courts which deal exclusively with matters pertaining to juveniles have no power to make orders for access.

Statistics of offences committed by young people supported the view that something had gone wrong. The number of children under the age of 17 dealt with (either by the courts or by police caution) for indictable offences rose from 165,000 to 205,000 between 1969 and 1973. At the same time, the degree of seriousness of the offences increased and by 1975 boys and girls aged 10–16 were responsible for nearly one-sixth of all offences of personal violence, one-fifth of all theft and handling, a quarter of criminal damage, 30 per cent of robberies and 45 per cent of burglaries.

A further disturbing phenomenon was that as the degree of seriousness of the offences rose the age of criminality decreased. Over the twenty-year period 1955–75 the increase in offending was greater among those aged 17–20 than among those aged 14–16; but in the period 1969–75 the increase was greater among those aged 14–16.[9] It is interesting to note that the lowering of the average age at which offences are committed has coincided with a policy of raising the age of criminal responsibility. The youngest age at which a child could be prosecuted under the 1933 Act was eight. In 1960 the Ingleby Committee recommended that the limit be increased to 12. The Children and Young Persons Act 1963 raised it to 10, where it remained, though provision was made in the Children and Young Persons Act 1969 to raise it further, first to 12 and then to 14. Since 1969 opinion has hardened against raising the prosecutable age; though the idea of fixing it at 12 is not a novel one. The Saxons held that a child under 12 could not be guilty of crime but this limit was reduced by the Normans to 7, where it remained for nearly nine centuries.

Public alarm at the apparent increase in violent crime and hooliganism among the young tended to polarise the issue on political lines. Mr William Whitelaw, when Shadow Home Secretary, in a letter to *The Times*, argued that the courts should have at their disposal a wide range of treatment including power to lock up those who do not respond to non-custodial measures; and his criticism of the Government was 'that they have failed to distinguish between those young offenders who can be treated outside secure units and those who clearly need to be put in secure units both for their own good and for the protection of the general public'.

The level of serious child crime in the 1970s undoubtedly reached alarming proportions, but it should be seen in its proper perspective. It was not a new phenomenon. Socrates complained that the young were contemptuous of authority and tyrannical towards their teachers. There have been many notable rises in juvenile crime in the past, and curiously there were marked manifestations after each of the previous Acts, of 1908 and 1933, which introduced progressive measures for dealing with young offenders; though there is no evidence to connect this with the provisions of the Acts themselves. Young people are not naturally wicked but like all young creatures they have an urge for self-expression and excitement. There is special excitement in doing something that is known to be wrong, and the excitement increases with the risk of being caught. Much of the present trouble devolves from failure to sublimate the surplus energy of the young. The vast majority respond to sensible guidance and discipline. There are a few, however, who do not, and who become a menace to their fellow citizens, and it was with this minority that the authorities were unable to deal after 1969.

Not all the blame for the rising crime rate can be placed on the 1969 Act. Juvenile crime was already rising before 1969 and this trend was not unique to the United Kingdom. It was to be seen in all industrial nations. The causes seem to lie largely in urban industrial society. Many of my colleagues in the Commonwealth Magistrates Association, particularly those from Africa, claimed that there was virtually no juvenile crime in their countries before they were blessed with Westernisation. This was largely due to family influence. The family was responsible for the conduct of its children and, in exceptional cases, when the family failed to exercise effective control, responsibility rested with the tribe. With the coming of Westernisation family ties weakened, particularly in urban industrial areas, and juvenile crime increased. In Hong Kong, which has one of the highest rates of juvenile delinquency, crime among the young used to be very low when Chinese family discipline was strong, but this has been eroded. The two largest contributing factors to the crime increase in Hong Kong are thought to be weakening of family influence and the mass erection of high-rise flats. Undoubtedly the family is of vital importance in the pattern of juvenile crime. When sitting as a juvenile magistrate I have noticed that it is rare for the court to have before it a child from a section of the community where family discipline is strong; Jewish children being a particular example. Unfortunately family influence has been weakened not only by the behaviour of some parents and by the increase in the divorce rate and in the number of one-parent families, but even more by modern social conditions.

The White Paper *Children in Trouble*, on which the 1969 Act was based, said that 'the aims of protecting society from juvenile delinquency and of helping children in trouble to grow up into mature and law abiding persons are complementary and not contradictory'. Few would quarrel with that philosophy, but the Act was not well handled and lack of facilities denied it a fair trial. Its implementation was also made more difficult because it coincided with the amalgamation of the children's departments and the transfer of responsibility from the Home Office to the DHSS. This was followed in 1974 by the reorganisation of the local authorities upon whom responsibility now largely rests. Many of the defects amounted to teething troubles which could resolve themselves in time and there was support for this view in that from 1975 there was a decline in the number of young persons convicted of indictable offences. Nevertheless, majority opinion had come to accept the need for a reappraisal of the 'children in trouble' philosophy which, in its 1969 application, tended to submerge the law-and-order element in preoccupation with the welfare of the juvenile offender. It remains to be seen how effective subsequent legislation, particularly the 1982 Act, will be. Fundamentally, a great deal of the trouble must also have been due to the attitude of a society which encouraged the young to denigrate authority. For two decades society leaned over backwards to give the younger generation independence and to treat them as sophisticated adults at the earliest possible age. In many cases the price that was paid was loss of self-discipline.

9 Quarter Sessions and the Crown Court

The last day of December 1971 saw the demise of the courts of Quarter Sessions after more than 600 years of eventful history. It also marked a turning point in the shifting fortunes of the lay justices in that, for the first time, they were given full jurisdiction in the highest criminal court of trial in the land.

Since 1362 county justices had held quarterly meetings at which justice was dispensed and the local government of the land administered. The scope of the justices' powers at Quarter Sessions was considerable. There were few criminal offences they could not try when sitting judicially and, until 1842, they could impose the death penalty. As administrators they were, until 1888, the precursors of the county and district councils, as was shown in Chapter 1.

By 1947 the work of Quarter Sessions consisted mainly of trying indictable offences (except the most serious, which went to Assizes), hearing appeals against conviction or sentence by magistrates at Petty Sessions and hearing rating and licensing appeals.

In each county appeals were heard by committees of not less than three and not more than twelve justices elected by their colleagues, but there was no limit on the number who could sit for trials, although two were sufficient to form a quorum. Sometimes over 100 turned up and it was not uncommon for 40 or more to crowd on to the bench, causing a major upheaval whenever the court had to adjourn and at best presenting an undignified scene with much whispering and passing of papers. Although this caused delay the consequences were less serious in those days than they would have been later because the work load was not heavy and any case which was expected to last for more than a day or two was committed to Assizes. The Royal Commission of 1948, however, recommended that not more than eight justices, in

115

addition to the chairman, should adjudicate at Quarter Sessions and this was implemented in rules made by the Lord Chancellor in 1950.[1] This led to some acceleration in the disposal of cases but it had no noticeable effect on Assizes, which continued to be burdened with the longer cases. There was also no appreciable reduction in the number of justices who came to Quarter Sessions even though they could not all adjudicate. Most of them wished to attend the administrative meetings which usually coincided with sessions and they also welcomed the opportunity to meet their colleagues over lunch, which was normally provided by the county council.

With a view to transferring some of the work load from Assizes to Quarter Sessions an Act had been passed in 1938 extending the jurisdiction of Quarter Sessions when they were presided over by a legally qualified chairman or deputy chairman.[2] To be legally qualified for the purpose of the Act it was necessary for the chairman to hold or have held high judicial office,[3] or to be a barrister or solicitor of not less than ten years' standing appointed by the Sovereign on the recommendation of the Lord Chancellor following an application by the sessions. Whenever such a person presided the sessions could try a number of offences which would otherwise have had to go to Assizes. The initiative for these appointments rested with the sessions themselves but it was my duty as Secretary of Commissions to persuade every sessions to have at least a legal chairman and if possible one or more legal deputies so as to provide effective relief to Assizes. In 1947 there were still three counties[4] with no legal chairman and seventeen with no legal deputy chairman, but by 1951 all had legal chairmen and only seven were without a legal deputy.

Except in London and Lancashire, chairmen and deputy chairmen were appointed for a period of three years under a warrant which stipulated that the Lord Chancellor might terminate the appointment prematurely if he thought this desirable for any reason. The Chancellor could therefore decline to renew an appointment at the end of the period if the person concerned had not proved satisfactory and in exceptional circumstances he could remove him in mid-stream. Seldom in modern times have there been such omnipotent powers over the judiciary; but the arrangement seemed necessary as a subtle way of eliminating dead wood, of which there had been many earlier instances. In the event the Lord Chancellor seldom found it necessary to exercise these powers. Only one deputy chairman was removed before his time had expired and about a dozen were not reappointed for a second term because of some personal inadequacy, sometimes amounting simply to an inability to establish a good working relationship with their justices.

Chairmen and deputy chairmen appointed under the 1938 Act could be remunerated at rates which, except in London and Lancashire, were agreed between Quarter Sessions and the county council with the approval of the Lord Chancellor. In 1947 the chairmen in ten counties were remunerated, the rates ranging from £2500 for the whole-time chairman of London sessions to £31 for the part-time chairman in Shropshire, who sat six days a year. These sums may be compared with the salaries paid at that time of £5000 to a High Court judge and £3500 to a Permanent Secretary in the Civil Service. In the ensuing years salaries at Quarter Sessions were gradually raised at the instigation of the Lord Chancellor, but he and his staff had a thankless task in reconciling the thrift of county councils with the financial loss sustained by a legal practitioner when undertaking this work.

The office of Chairman of Quarter Sessions carried no personal title, but by 1960 the rising importance of the criminal jurisdiction exercised by whole-time chairmen led to proposals that they should be given the same style as County Court judges, who were addressed as 'His Honour Judge . . .'. This move was partly inspired by the hope that the enhanced personal status might improve the reputation of the sessions (which up to then had not been as high as that of the County Courts) and encourage abler applicants to seek appointment. These proposals were accepted in respect of chairmen and also deputy chairmen in 1966, but before they were announced one or two unfortunate lapses occurred among the deputy chairmen and the moment seemed inopportune to confer a distinction upon them. It was not until 1969 that the Queen declared that every salaried, whole-time chairman and deputy chairman of Quarter Sessions should 'be called, known and addressed by the style and title of "His Honour" prefixed to the word "Judge" before his name'.[5]

At the end of the war most of the 62 county Quarter Sessions (49 in England and 13 in Wales) still sat only 4 times a year and 38 of them did not average more than 3 days at a time. In 1947, 22 sat for 10 days or less and the total sitting days for all Quarter Sessions in England and Wales other than London was 1134.

London, Lancashire and Middlesex were the only places having 'whole-time' sessions, though they were not whole-time in the modern sense of the word.[6] Quarter Sessions remained to the end essentially part-time courts.

A number of boroughs enjoyed the right, originally under Royal Charters and later under the Municipal Corporations Acts 1835 and 1882, to hold separate Quarter Sessions, but no justices sat in these courts, which consisted of a single judge, known as a Recorder, who was a practising member of the Bar of at least ten years' standing and held office on a part-time basis. Unlike county justices, those in the boroughs never adjudicated at Quarter Sessions; the nearest they came to doing so was when the Children and Young Persons Act 1963 required Recorders to sit with two justices as assessors when hearing appeals from the juvenile court. This provision was a concession to the view that justices who had served in the juvenile courts had experience and understanding of juvenile problems which were not possessed by a Recorder. The justices often felt that the Recorder also lacked an understanding of local problems when he heard appeals from their adult courts. A frequent source of grievance among borough justices was that when they imposed heavy penalties in response to public feeling and exhortation by Ministers these were reduced by the Recorder on appeal.

Before 1835 boroughs appointed their own Recorders under the authority of their charters but the Municipal Corporations Act of that year placed the power of appointment in the Crown.[7] By custom this was made on the recommendation of the Home Secretary but in 1949 the Justices of the Peace Act transferred responsibility to the Lord Chancellor.

As in the counties, most borough Quarter Sessions operated on a part-time basis, but the City of London, and after 1956 Liverpool and Manchester, had whole-time Recorders who exercised the jurisdiction of a Commissioner of Assize. Those in Liverpool and Manchester were appointed on the Lord Chancellor's recommendation under the Criminal Justice Administration Act 1956 and sat in Crown Courts which the Act created but the Recorder of London remained the only judge to be appointed by the municipal authority under its charters, though in 1964 the City of London (Courts) Act reconciled tradition with modern constitutional practice by providing that he should not exercise any judicial function unless he was 'appointed by Her Majesty to exercise such functions'. The City were thus forced to choose someone who had been approved by the Lord Chancellor.

Recorders held office during good behaviour until in 1956 the Criminal Justice Administration Act gave the Lord Chancellor power to dismiss for inability. This was never exercised. There were occasions when a Recorder's conduct did not meet with the Lord Chancellor's approval but these did not amount to inability or misbehaviour within the meaning of the Statute. The most common situation of this kind was where a Recorder was unduly severe or lenient in his sentencing. As in the case of justices it was not open to the Lord Chancellor to direct Recorders on the level of penalties they imposed, but excessive leniency could be as much a miscarriage of justice as excessive severity and whereas the latter could be cured by the Court of Appeal there was no remedy for a grossly inadequate sentence. Where, therefore, a Recorder was clearly out of line with public thinking and with the views of the rest of the judiciary, successive Lord Chancellors considered it their duty to draw the matter to his attention. Lord Hailsham wrote to a Recorder who had expressed an aversion to custodial sentences:

I appreciate the sincerity of your belief that a judge should do everything he properly can to keep people out of prison, but there are two matters the importance of which you underestimate; example to others and the desirability of consistency between court and court.

During the twenty years prior to 1972 four recorders who followed a consistent course of gross leniency were sent for by the Lord Chancellor and each responded, at least to some extent, to the advice he received.

A Recorder's salary was paid by the borough council but for many years the amount varied considerably, depending more upon the council's generosity than upon the size of the borough or the volume of work. From 1962 the remuneration was fixed by the Lord Chancellor after consultation with the council, the rate being based on the borough's population. In most cases the amount fell far short of compensating the Recorder for what he lost in briefs while attending sessions, and a further disadvantage was that he had to pay his own travelling expenses without income tax relief. This unfair rule was established by the decision of the House of Lords in 1926 in Ricketts v. Colquhoun,[8] which upheld the Inland Revenue's contention that a Recorder's work did not begin until he was seated on the bench, even though he would have been entitled to tax reimbursement had he attended the same sessions as counsel. Heated battle between the Lord Chancellor's Office and the Revenue raged over this issue for many years but the Revenue refused to capitulate even when a Royal Commission and an Interdepartmental Committee[9] recommended that the rule should be abrogated.

In spite of these tribulations there was no shortage of applicants for Recorderships, for a number of reasons: they provided an opportunity to give service to the community; there was some prestige attached to the office, which could assist rather than hinder a practice; and a Recordership was also a stepping-stone to a whole-time judicial appointment.

No records were kept of the number of days sat by Recorders but usually the sessions were shorter than those in the counties. It rested with the Recorder to fix the dates of his sittings and, as the majority had busy practices, it was not surprising that some tended to select dates immediately after those of the county sessions when there would be little work left over. The Justices of the Peace Act 1949 sought to eliminate those Recorderships which were unproductive and with this object it provided generally for the abolition of every borough Quarter Sessions serving a population of less than 20,000. There were thirty-one of these, but the Act contained a saving clause which enabled a Recordership to be retained if the Lord Chancellor was satisfied that this was desirable for historical or geographical reasons and having regard to the assistance which the court had given or was likely to give to the administration of justice in the county. Responsibility for deciding the fate of the smaller boroughs was entrusted to a committee of three, comprising the Attorney-General (Sir Hartley Shawcross, as he then was), Phillip Allen of the Home Office (who later became Permanent Secretary) and myself. It was no easy task, especially when it came to assessing historical interest. Many small boroughs drew our attention to their fascinating histories, and at Richmond in Yorkshire we were met with the cry 'What William Rufus set up, William Jowitt shall not pull down!' Proof that Rufus had nothing whatever to do with the matter did not dampen their ardour; but alas it availed them little and Richmond lost its Recordership. Another small borough,

Abingdon, produced evidence, which no one succeeded in refuting, that it had nearly twice the population shown in the Registrar General's estimates. Abingdon was peculiar in many ways. The Recorder, Stephen Benson, had held office for far longer than any other Recorder and his sessions were always preceded by the arrival of a little train which came puffing down from Oxford carrying in its three coaches the Recorder, the Clerk of the Peace who had come to meet him, the Bar, solicitors, various camp followers and, bringing up the rear, the prisoners, or sometimes the one and only prisoner. We were glad to find that Abingdon sessions also disposed of an appreciable amount of work and we felt justified in reprieving its Recordership. In all, a total of 8 small Recorderships were retained and 23 abolished[10] leaving 93 boroughs with Quarter Sessions which survived until 1971.

In the 1960s the volume of work in the higher criminal courts was increasing rapidly and the part-time system which had worked well for centuries was becoming inadequate in spite of attempts to patch and rejuvenate the creaking structure. In 1960 a survey by the Home Office Research Unit showed that at courts which were in continuous session, like the Crown Courts in Liverpool and Manchester, the bulk of cases were heard within eight weeks of committal whereas at Assizes and part-time Quarter Sessions some had to wait for four months or more. In the following year, the Streatfeild Committee advised that the time between committal and trial should not be more than eight weeks.[11]

With a view to relieving pressure on Assizes the jurisdiction of Quarter Sessions was further extended by the Criminal Justice Administration Act 1962, and more sessions began sitting on a virtually whole-time basis. This increased the difficulty of ensuring the presence of a sufficient number of justices (there had already been occasions in 1961 when Middlesex sessions were unable to rely upon a complete team each day) and the 1962 Act therefore provided that a legally qualified chairman or deputy chairman might sit alone if justices were not available. These measures served only to postpone the inevitable crisis and the reckoning came in the mid-1960s when arrears at Assizes became unacceptable. Drastic reform of court structure and administration could no longer be postponed.

In 1966 a Royal Commission was appointed to enquire into the arrangements for the administration of justice at Assizes and

Quarter Sessions outside Greater London, and to report what reforms should be made for the more convenient, economic and efficient disposal of civil and criminal business. Every previous enquiry into the administration of the courts had been chaired by a lawyer, but Lord Gardiner took the view that lawyers did not excel as administrators and that on this occasion knowledge and experience of administrative techniques were essential. The choice for the chairmanship of the Royal Commission therefore went to Lord Beeching, Deputy Chairman of Imperial Chemical Industries and former Chairman of British Rail.

The Report of the Beeching Commission[12] is one of the most readable blue books to be published in recent years and it contains a remarkably clear prescription for the ills that it was set up to examine. The Commission found that the circumstances for which the courts, as they then were, were devised no longer existed and had not done so for a long time, and that the defects resulting from a failure to change the system had been made more serious by a recent sharp increase in civil and criminal business. They went on to say that many Quarter Sessions were attempting to dispose of a full-time load with part-time resources, and that dependence upon part-time judges, whose availability was subject to pressure from their other occupations, led to bunched sittings of the courts with resulting overloading of the Bar and others providing services to groups of courts. The Commission's recommendations were based on two main propositions: firstly, that all criminal courts, including Quarter Sessions and Assizes, above the magistrates' courts should be abolished and their jurisdiction merged in one new whole-time court to be known as the Crown Court, which would have jurisdiction throughout England and Wales; and, secondly, that a new unified court service should be created under the Lord Chancellor for all courts, both civil and criminal, except the magistrates' courts. The old judicial offices of chairman and deputy chairman of Quarter Sessions, Recorders and County Court judges were to be replaced by two new types of appointment: Circuit judges and new-style Recorders.[13] These recommendations involved the most comprehensive reforms in judicial administration since Henry II introduced the Assize system in the twelfth century. They were accepted and implemented in record time.[14]

The Beeching Commission was concerned with the higher criminal courts and the civil courts; its terms of reference did not embrace the structure and administration of the magistrates' courts. On the other hand, the Courts Act as it finally emerged made a substantial impact on the justices by giving them a new role in the higher criminal courts and also by introducing procedural changes which extended to the magistrates' courts.

The Commission, after considering whether justices should play any part in the new Crown Court, recommended that they should be encouraged to sit with certain of the judges but that they should do so only as assessors and not as full members of the court. This half-hearted compromise was reached after intense argument, but it is doubtful whether it could have worked because few justices would have consented to sit merely as assessors. Moreover, the Commission's principal reason for recommending that justices be associated with the work of the Crown Court was to provide them with a useful training forum, which was illogical because if justices were there merely to learn they ought not to have been able to influence the proceedings even as assessors. The Magistrates' Association resisted the Beeching Commission's recommendation and urged that justices should be full members of the court. Lord Gardiner, the Lord Chancellor, accepted the Association's view subject to their being able to satisfy him that justices could give the time that would be needed in attending the Crown Court. In a memorandum submitted to the Lord Chancellor in March 1970,[15] the Association concluded that, subject to certain adjustments, the inclusion of justices as full members of the Crown Court should operate satisfactorily. The Association's proposals were accepted by Lord Gardiner, and subsequently by Lord Hailsham when he became Lord Chancellor in June 1970, and the necessary provisions were included in the Courts Act 1971. They were based on the understanding that the justices themselves were desirous of acquiring these additional functions and that they were capable of discharging them. The Act provided that all appeals and committals for sentence from magistrates' courts should lie to the Crown Court and that, when hearing them, the Crown Court should comprise four justices (the number could be reduced in certain circumstances) with a Circuit judge or Recorder as chairman.[16] Justices were eligible to sit in trials, though only for certain classes of offence to be specified by the Lord Chief Justice with the concurrence of the Lord Chancellor. In the event directions were made limiting the presence of justices to those cases which would normally be allocated for trial by a Circuit judge or a Recorder and not by a High Court judge, which meant that generally speaking justices would take cases similar to those which had previously come to them at county Quarter Sessions. The judge had a casting vote, both at appeals and trials, but only if the court was equally divided. The judge may therefore be outvoted by the justices, but this seems to be a rare occurrence.

The Act applied equally to county and borough justices so that, for the first time, borough justices were empowered to sit in a higher court than Petty Sessions. The sudden eligibility of about 12,000 additional magistrates to serve on a tribunal of which they had had no previous experience created difficulties which would have been more easily surmounted if we had had time to integrate the borough justices more slowly. The Act also took the progressive step of giving the Crown Court jurisdiction over the whole of England and Wales so that an offence committed in any part of the country could be tried in any court centre. This was another break with the former localised approach to the administration of justice. Quarter Sessions could only try cases arising in the county. A similar extension of jurisdiction in Petty Sessions would have been salutary because a large proportion of offences were no longer committed in the area where the offender lived, as had been the case in the past; many motorists infringed the traffic laws far from home, while thieves seldom fouled their own doorsteps.

The principal object of the 1971 Act was to establish a streamlined court structure with supporting services which would dispose of criminal and civil business as expeditiously as possible. In the early stages the result was highly successful and, within a year of the Act coming into force, the period between committal and trial in criminal cases in the Crown Court outside London had been reduced to under eight weeks, but thereafter arrears again began to accumulate owing to a further staggering increase in the volume of work. Days sat at Assizes and Quarter Sessions amounted to 6966 in 1957 and 17,930 in 1967; those spent in the Crown Court in 1974 were 45,007. Between 1967 and 1975 committals for trial increased by 130 per cent. This flood of business (due not only to more crime but to many more minor offences coming before the Crown Court and to cases taking longer to try) could be contained only by the provision of more courts and more staff, which was out of the question during the period of financial stringency, or by the transfer of work from the

Crown Court to the magistrates. The latter course was the subject of the enquiry by the James Committee mentioned earlier.[17]

With hindsight it can be argued that the Act of 1971 went too far in giving justices full jurisdiction in the Crown Court and that it would have been better to limit their role to hearing appeals and committals for sentence and perhaps pleas of guilty. If this was so the fault was mine. I was of the opinion that the Magistrates' Association's proposals were viable and I advised that justices should be given full jurisdiction in both appeals and trials. My principal reasons were as follows. (1) As pointed out by the Royal Commission, it was of considerable benefit to justices to have experience of sitting in a higher court. It broadened their outlook, extended their knowledge of court procedure and gave them experience of higher standards of chairmanship and advocacy than were normally to be found in the magistrates' courts. (2) It was generally conceded that justices, with their training and experience in penology and sentencing techniques, could play a valuable part in assisting the professional judge when it came to sentencing,[18] especially when, as was more likely then than it had been in the past, the judge did not have local knowledge of the area. (3) Judges necessarily lead more isolated lives than do justices, and there was ample evidence that magistrates could exercise a useful restriction on any idiosyncrasy of a judge or Recorder. (4) The participation of justices in hearing appeals should avoid the friction which had previously occurred between borough benches and their Recorder. (5) The identification of the ordinary citizen with the dispensing of justice in the higher tribunals seemed to be an acceptable philosophy in line with current thinking. (6) Previous experience of the performance of justices at county Quarter Sessions suggested that, with adaptation, similar courts could with advantage be fitted into the structure of the new Crown Court.

My counsel was accepted by the consecutive Lord Chancellors, Lord Gardiner and Lord Hailsham, and subsequently by the Home Secretary, Mr Roy Jenkins. Responsibility for decisions rests with Ministers but if in this case the decision was wrong I was to blame for the advice I gave.

I confess to misjudging the extent of the differences between Quarter Sessions and the Crown Court, though in mitigation I would plead that these differences could have been greatly modified and made more acceptable to the justices if we had had.

the chance to prepare the ground gradually and to introduce the new system after a reasonable period of explanation and discussion with all concerned, including the judiciary, the staff and others involved in the work of the courts. Instead, there was a frantic dash to implement Beeching before a public outcry broke over the law's delays.

The differences which emerged in practice between the Crown Court and Quarter Sessions were due to four factors. Firstly, trials before justices in the Crown Court lasted longer than they did at Quarter Sessions because the Crown Court was doing what Beeching intended it to do: High Court judges were no longer burdened with long cases that were suitable for trial by a judge or Recorder sitting with justices, whereas previously most long cases had been committed automatically to Assizes although many could have been dealt with by sessions. Secondly, Quarter Sessions sat only periodically and began on a fixed date, whereas the Crown Court was in continuous session and the work ran on from day to day. Thirdly, the legally qualified chairmen and deputy chairmen of Quarter Sessions almost invariably had considerable experience of criminal trials and recognised the problems inherent in sitting with laymen, whereas in the Crown Court it was not uncommon for justices to sit with a Recorder who had had less experience of sentencing than they themselves, though he would not admit it. Fourthly, the facilities provided for justices in the Crown Court often fell short of those to which they had been accustomed at Quarter Sessions, where they met in a convivial atmosphere and everything was done for their convenience. It was impossible to achieve the same standard in most Crown Court centres, and in some not even refreshments were available.

At Quarter Sessions a justice could usually assume that any trial in which he sat would be concluded within the day or that special arrangements would be made to deal with the few cases which lasted longer. In the Crown Court a justice who had arranged to sit on a certain date often found either that all cases had already begun on a previous day or that the trial in which he sat ran over for two or three more days. If he was unable to stay to complete it he felt that he had wasted his time because he was not present at the moment when the justices exercised their paramount role of deciding sentence. This state of affairs was even more unsatisfactory to the accused, whose trial might begin with a full court of judge and four justices all of whom might drop out during the first and second day, so that by the third day the judge was left sitting alone, and the unfortunate prisoner was left wondering whether anyone would bother to finish trying him at all. In some places Crown Court staff tried to avoid the difficulty by not calling upon justices to sit in long cases (judges were empowered to sit alone if justices were not available) but it is not always possible to estimate the length of a case and it could be said to be wrong in principle for the same type of offence to be tried by a court which sometimes included justices and sometimes did not, so that the severity of the sentence might be thought to vary accordingly. In some areas only justices who could undertake to sit for several days consecutively were summoned to attend, but this tended to limit the composition of the courts to a small residue of retired, elderly justices with a large preponderance of women.

With a view to increasing the supply of experienced justices with ample time at their disposal, an innovation was introduced in 1974 whereby justices on the Supplemental List might continue, if the Lord Chancellor so approved, to serve in the Crown Court until they reached the age of seventy-two. This was a joint idea of Baroness Macleod and myself and, with her support, it was implemented in the Administration of Justice Act 1973. To those who posed the obvious question why, if a justice was too old to serve in the magistrates' court, he was not too old to remain in the higher courts, there was a threefold answer. (1) In the Crown Court pressure on the bench was less and the pace was slower than in the magistrates' courts. (2) Cases were presented to the Crown Court by counsel on both sides, whereas magistrates' courts, more often than not, had to deal with unrepresented parties who frequently had difficulty in making themselves understood. (3) Justices in the Crown Court invariably sat under the chairmanship of a judge or Recorder.

The Lord Chancellor and the Lord Chief Justice would have liked to disqualify all justices from sitting in the Crown Court until they had served in Petty Sessions for at least five years. In the absence of any limitation it was possible for a majority of newly appointed justices to overrule a judge on sentence or to reverse the decision of an experienced petty sessional bench on appeal. A qualifying period would, however, have reduced still further the number of justices available to attend, and the furthest the Lord Chancellor felt able to go was to ask that no justice should be called on to adjudicate in the Crown Court unless he had completed both stages of his basic training and, in so far as it was practicable, had at least two years' experience as a magistrate.[19] He added later that in no circumstances should a justice with less than two years' service hear appeals or deal with committals for sentence.

The essential differences between county Quarter Sessions and the Crown Court would not have been felt so acutely by the justices had it not been for ancillary changes in the chairmen and officers of the courts. Quarter Sessions met under the chairmanship of a prominent county figure, often a High Court judge, whom the justices knew personally and with whom they discussed their problems frankly and with confidence. The Beeching Commission foresaw the need to fill the gap created by the abolition of the office of chairman and recommended that members of the Circuit bench should be allocated to groups of petty sessional divisions with a view to the justices being able to turn to them for help and advice. This recommendation was accepted and judges, known as liaison judges for want of a better title, were appointed in every area. For the first few years most of them were also placed on the commission of the peace and were co-opted as members of the Magistrates' Courts Committees for their respective areas. Many played a valuable role in indoctrinating the new justices, but the success of the scheme varied considerably. Much depended upon the personality of the judge, but he could not fully replace the chairman of Quarter Sessions as the captain of the county team, for his position could never be that of leader and focal point of the county magistracy in the manner of the former chairman. The primary role of the liaison judge was to smooth the relationship between the Crown Court and the magistrates, but attempts to draw up a precise list of their duties were defeated by inability to devise a code which would be universally applicable. In the field of training, for example, there are wide differences between the requirements of different areas as well as between the ability of different judges to meet demands.

An equally significant change occurred in the court staff. At Quarter Sessions they were part of the county and had a special loyalty to their justices, who knew them all as individuals. The 1971 Act destroyed local loyalties and transferred control of administration from the justices to a national court service. At the outset most of the Crown Court staff, like many of the judges and

Recorders, had had no experience of working with justices and there was much misunderstanding, giving rise to resentment on both sides.

A notable casualty of the Courts Act was the Clerk of the Peace, whose office dated from the fourteenth century. He was the principal officer of Quarter Sessions both in counties and in boroughs, but in counties was far more than the officer in charge of the court. In all but five counties outside London he was also clerk of the county council. In addition, he was usually secretary of the Advisory Committee and clerk to the Standing Joint Committee, the Magistrates' Courts Committee, the confirming and licensing authority and the lieutenancy, as well as holding every other county office that was worth having. Such plurality may have been wrong in principle but it had its advantages. It meant that the principal administrative officer had a profound knowledge of all aspects of the judicial system in the county and could act as an effective link between the various authorities responsible for both Quarter Sessions and Petty Sessions. Potential sources of friction were avoided or defused by the action of the Clerks of the Peace, whose departure created a vacuum which has not been entirely filled.

Many of the Crown Court teething troubles were resolved and in some areas, principally the rural counties, the new system worked well apart from justices having to travel greater distances to their courts than they had done to Quarter Sessions; but in many places there remained dissatisfaction among the magistrates and frustration among the staff, who were inclined to regard magistrates as an unnecessary nuisance. While considering how these problems could be resolved the Lord Chancellor, in common with his colleagues in the Government, was under pressure to reduce expenditure and although the amount spent on justices attending the Crown Court was only a drop in the ocean of the national economy it was such drops as these that had to be justified. In 1976 £92,635 was paid to magistrates for travel, subsistence and loss of earnings when sitting in the Crown Court. Administrative costs brought this total to approximately £110,000. If justices had sat only for appeals and committals for sentence the amount saved would have been between £50,000 and £65,000. There was the further consideration that courts dispose of their work slightly more rapidly when a judge sits alone than when he has justices with him.

In these circumstances the Lord Chancellor asked the Magistrates' Association in 1976 to identify the difficulties which were causing concern to many of their members and to consider whether the existing rules might be amended so that justices should no longer be called upon to sit for trials.[20] Unfortunately, this was interpreted by some as a Machiavellian scheme to deprive justices of the right to sit in the Crown Court, with the result that a decidedly blurred picture emerged from the enquiry conducted by the Magistrates' Association at the Lord Chancellor's request. All that could be said for certain was that about one justice in every four was dissatisfied with some aspect of the Crown Court system but that the great majority of justices wanted to continue to sit in trials.

Neither the Lord Chancellor nor the Lord Chief Justice was prepared to curtail the justices' role in the Crown Court against their wishes and it is improbable that any significant change will occur in the foreseeable future; but much remains to be done if the justices are not ultimately to lose at least part of what they gained in 1972. On the other hand, if remedies could be found for the present deficiencies there could be a movement in the opposite direction, and if the justices were minded to accept additional responsibility their jurisdiction might one day be extended further.

The 1971 Act presented a challenge to the justices and it was up to them whether they accepted it or not. One could well understand it if they felt that their public duties were already onerous enough. No one could blame them if they called a halt. But the challenge was there, offering a chance for the layman to play an even greater part in the administration of justice than ever before. I like to think that what was done in 1971 constituted the beginning of a new era, of almost unparalleled scope, in the long history of the Justices of the Peace.

10 Sentencing

Penology and the treatment of offenders are wide and complex subjects which lie outside the scope of this book except in the context of their impact on the work of the courts. They come within the domain of the Home Secretary rather than of the Lord Chancellor. This chapter is therefore concerned with the subject principally from the viewpoint of the sentencer.

When passing sentence the court is discharging its constitutional function of maintaining the law of the land, and the problem of how to deal with a convicted criminal is one of the greatest challenges to the judiciary. Many consider that sentencing is the most exacting function a judge has to perform. Certainly no part of the judicial process is more important, and there is none which excites greater public interest, involving as it does issues of the greatest moment for both the convicted person and for the community as a whole. The court has the twin functions of preventing crime in the interest of the public and of safeguarding the offender from oppressive or secretive sanctions. Sentencing is a subjective art involving the reconciling of the seemingly irreconcilable in the diverse aims of punishment, retribution, deterrence, reform and rehabilitation.

Ideas about the treatment of offenders have varied greatly during the 600-year history of the Justices of the Peace. For centuries the prime concern of the courts was to inflict punishment on the wrongdoer. Justices did not have the power to order some of the more exquisite tortures which were the privilege of judges of Assize, but up to the middle of the nineteenth century they could impose penalties of death or transportation and, although they ceased to exercise their power of capital punishment some time before it was formally abolished in 1842, they continued to make savage orders for transportation. As late as 1830 Wiltshire Quarter Sessions sentenced a man to fourteen years' transportation for stealing a wooden plank, valued one shilling, the property of a local justice who sat on the bench which sentenced him.

Imprisonment as a punishment was used very rarely until the nineteenth century. Before that all serious crimes involved death or transportation, and prisons were used only to house debtors or those awaiting trial, or as a staging post to the gallows or the convict camp. In 1800 there were still some 200 offences carrying the death penalty but by the middle of the century it had been abolished for everything except treason, murder, piracy and arson of certain Crown property (it ceased to be the penalty for murder in 1965). Meanwhile transportation, which thrived when the American colonies and later Australia provided ample scope for penal settlements, became less readily available and was finally abolished in 1857. Imprisonment suddenly became the only option for many offences, but prison conditions had long been appalling. John Howard had drawn attention to the unsatisfactory situation in 1777 but there had been no great change by the middle of the following century, though there were some improvements initiated by Elizabeth Fry and by some of the justices responsible for local prisons. A big step forward was taken in 1878 when the prisons, which until then were privately owned, were taken over by the state, but imprisonment was still regarded purely as a punishment and a deterrent and the regime involved the crank, treadmill and other devices. A new era began in 1895 when the Gladstone Committee proposed that imprisonment should also be used to reform and rehabilitate the criminal, though for some time little progress was made in this direction except in the case of young offenders, to whom reformative treatment was applied through Borstal institutions (introduced in 1908), and it was not until after the last war that these measures were extended to the adult criminal.

The last forty years have witnessed greater changes in penal policy and a far more enlightened approach to sentencing than any other similar era in our history. The period was marked by increasing limitations on the courts' powers to impose sentences of imprisonment and by experiments in alternative methods of disposal. Under the Criminal Justice Act 1948 magistrates were not permitted to send anyone under the age of 17 to prison and they could not impose a prison sentence on a person aged 17–21 unless no other method was appropriate and they recorded their reasons. Similar limitations were placed on magistrates' powers to imprison a first offender over the age of twenty-one by the First Offenders Act 1958. These measures had no noticeable effect on the prison population, which began to rise. In England and Wales it remained fairly static at just over 20,000 until 1950, when it started to climb, and by 1977 it had reached 42,000. It continued to rise until 1980 when industrial action by prison officers led Parliament to pass the Imprisonment (Temporary Provisions) Act giving the Home Secretary power to suspend prison sentences for a limited period. This proved unnecessary because the courts themselves reduced the number of their custodial sentences to meet the situation and the numbers in prison began to fall. At the conclusion of the emergency, however, the numbers again increased, stimulated by serious public disorders in July 1981, and the prison population rose to a record 45,500. This was higher than almost any other country in Western Europe. France, for example, with a slightly larger overall population had only 38,000 persons in prison; though it should be recognised that crime is chiefly a product of large cities, in which England abounds. Faced with this situation the Government came to look upon the reduction of the prison population as an end in itself, especially in the light of the increasing cost[1] (in 1978 the annual cost of keeping a person in prison was £5800, by 1982 it was £10,000). The Government therefore intensified its efforts to limit the courts' scope in custodial sentencing, and further restrictions were added by the Criminal Justice Act 1961 and the Criminal Law Act 1977.

A more realistic approach, however, was adopted during the passage of the Criminal Justice Bill in 1982 when the Government resisted strong pressure to curtail the sentencing discretion of the courts in order solely to reduce the prison population. Those who demanded this limitation claimed that the overcrowding of the prisons was all the fault of the courts, especially magistrates. This was totally untrue. The prisons were overcrowded because of the increase in serious crime and because successive governments had failed to do anything to increase accommodation. Between 1918 and 1959 not a single purpose-built prison was constructed in England and Wales. The magistrates were in fact less to blame for the appalling conditions in the prisons than almost anyone. The Magistrates' Association were among the first to draw attention to the deteriorating situation and to propose ways of dealing with it. Published statistics show that the Crown Court is far more likely to imprison for a summary offence than a magistrates' court. It is very rare for magistrates to impose a custodial sentence save in cases of violence, burglary, serious fraud and drugs – which are precisely the types of case in which the Court of Appeal have stated that imprisonment is normally the appropriate sentence. When the Lord Chief Justice pronounced upon the proper length of prison sentences in R. v. Bibi (1980) there was immediately a striking reduction in the average length of sentence imposed in magistrates' courts. Lord Lane's dicta laid down that imprisonment should be avoided if possible, but if unavoidable it should be for as short a period as possible.

One result of restrictions on sentencing was to increase the population of the Borstal institutions which catered for young offenders aged seventeen to twenty-one. Magistrates' courts could not sentence offenders directly to Borstal (except in Northern Ireland). If they considered Borstal to be the appropriate treatment they might commit them to a higher court for an order to be made. Many young adult offenders who would previously have been sent to prison began to arrive in the Borstals, which became overcrowded, and among the inmates were many difficult types for whom the system was not originally intended. Borstals were designed for the more simple society of the pre-war years when, judging by their low reconviction rate, they were reasonably successful. Overcrowding meant that time spent in Borstal had to be reduced and many were discharged before their training was completed, with the result that the system became discredited.

Young adult offenders, who potentially constitute a particularly delinquent group, were the subject of an enquiry by the Advisory Council on the Penal System under the chairmanship of Sir Kenneth Younger whose report, published in 1974, gave a very full account of the system and its evolution. It put forward proposals for a shift from custody to treatment in the community and it recommended that imprisonment, Borstal and detention centres for young adult offenders should be discontinued and replaced by two new sentences: one custodial in a Prison Department establishment designated by the Home Secretary, the other non-custodial, which would amount to release under supervision in the community. These recommendations were not accepted but in 1982 the Criminal Justice Act abolished Borstal training and imprisonment for offenders aged under 21. These were replaced by new determinate sentences. In broad terms the courts are now able to impose detention centre orders on young men from three weeks to four months in length. When longer sentences are necessary the court can impose youth custody. A youth custody sentence is usually served in the same institution which was previously used for borstal training. As yet one cannot say whether the change is purely cosmetic or will prove to be of substance. One clear change, however, is that magistrates can send an offender straight to youth custody whereas previously they were obliged to commit to the Crown Court for a Borstal sentence.

It was natural that anxiety over the size of the prison population which coincided with rising concern for the liberty of the subject should focus attention on the number of persons remanded in custody awaiting trial. During the ten years 1966–75 the number of those not bailed while on remand rose by 50 per cent compared with a rise of only 20 per cent in the total daily population of all prisons. During 1981 44,000 males and 2500 females were remanded in custody untried. Large numbers of those so remanded did not subsequently receive custodial sentences. Those who have never had to administer justice usually assume that there is no great difficulty in deciding whether or not to grant bail. In fact it is one of the most difficult tasks facing the court. For magistrates it was made no easier by frequent encouragement from the Home Office to grant bail almost as a matter of course when, if they did so and the defendant absconded, they were reprimanded by the higher courts and accused by the police of making their task impossible. A study by the Metropolitan Police in 1977 showed that, excluding juveniles, about 4000 persons absconded from bail in the London area in a year and 3000 indictable offences were committed while on bail. On the other hand, at remand stage the defendant is presumed innocent and remands in custody are the only circumstances where, contrary to Magna Carta, a person can be confined for an appreciable period in peacetime without trial. The task of the bench is to balance the rights of the public against the rights of the individual and the crux of the problem is that the decision must inevitably be based on probability and not certainty. It is a forecast of the future and not an assessment of past conduct and it must be made at a stage when information is limited.

Until 1967 bail had to be applied for and magistrates had an almost unfettered discretion. The Criminal Justice Act 1967 provided that bail should not be refused except on one or more of a number of listed grounds and that the reason for refusal should be given if the defendant was not legally represented or if his representative asked for it. Remands in custody declined considerably after 1967. The 1967 Act was replaced nine years later by the Bail Act 1976 which went still further and provided that a defendant awaiting trial or remanded for enquiries pending sentence should be granted bail unless he fell within one of the exceptions set out in the Schedule. The effect was to create a statutory presumption in favour of the grant of bail which had to be considered whether or not an application was made.

While steps were being taken to curtail the courts' powers to send people to prison curious mutations were taking place in informed opinion on the proper length of prison sentences. For nearly twenty years from the end of the war penology was dominated by the reformative philosophy which had begun with the Gladstone Report, with the result that sentencing policy was engrossed in reform and rehabilitation to the exclusion of other previously accepted objectives such as deterrence or retribution. This approach was characterised by insistence on long prison sentences because a short sentence did not allow sufficient time for custodial training to be effective. In 1913 over 80,000 prison sentences were for two weeks or less and in 1947 such sentences were still common but by 1960 they had dropped to around 3000. Magistrates were regularly discouraged by the Lord Chancellor and the Home Secretary from imposing short custodial sentences, and when the Lord Chief Justice held his first sentencing seminar for High Court judges in 1963 they were exhorted to follow the same practice. Twelve years later courts were being urged to shorten their sentences and the long prison sentence was anathema. Expert opinion had come to doubt the reformative value of custodial treatment, and official policy, stimulated by the spectre of an unmanageable prison population, underwent a complete *volte-face* on length of sentence. If anyone was to be sent to prison at all, it had to be for the shortest possible term, emphasis being laid on the initial shock-effect.[2] In 1967 the Criminal Justice Act provided for prisoners to be released on licence after serving one-third of their sentence (or twelve months, whichever was the longer), subject to recommendations by local review committees in each prison and by a national Parole Board. In 1968 the automatic remission of detention centre sentences was raised from one-sixth to one-third and in 1975 the Home Secretary annoyed magistrates by raising it for junior centres to a half. There was a greater inclination than there had been for centuries for the executive to become involved in the sentencing process.

In the 1960s there was also a growing body of opinion which regarded all imprisonment as futile except for the dangerous criminal who needed to be kept out of circulation. Many still attached importance to the deterrent effect on potential offenders of the prospect of imprisonment though there was evidence to show that speed and certainty of detection and conviction were greater disincentives than the ultimate sentence. Clearly, resort should not be had to imprisonment if it could reasonably be avoided. (No one who has not had experience of penal institutions can fully appreciate the traumatic effect of the clanging door and the key turning in the lock.) The search for alternative methods of disposal, which had begun just after the war, was intensified and the magistrates were presented with an increasing variety of options.

Up to the end of the war magistrates had regarded sentencing with considerable complacency. Their principal options were imprisonment, corporal punishment, fine and probation. From 1948 onwards they were obliged to adjust to constant changes in sentencing policy and to apply many new methods of disposal. The new era began with the Criminal Justice Act 1948 which, *inter alia*, abolished corporal punishment (except in prisons, where it survived until the Criminal Justice Act 1967), replaced the Probation of Offenders Act 1907 and provided new methods of disposal in lieu of imprisonment. Among the most important provisions of the Act were the establishment of attendance centres and detention centres for young offenders. Those aged twelve (reduced to ten in 1961) to under twenty-one could be obliged to attend an attendance centre for certain hours which did not interfere with school or work. The regime provided 'physical exercise and useful occupation'. The centres were open on Saturdays and were recognised as particularly useful for dealing with young hooligans at football matches. No attendance centre was provided for girls because at first there was an insufficient number of girl offenders to make it worth while, but from the late 1960s there was an alarming upsurge in delinquency, including criminal violence, among girls which presented a new challenge that could not be met effectively by the courts owing to lack of suitable facilities.

Detention centres, for offenders aged over fourteen and under twenty-one, provided residential training for periods of three or six months according to the age of the offender. They were intended to give a short, sharp shock with hard work and discipline, and offenders could be sent to them for periods of three to six months. The courts regarded detention centres as a valuable form of disposal and would have liked to see them extended to adult offenders, but only a small number of centres were set up even for those under twenty-one and the courts' attempts to make use of them were frustrated by lack of availability. (Similar problems arose in the case of attendance centres.) The concept of detention centres when first introduced was based on the wartime 'glasshouse' principle of punishment, but as the years passed the authorities came to favour a less rigorous regime. In 1967 the Advisory Council on the Penal System[3] reviewed the operation of the detention centre principle and redefined its aims and philosophy. The council's recommendations, which were accepted by the Home Secretary, resulted in the 'short, sharp shock' principle being abandoned and replaced by emphasis on rehabilitation, but the pendulum seems to have swung again recently towards an evaluation of the more harsh regime.

The 1948 Act also enabled a court to discharge an offender without punishment on condition that he committed no further offence within a specified period. This useful option was widely used by magistrates.

Throughout the period Parliament was reluctant to increase the severity of the penalties which could be imposed by the summary courts, but, recognising that this sometimes resulted in offenders receiving inadequate sentences, they provided in the 1948 Act and the Magistrates' Courts Act 1952 that where, in a particular case, magistrates were of the opinion that their powers were inadequate they could commit the accused to a higher court for sentence. Although considerable use was made of this power magistrates were sometimes reluctant to avail themselves of it because they found that the higher courts imposed a lower level of penalty than they could have given themselves.

The Criminal Justice Act 1967 (which abolished the sentences of preventive detention and corrective training available to the higher courts) enabled courts, when passing a sentence of not more than two years' imprisonment, to suspend the sentence for from one to three years, after which it would lapse unless the offender was convicted of another offence within the period. After the introduction of suspended sentences other forms of penalty, financial as well as custodial, diminished steadily, but this was due partly to the courts wrongly using the sanction in cases where, before 1968, they would have imposed a fine or a conditional discharge instead of imprisonment.[4] In the retiring room one sometimes heard justices remark: 'I don't think he should go to prison but it will do him good to have it hanging over his head.' Some suspended sentences which ought not to have been imposed in the first place had to be activated when the offender committed another offence, with the result that ultimately more instead of fewer offenders finished up in gaol. Yet, in spite of this, the process was carried a stage further by the introduction of partly suspended sentences in the Criminal Law Act 1977. This was an integral part of the Government's desperate efforts to clear the prisons, but obviously it could result in more rather than less time being spent in custody under the 'taste of prison' syndrome. There was therefore some disenchantment with the whole concept of suspended sentences and an attempt was made to defuse the controversy in the Criminal Justice Act 1982 which reduced from six to three months the minimum sentence to which partial suspension may apply and reduced to 28 days (from one quarter of the sentence) the minimum period that must be spent in custody. It is felt by many that this still does not go far enough and that, in the interest of shorter time in custody, the period to be served should be limited to a small fraction of the total sentence. Three or four weeks is quite enough for the 'clang of the prison gates' effect to be achieved.

A noticeable feature of the years following the 1967 Act was the diminished use of probation orders in favour of other non-custodial sentences. In 1963 probation orders accounted for 78 per cent of the average probation officer's case load, while ten years later it was only 41 per cent. The drop was due partly to the diminished confidence of some magistrates in the probation service which was passing through a critical stage. The atmosphere is now changing and courts are reverting to greater use of probation orders.

The Criminal Justice Act 1972 provided a number of new options. It introduced criminal bankruptcy for the purpose of preventing convicted criminals from profiting from their crime, it empowered courts to confiscate property (including vehicles) used in the course of a crime, and it enabled the courts to defer sentence for up to six months to see how the offender conducted his life in the meantime. The 1972 Act also introduced two new non-custodial methods of treatment: community service orders and day training centres. The community service order was inspired by the 1970 Report of the Advisory Council on the Penal System under the chairmanship of Baroness Wootton and was one of the most promising developments in the social history of the era. It was introduced with the primary purpose of providing a constructive alternative for those offenders who would otherwise have received a short custodial sentence. Offenders aged seventeen and over who had been convicted of an offence punishable with imprisonment could be ordered to carry out unpaid work of service to the community during their spare time, up to a maximum of 240 hours. The order deprived the offender of his leisure-time but did so for a constructive and outward-looking purpose and gave him an opportunity to make reparation to the community against which he had offended. The new system began hesitantly in six experimental areas but, with growing confidence from both magistrates and the probation service, the number of referrals rapidly increased as facilities became available and they rose from about 5000 in the first year to 12,133 between December 1976 and November 1977. During the six years from the inception of the scheme in 1973 the number of persons given community service orders was 105,000. The failure rate was between 15 and 20 per cent. Over half the referrals were in respect of persons under 21.

Community service was the success story of the 1972 Act and it was extended to offenders aged 16 by the Criminal Justice Act 1982. The Act also enabled the court itself to lay down the regime which the youngster was to follow. Previously this rested largely with the social workers or probation officers, and the courts, through lack of confidence, often imposed a custodial sentence where it was not really necessary.

An important feature of the community service order was that it gave an offender a sense of responsibility, which is one of the most important elements in the war against crime. An interesting example of this occurred in Northern Ireland when the age for jury service was lowered from twenty-one to eighteen in 1975.

Northern Ireland still makes considerable use of the jury in civil cases and the authorities feared that there might be a miscarriage of justice if juries included numbers of irresponsible youngsters, many of whom were involved in the contemporary disturbances. The reverse was the case. For the first time these young people, who up to then had regarded the courts as instruments of the Government for imposing punishment, came to realise that courts were there to resolve the problems of the ordinary citizen, and they quickly accepted the responsible role which they as jurors were required to play; many even proved to be fairly adept at assessing damages. There was evidence to suggest that these young people retained their new sense of responsibility after they left the court and returned to normal life.

Day training centres, also introduced by the 1972 Act, were intended as an alternative to imprisonment for the socially inadequate recidivist for whom other methods of disposal seemed to have failed. Men and women between the ages 21 and 45 could be required to attend the centres five days a week for about eight hours. Experimental centres were established in four places, centrally funded by the Home Office. Attendance at a centre was effected as a condition of a probation order and the period of attendance was limited to 60 days. Those involved in the centres, including most ex-trainees, thought them beneficial, but one-year reconviction rates varied from 40 to 65 per cent and the centres suffered from a general disenchantment with the concept of 'therapeutic' sentencing. In 1982 the new Criminal Justice Act replaced them with locally funded 'day centres' and courts were allowed to make probation orders requiring attendance at such centres for not more than 60 days. It remains to be seen whether the new scheme, funded by local probation committees, can be justified in the light of the previous disillusionment with day training centres.

The 1982 Criminal Justice Act contained a number of other important new provisions. One novelty, which had been conceived by the Magistrates' Association, was the 'curfew'. The Act enabled courts, with the consent of a juvenile offender and his parents, to require him to remain at home for up to ten hours between 6 pm and 6 am on up to thirty nights during the first three months after a supervision order has been made. This innovation was opposed by some social workers and probation officers and also by the police who thought that it would require frequent random checks of the offender's home. This was not, however, the intention. The object was to keep youngsters who were prone to hooliganism off the streets at night. If someone appeared on the streets in breach of an order the police could arrest him without having to wait for him to commit a breach of the peace. If, on the other hand, he did not appear in public there was no need in the public interest for checks to be made on his house to ensure that he was at home.

Another provision which was included in the 1982 Act at the instigation of the Magistrates' Association was the residential care order, already mentioned in the context of the juvenile courts.

Many of those who appear in the courts are mentally ill and one of the most difficult tasks of magistrates is to decide how to deal with them. Under the Mental Health (Amendment) Act 1982 magistrates have jurisdiction to deal with the mentally disordered by way of hospital orders, probation and restriction orders. There are four types of mental disorder which can be compulsorily admitted to hospital.

When it came to non-custodial sentences the posture of Parliament and of the Government was the opposite to that adopted towards imprisonment. There was no question of discouraging magistrates from exercising their powers to the full; on the contrary, the fear that they might be too lenient led to proposals that minimum penalties should be fixed by Statute, and although these were not implemented they were reflected in compulsory disqualification for certain driving offences under the Road Traffic Acts.

In the 1960s and 1970s there was a rising stream of guidance from government Departments on how magistrates should exercise their sentencing powers. The Lord Chancellor was reluctant to support this proclivity and was careful to point out that in his executive capacity he had no authority to tell courts how they should exercise their discretion; but under mounting pressure from his colleagues and the public he sometimes took the opportunity in a speech to draw attention to the need for 'realistic' sentences. On these occasions his comments were usually directed to the level of fines. Fines are the most usual penalty in magistrates' courts and in 1976 they were imposed on 98 per cent of those convicted. For a time many magistrates did not take account of the fall in the value of money, with the result that the level of fines became unrealistically low. Magistrates also failed to appreciate the significance of certain types of offence which began to occur with greater frequency than before. Examples were harassment of tenants by landlords and various new phenomena in the realm of traffic offences such as the overloading of lorries. To overload a lorry even by a seemingly small amount could constitute a serious danger and might also enable the cargo's owner to increase his profits by thousands of pounds. In some cases Parliament indicated what it regarded as appropriate increases in monetary penalties by raising the maximum fine for certain offences, the last occasion being the Criminal Law Act 1977 which also enabled the Home Secretary to vary fines by order to take account of inflation. There were divergent views on the extent to which courts should follow this lead and the effect of such statutory changes was not always very marked, but the Magistrates' Association reflected the rises in their lists of 'starting points' for penalties referred to later. These lists and periodic guidance from the Lord Chancellor made magistrates more inflation-conscious, particularly in respect of penalties for the more common offences. Thus, the average fine for speeding rose from £6·8 in 1967 to £9·6 in 1972, £17·7 in 1975, £20·04 in 1977 and £29 in 1981. The increase between 1967 and 1972 was in line with changes in the Retail Price Index. The average fine exceeded the Index in 1975, but this was mainly as a result of large increases in maximum fines under the Road Traffic Act 1974, and after 1976 the increase in fines dropped behind the rate of inflation. Between 1977 and 1981 the average annual rate of increase for fines in motoring offences was 10 per cent compared with 13 per cent inflation.

The maximum fines that magistrates could impose for indictable offences triable summarily with consent was fixed in 1925 at £100 (and/or six months' imprisonment). This was not changed until 1967 when the figure was raised to £400 and in 1977 to £1000. There were a few exceptions to this limit of which the most notable were offences against foreign currency and fishing regulations. Under the Fishery Limits Act 1976 penalties of up to £50,000 could be imposed on summary conviction for breaches of fishery regulations. In 1973 the City of London justices, in DPP v. Stanley and Others which took four weeks to try, imposed fines of £300,000 (£200,000 on one charge and £100,000 on a second) on two companies for offences under the Exchange Control Regulations, the financial penalty in such cases being limited only by the sums involved in the illegal transaction. These proceedings could have been brought before the Crown Court but the City magistrates, who were able to field a full team of financial experts, were thought to be the better tribunal. All fines are now, with minor exceptions, on a five point scale set out in the Criminal Justice Act 1982.

A fine is potentially the most promising alternative to a custodial sentence, but this depends upon prompt and effective enforcement measures. At the end of 1976 the amount of unpaid fines amounted to about £15 million; six years later it was nearly £40 million[5] (but this included fines not yet due because the court had allowed payment by instalments). It follows that fine enforcement is a crucial element in the function of every court, yet it is usually given low priority. The success rate varies from court to court and a Home Office study in 1982 revealed that performance was closely related to efficient organisation and the quality of the staff engaged in collection and also to the speed with which action is taken after default.

In default of payment of a fine magistrates have power to order imprisonment and about 20,000 defaulters are jailed each year, but the courts are under increasing pressure not to impose this sanction. The fact remains, however, that if the fine is to be a valid penalty it must be enforceable and no alternative to imprisonment as a last resort has yet been devised for this purpose. The subject was examined in 1981 by a NACRO group headed by Lady Howe (a London justice and wife of the Chancellor of the Exchequer) who came firmly to the conclusion that prison should be retained as a final sanction for those who wilfully refuse to pay fines.

It is of even greater importance to get the fine right in the first place. Fine default increases with the offender's inability to pay and the growing number of unemployed coming before the courts makes it essential to fix fines realistically. Magistrates are required by the Magistrates' Courts Act, 1952 and subsequent legislation to take the offender's means into account before imposing a fine, but some courts are too rigid. This is particularly so where the defendant is convicted of a number of traffic offences arising from a single incident. Some courts normally impose for each of these offences the full norms set out in the Magistrates' Association's guidelines which, when added together, amount to an excessively high total. In some cases it is impossible for the court to assess the offender's means because he pleads guilty by post. A solution to this might be the system of 'day fines', which operates successfully in West Germany and Sweden, whereby the court imposes a fine, not in terms of a cash sum, but of a number of days' income of the offender.

A number of civil matters were enforceable in the magistrates' courts by imprisonment. Civil debts incurred in a County Court were enforceable in this way until the procedure was abolished by the Administration of Justice Act 1970, but it remained possible for magistrates to imprison in default of payment of maintenance orders and of rates and taxes; though in 1969 the Payne Committee[6] recommended the establishment of enforcement offices to deal with enforcement of civil debts and fines. The Attachment of Earnings Act 1971 was calculated to reduce the number of committals to prison for non-criminal matters but it by no means eliminated them, and from 1974 the receptions of non-criminal prisoners began to rise.

In the last twenty years an additional problem has been created by the increasing public addiction to hire purchase. The population has been persistently tempted by industry to live beyond its means and is the normal experience of magistrates' courts to be asked by a defendant with a good income for time to pay because of his hire purchase commitments. In his view the last thing that should be a charge on his resources is a penalty imposed by law.

Preoccupation with the treatment of offenders diverted attention from those who suffered from their depredations. Much thought was given to the offender but comparatively little to his victim. One frequently heard bitter complaints from those who had been assaulted or whose homes had been broken into that the culprits were treated leniently while their own loss and suffering was ignored. To some degree this situation was met by the Criminal Injuries Compensation Scheme introduced in 1964 which, although it did not have any impact on the offender, enabled *ex gratia* payments to be made out of public funds for personal injury directly attributable to a crime of violence. Until 1972 magistrates had very limited powers to order compensation in cases of personal injury. Prior to the Criminal Justice Act 1972 courts could not award compensation unless the injured party applied for it, and usually he did not. The Act made sweeping changes in the law, bringing the courts into line with public opinion, and it removed any need for an application by the victim before the court could order compensation up to a maximum of £400 in respect of each offence. After the Act a majority of offenders convicted of property offences were ordered to pay compensation but there was no similar increase in orders made in respect of offences of violence against the person.[7] Among the reasons for the infrequency of awards were the offender's inability to pay, the insistence of the divisional court.that compensation should be ordered only in the clearest cases (otherwise the victim should be left to take proceedings in the civil courts) and the difficulty experienced by magistrates in assessing the cost of the victim's injuries. In a number of speeches to magistrates the Lord Chancellor pointed out that the victim and the public were entitled to see that the criminal did not profit from his crime and he urged magistrates always to consider compensation where it seemed appropriate and where the assessment of damage was not complicated. There was some response to this appeal and the number of compensation orders increased: about 27,000 were made in 1976. In 1978 the Magistrates' Association issued guidelines[8] to assist magistrates in assessing compensation and to secure reasonable uniformity. In 1982 the Criminal Justice Act continued the process started by the 1972 Act. It enabled a court to make a compensation order as a sentence in its own right and not just as an adjunct to another sentence, and it gave compensation priority over a fine where an offender could not afford to pay both.

The magistrates themselves were among the first to draw attention to the unfair position of a defendant who was not legally aided and had to pay the costs out of his own pocket if he was acquitted. The costs of a defendant cleared of a summary offence may be awarded against the police, but magistrates are reluctant to take this course lest it be thought that they are criticising the police for bringing the case. The Metropolitan Police have long regarded costs against them as an indictment of themselves. The Magistrates' Association have sought to solve the problem by urging, so far unsuccessfully, that all costs should be paid out of central funds (as in Scotland where the prosecution is in the hands of the Procurator Fiscal). A solution may now be in sight following a recommendation of the Royal Commission on Criminal Procedure in 1982 that all prosecutions should be removed from the police and placed in the hands of Crown Prosecutors who, though appointed for each police area, should be totally independent of the police and separately funded.

A further problem is that the police, faced with growing economic stringency, have recently been pressing magistrates to award them a fixed sum to cover administrative expenses in every case of conviction. This has been condemned by the Magistrates' Association as being unfair but about 40 per cent of courts have complied with the police request.

Thirty years ago a large proportion of crime was against property. By 1977 there was far more violence and there had been a steep increase in cases of fraud. New phenomena had appeared in the forms of drug offences and shoplifting; the latter in particular posed peculiar psychological questions and the courts needed to distinguish between greed, exhibitionism, mental depression and inadvertence. I referred (page 86) to traffic offences as being the most prolific source of work for magistrates and I mentioned extension of the fixed penalty system as a palliative in that context. In the sphere of sentencing, traffic cases present an extra dimension in that they may involve disqualification of the driver in addition to the more orthodox penalties. The Road Traffic Act 1972 introduced a new procedure whereby magistrates were required to disqualify an offender for at least six months when he was convicted of a third endorsable offence within three years unless there were mitigating circumstances. This 'totting-up' procedure was in turn replaced by a 'penalty points' system under the Transport Act 1981 (which also made the wearing of seat belts compulsory). If an offender incurs 12 points or more within three years the court must disqualify unless satisfied that there are sufficient mitigating circumstances. The number of points to be incurred for each offence is fixed by statute, with certain exceptions[9] where the gravity of the offence may vary greatly. Careless driving, for example, may range from inadvertence to the verge of recklessness. It must be recognised, however, that variable points add to rather than reduce the work of the courts because offenders will contest the number of points awarded against them.

It was in sentencing motoring offenders that divergent views among the magistrates became more apparent than in other types of case and the motoring public, being highly articulate, was not slow to voice its disapproval. Dr Roger Hood, in an interesting and far-ranging study of magistrates' sentences in motoring cases in 1965–7[10] noted widely differing assumptions and came to the conclusion that magistrates 'never really thought through their attitudes'.

Of the complaints received by the Lord Chancellor about magistrates' courts, 90 per cent related to sentencing and almost all of these alleged either undue leniency or disparity. In nine out of ten of these cases enquiry showed that there was a sound reason for the magistrates' decision. Unfortunately, the public is seldom aware of all the facts of a reported case, nor do they appreciate the principles which properly influence a court to deal with one offender in a different way from another. The facts of each case are rarely the same and the court must take account of the means and previous record of the accused. There was much indignation when a bench fined a motorist £100 and disqualified him for twelve months for careless driving and on the same day conditionally discharged some one who indecently assaulted a child. Press reports had not disclosed that the driver was a wealthy businessman with a number of previous convictions while the assault had been committed by an old pensioner in his dotage who, until then, had led a blameless life. Nevertheless magistrates, like other human beings, vary in their views on many subjects, including sentencing, and in this respect Justices of the Peace do not differ from professional judges.

In 1962 the Magistrates' Association began to consider ways of avoiding undue disparity of sentence, and in 1964 they prepared a list of what they then termed 'basic penalties' for the principal motoring offences. This was intended to give an indication of what would be appropriate where there were no aggravating or mitigating circumstances. The Association emphasised that the suggestions were subject to variation according to the means and previous record of the offender and the circumstances of each case. In 1965 the list was submitted to the Lord Chancellor and the Lord Chief Justice, who gave their approval, and it was then circulated to the Magistrates' Association's members. The list was soon under attack on the ground that it attempted to fetter the court's discretion. Lord Gardiner defended the Association, pointing out that the critics could not have it both ways. They cavilled at disparate sentences yet condemned the magistrates' reasoned attempt to secure a degree of uniformity. The Association issued further lists (of what they later termed 'starting points', to emphasise that they were not attempting to lay down standard tariffs) to take account of inflation and statutory increases in penalties. In the light of these guidelines many benches drew up their own lists of 'norms', not only for traffic penalties but also for other common types of offence. There was reason to think that these steps, together with the sentencing exercises referred to in Chapter 6, went some way towards eliminating gross disparity; but there were still marked variations, not so much between magistrates on the same bench as between benches in different parts of the country, though these could often be justified by differing local conditions and the prevalence or otherwise of certain types of crime in the area, and also by the extent to which the police cautioned the least serious offenders instead of bringing them to court.

Leniency was an even greater source of complaint than disparity. Rarely did anyone other than a convicted defendant claim that a penalty had been too harsh. Public indignation at an apparently inadequate sentence suggested that what weighed most in the mind of the community was deterrence and retribution.

Here again published reports were often misleading. In 1975, a weekend newspaper printed an article attacking magistrates for inadequate sentences and gave what were alleged to be four examples of cases where the court ought to have imposed imprisonment. On being challenged by the Magistrates' Association the writer was unable to give details, but further investigation showed that one case had been heard in the Crown Court, in another the magistrates did not have power to imprison, and in a third, where a man had been fined £20 for assault on the police, the article did not reveal that the assailant had also been ordered to pay £150 to the constable. At about the same time that this article appeared Sir Robert Mark, Commissioner of Police for the Metropolis, was widely reported as having censured magistrates for encouraging criminal activity by their inadequate sentences. I asked him to let me have details and it was found that in most of the instances he cited there was a reasonable explanation of the level of sentence, and furthermore two of the cases had been tried in the Crown Court when justices were not present, another was an appeal where the Crown Court had reduced a heavier penalty imposed by the justices and all but one of the remainder were decisions of Metropolitan Stipendiary Magistrates.

Justices of the Peace were not basically more lenient than other courts. A study carried out by my office in the London courts in 1957 showed that their average fines for a number of offences were slightly higher than those of the stipendiaries. Circuit judges received their share of criticism for leniency and even the Court of Appeal (Criminal Division) did not escape when in 1977 it reduced the sentence on a rapist in R. v. Houldsworth. However, Justices of the Peace differed from other members of the judiciary in tending to focus their attention on the defendant who stood before them to the exclusion of other considerations. Crown Court judges often commented that the first reaction of justices who sat with them was to ask themselves what was best for the defendant and to concentrate on statements by the probation officer and defence counsel. The judge, on the other hand, began by considering the public interest and the gravity of the crime and went on to review any aggravating or mitigating circumstances, and only then did he address himself to the possibility of doing something to help the defendant. Some justices might therefore have been criticised for over-reacting to defendant welfare. They were tempted to regard themselves as welfare officers, whereas their function was to maintain and vindicate the law. It is also true that some justices had a pathological revulsion against imprisonment but in this respect they did not differ from some professional judges.

The rising incidence of criminal activity (which was in evidence throughout the world), could not have been due solely to the failure of therapeutic measures adopted by the courts or by the police or social services. Crime is a product of the cultural, physical and social environment in which it occurs and its control and prevention depends far less on the sentences imposed by the courts than is generally recognised. In any event, courts cannot produce a panacea of their own. They are bound by the law and are obliged to apply policies laid down by the legislature, but neither the legislature nor the criminologists have yet found a cure for generic crime although the subject has been debated since Aristotle's *Ethics*, and an analysis by S. R. Brody in 1976 showed that results of survey confirmed that little can be done to cure criminals.

It is against this sombre background that magistrates have had to perform their sentencing duties. Even if all sentences were ineffectual magistrates would still have the task of maintaining the credibility of law and order, but there is no doubt that, as deterrents, sentences can have an impact on the commission of specific offences. A marked drop in the incidence of some types of offence has followed a raising of the monetary penalty and the introduction of imprisonment (now repealed) for soliciting by the Street Offences Act 1957 resulted immediately in the streets being cleared in the manner intended. Nevertheless, before the courts can be sure of imposing the most efficacious sentences a good deal more needs to be known about the effect of sentences and about individual offenders. In 1961 the Streatfield Committee[11] recommended that sentencers should be provided with information about the results of their sentences, but little has been done in this direction. During the past twenty years there has been greater awareness of these needs and much more research than ever before, but so far studies have been mainly directed towards crime rather than criminality and have been of little help to the sentencer.

Magistrates are also at a disadvantage in having to dispose of offenders, because only a minimum of information about the accused and his background is available. Day after day they try hundreds of cases knowing very little about the defendant, who often is not even present in court. The Streatfeild Committee, which was the first large-scale review of what sentencing is for, stressed the importance of pre-trial reports, but time and cost did not allow these to be used by magistrates to the extent possible in the Crown Court, and even the Crown Court cannot be sure how the offender will react to treatment. These considerations have led some authorities to conclude that sentencing should be taken out of the hands of the trial court and transferred to a separate body which, after conviction, would have an opportunity to review the whole of the offender's background and to adjust the treatment accordingly. Proposals on these lines were fashionable for many years prior to 1970 but recently seem to have lost favour,[12] and such procedure would be unacceptable for most cases coming before summary courts, where the accused usually wants the matter to be disposed of as soon as possible.

11 Conduct and Removal

Magistrates, both lay and stipendiary, have always had to work under a fairly constant stream of criticism. It is ironical that, notwithstanding their improved standard of conduct and efficiency, public censure has, if anything, increased over the last thirty years. This is probably due to a more critical approach to all public institutions and to the unpopularity which magistrates have incurred by having to deal with an increasing volume of offences not regarded by the public as 'crimes', such as motoring cases or failure to have a television licence. Those who commit such breaches of the law tend to feel a grievance against the courts which convict them, and the offenders include large numbers of the more well-to-do members of society who, unlike the criminals of earlier days, are well able to make their voices heard.

For a long time there was a reluctance among Englishmen to criticise judges of the higher courts or to expose their failings and shortcomings to public gaze. This inhibition has never been so strong in the case of Justices of the Peace, partly no doubt because the would-be attacker knew that the higher courts had teeth with which to bite back whereas the magistrates had no power to commit for contempt nor, it was believed, would magistrates receive the same protection from authority as the judges. In the last twenty years the position has changed and today there is proportionally more public censure of professional judges and Stipendiary Magistrates than there is of justices. Lord Hailsham, writing in 1976, remarked: 'By far the bitterest complaints I have received as Lord Chancellor were about professional judges and magistrates and not about lay magistrates.'[1] This may be due partly to the fact that most individual justices have less opportunity than the judges and stipendiaries to say and do things which attract public attention when they are on the bench, but there is also a general change of attitude towards the courts of justice and particularly towards the sanctity of the higher courts, which are no longer immune from the general predilection for knocking authority. It is the task of the Lord Chancellor to see that proper steps are taken, and are generally known to be taken, to deal effectively with genuine errors and omissions, while at the same time ensuring that the judiciary are not subjected to undue interference.

There are considerable differences between the tenure of office of Stipendiary Magistrates and lay justices. Stipendiaries, whose terms of service are explained in a later chapter, are subject to conditions similar to those applicable to other members of the lower professional judiciary and may be removed by the Lord Chancellor for inability or misbehaviour. Justices hold office at pleasure and may legally be removed by the Lord Chancellor at any time without showing cause; but today no Lord Chancellor would dismiss a justice without giving a sound reason.

The machinery for disciplining justices rests exclusively with the Lord Chancellor, who may admonish, suspend or dismiss. Acting on behalf of the Crown he may remove a justice at his absolute discretion, but this power has come by constitutional usage to be exercised in a judicial manner, and as head of the judiciary the Lord Chancellor is uniquely placed to exercise this function.

It is a rare event for a permanent member of the professional judiciary to be obliged to give up office, save on grounds of ill health, before reaching the statutory retiring age. Since the Act of Settlement in 1700, which finally established security of judicial tenure, only one superior court judge has been dismissed, though many attempts have been made to remove others. On the other hand, it is fairly common for a Justice of the Peace to be required to relinquish his appointment. Usually this occurs in circum-stances which impute no blame to the individual, as where he is unable to fulfil his undertaking to do a fair share of the work[2] or where he becomes residentially disqualified by moving to a different area. As has been said, the Lord Chancellor receives annual reports from his Advisory Committees on the attendance of justices in their respective areas, and anyone who, without good cause, has not sat on at least twenty-six occasions is required to resign. Pressure of other work, whether of a public or private nature, is not an acceptable ground for absence. About 1 per cent of all justices on the Active List are obliged to resign each year because they are unable to complete the minimum number of court attendances and a further 1 per cent become residentially disqualified.

There are other cases, however, where a justice's conduct calls for disciplinary action or where he acquires a reputation which raises doubts as to his fitness to remain on the bench. The Lord Chancellor's approach to all these cases is based on the hypothesis that the independence of the magistracy must be maintained and that no justice should be removed, suspended or reprimanded except for substantially indisputable cause. Independence requires some tolerance of magisterial behaviour, and conduct which would exclude a person from appointment does not necessarily justify removal if it occurs after he has become a magistrate. The retention on the bench of a few unsatisfactory or ineffective justices is, in the words of the Royal Commission of 1948, 'the price that has to be paid for the principle of security of tenure'. It is in the public interest that judicial independence be preserved and therefore no judge or magistrate is removed from office unless this course is unavoidable in the public interest. When, however, such a situation does arise the reputation of the bench takes precedence over the reputation of the individual justice; the overriding consideration being that public confidence in the administration of justice must be preserved. The test of public confidence has often been the yardstick by which judicial misconduct has been measured during debates in both Houses of Parliament. This means that, although an ineffective justice may be allowed to remain a magistrate if he can be carried by his colleagues without unduly inflaming public opinion, conduct which clearly tends to undermine confidence in the bench will result in disciplinary action.

It is not always easy to draw the line, but the policy sometimes operates harshly on justices who find themselves, through no fault of their own, in a position which is open to criticism. An extreme example of this was the case of a lady justice in Herefordshire who happened to have the same unusual surname as myself, though she was not a relative. Her husband was the proprietor of a garage which was prosecuted for a breach of certain regulations. There was little doubt that the offence had been committed by an employee without Mr Skyrme's knowledge, but he died before the case came to court and the garage passed to his widow. Mrs Skyrme had had no previous connection with the garage but, as owner, she was convicted. The Lord Chancellor took the view that as the matter had received some adverse local publicity it would be detrimental to the reputation of the bench if Mrs Skyrme, although morally blameless, were to remain a magistrate, and she resigned. A similar line was taken in a number of cases where the spouse of a justice had fallen foul of the law. In the mid-1970s, three women magistrates whose husbands had been convicted of offences relating to the Poulson affair were required to resign.

Cases which are deemed suitable for reprimand, without suspension or removal, arise most frequently where a justice is convicted of a minor motoring offence. In all such cases, except infringements of parking regulations, the justice receives a letter from the Lord Chancellor's Office drawing his attention to the importance of magistrates keeping strictly within the law. This letter sometimes arouses indignant reaction from magistrates, who take exception to the Lord Chancellor's rebuke for what is regarded as a trivial matter. On one or two occasions a justice convicted of a speeding offence has resigned in protest.

Cases involving suspension or dismissal cover a wide spectrum, from that of a justice who has been convicted of a serious offence involving moral turpitude to one where the justice's mental faculties have become impaired. Convictions of justices for serious offences are rare, seldom numbering more than half-a-dozen a year; but they are usually the easiest cases to deal with because, although every case of potential removal is considered by the Lord Chancellor on its merits, the court's decision to convict for a grave offence is assumed to indicate beyond doubt that the justice is not fit to hold office. On the other hand views change as to what amounts to a serious offence warranting intervention by the Lord Chancellor. An example is the change of attitude towards offences of driving under the influence of alcohol. For many years after the war any conviction of a justice for being drunk in charge of a motor vehicle, or more recently of driving with more than the permitted quantity of alcohol in the blood, resulted automatically in instant dismissal. Lord Hailsham, however, amended this rule. He suspended the justice from sitting during the period of his disqualification from driving, but at the end of that period he reviewed the case and, unless there were aggravating circumstances, he then allowed the justice to return to active duty.

There were many who thought that Lord Hailsham was wrong to modify his policy in this respect, especially in view of the serious consequences of drunken driving, but he had in mind the fact that professional judges did not lose their appointments when convicted of these offences and that, if anything, a higher standard of behaviour should be required of the judge than of the lay justice. To this it was answered that it is a serious matter for the judge to lose his office as this is his whole livelihood, whereas the termination of a justice's appointment is in no way detrimental to his gainful employment and need have little effect on his life. It was pointed out, further, that only a small proportion of a judge's work relates to traffic offences whereas they account for the major part of a justice's jurisdiction. Some judges do no criminal work at all, and it should not be difficult to arrange for a judge who has been convicted of a driving offence not to try any such cases himself, but it would be totally impracticable for a justice to perform his duties without handling cases of this kind. These arguments did not prevail and Lord Hailsham's policy was followed by Lord Elwyn-Jones.

Disregard of the law may be exhibited not only by a magistrate being convicted of an offence, but also by his refusing to apply the law to others. Every holder of judicial office may express an opinion that a particular law is a bad one but he must apply it none the less. The leading case on this point involving a magistrates' court arose in 1947 when the country was still subject to petrol rationing. Many people disapproved of the regulations governing the use of concessionary petrol and one of those who objected was the Chairman of the Carmarthen Bench, Colonel Delmer Davies-Evans, who showed his disapproval by imposing only a nominal fine of one shilling on a convicted motorist. I wrote to the colonel pointing out that it was his duty as a magistrate to apply the law as enacted by Parliament, however distasteful this might be, but he stuck to his guns, claiming that he and his colleagues had fulfilled their duty by convicting the defendant and that they were entitled to express their disapproval of the regulations by imposing a derisory penalty. In a subsequent interview with the press he said that he intended to continue to pursue this policy and, referring to the Act, said 'I am not going to play'. The Lord Chancellor removed him from the bench. The dismissal of the petrol-consumers' champion was met with an outburst of protest from the motoring population. The Member of Parliament for Carmarthen moved a motion on the adjournment in the House of Commons. In reply to the motion, the Attorney General, Sir Hartley Shawcross as he then was, explained at some length the constitutional principles governing the removal of magistrates and the policy in applying them. He stated that the

Lord Chancellor would never dismiss a justice for some isolated intemperate criticism of an Act of Parliament but he would be obliged to do so where the justice had allowed his dislike of an Act to influence his judicial administration of the law.

Twenty years elapsed after the Carmarthen incident before there were any further cases of refusal by justices to apply the law, and Wales again provided the setting. Towards the end of the 1960s the Welsh courts began to receive prosecutions for offences which were claimed to have been committed in support of the Welsh language. Many Welsh justices lived in Welsh-speaking areas and Welsh was their own mother language. It was a severe test of their dedication to their judicial duties when they were required to incur the odium of their neighbours and friends by convicting and sentencing persons whose offences had been committed in the cause of their native tongue. Much credit is due to the Welsh justices who steadfastly applied the law in these cases, but there were bound to be some who felt unable to do so.

In 1970 the chairman of the Welsh Language Society, Mr Dafydd Iwan, refused to pay a fine imposed by magistrates for daubing paint on English-language signs and was sent to prison in default. Some Welsh magistrates contributed towards the fine and secured Mr Iwan's release. One of these was a lady magistrate in Swansea who informed Lord Chancellor Gardiner that she was not prepared to impose penalties on people who, non-violently, broke laws which she considered to be unjust to the Welsh language. She persisted in this view and, after prolonged correspondence with the Lord Chancellor's Office, was finally removed from the bench by Lord Hailsham in 1972.

In 1972 the Bangor justices granted an absolute discharge to five persons who pleaded guilty to using television sets without licences and who explained that their motive was to draw attention to the inadequate programmes in the Welsh language. Lord Hailsham invited the Bangor justices to consider what would happen if everyone who disapproved of television programmes were excused payment for their licences, and he suspended the chairman of the Bangor bench from sitting while he reflected on the matter. The chairman, with some hesitation, agreed that he was at fault and undertook to apply the law in future; whereupon Lord Hailsham allowed him to resume sitting.

Refusal to implement unpopular laws has not been confined to Welsh magistrates. In 1975 a Humberside justice who objected to rate increases was dismissed for refusing to sign distress warrants in respect of persons who failed to pay their rates.

Sympathy for the oppressed is not a new characteristic of the human race but the occasions on which it has taken militant form have become more numerous during the present era of public demonstrations. Almost any section of the population may become involved in these activities and Justices of the Peace have sometimes appeared in a new role as contentious protestors. In particular, the presence of large numbers of wage-earners and trade unionists on the commissions leads to justices being involved in industrial disputes, including strikes. This is very different from the justices of previous centuries, who were to be found calling out the militia or appearing sword in hand at the head of their own retainers to quell a riot. The present phenomenon is not entirely new, however. During the General Strike of 1926 several justices were involved in clashes with the police and a few were arrested. When the strike collapsed these justices were treated leniently and most were allowed to remain on the bench.

During the past ten years these incidents have become more numerous. Several justices have joined picket lines – some outside the Grunwick factory – and others have organised and taken part in demonstrations on behalf of various causes. In cases where a justice took part in a peaceful demonstration which did not involve a breach of the law it was the Lord Chancellor's practice to ask him to consider whether what he was doing was compatible with his position as a magistrate, bearing in mind: (1) that a peaceful demonstration could lead to a breach of the peace even though this was not the intention of the participants; (2) that magistrates frequently had to try persons charged with offences arising from demonstrations, picketing and similar activities; and (3) as there were usually two sides to a question the identification of a magistrate with one side might destroy public confidence in the impartiality of judicial proceedings. The Lord Chancellor would also point out that no one was obliged to accept appointment as a magistrate, but if he did so he must also accept certain inhibitions on his freedom of behaviour which did not necessarily apply to others. Those justices to whom these considerations were put accepted the Lord Chancellor's view and either desisted from further action or resigned from the bench.

If, on the other hand, a justice who took part in a demonstration became involved in a breach of the peace, the Lord Chancellor would take disciplinary action. In 1969, Mrs Betty Bell, a Hampshire justice, participated in a demonstration protesting against a proposed increase in the admission fee to a public park. She and some of her companions appeared before a magistrates' court and refused to enter into recognizances to be of good behaviour, whereupon they were committed to prison. On appeal the order was revoked on a technical point, but Mrs Bell was suspended by the Lord Chancellor until the matter had been resolved. She subsequently gave the Lord Chancellor an undertaking not to take part in further activities of this kind and she was allowed to remain a magistrate.

The most difficult problems affecting tenure of office are presented by justices who have not been convicted of an offence nor involved in some specific incident but whose general standard of behaviour is alleged to be below what is expected of a magistrate.[4] Such allegations may relate to behaviour both in and out of court and range from mere ineffectiveness or physical incapacity to scandalous conduct.

Ineffectiveness may be due to an error on the part of an Advisory Committee in choosing a candidate who is found, after appointment, to be temperamentally or intellectually unfit to adjudicate, or it may arise from physical or mental deterioration after the justice has served for a number of years. Today, the process of selection is usually sufficient to eliminate the risk of ineffective appointments, and the few cases which slip through are accepted as the price that must be paid for ensuring judicial independence. Action is not justified unless the defect clearly affects the justice's work as a magistrate or the reputation of the bench. These situations when involving lay justices present greater difficulty to the Lord Chancellor than those of whole-time professional magistrates or judges because mental deterioration affecting judicial work is more apparent in a single judge sitting in court daily than it is in the case of a justice who attends only once a fortnight and always has colleagues with him on the bench. This is especially so when the justice is not chairman.

Mental deterioration due to advancing years has become a less serious problem since the introduction of the Supplemental List. In 1938 the Lord Chancellor issued a circular to all Advisory Committees suggesting that magistrates who had become incapable through old age or infirmity should transfer their names to a Supplemental List. Those whose names were on this list would remain justices and continue to enjoy the rights and privileges of the office but would not be summoned to attend court. The response to these proposals was disappointing and from 1940 every justice was required on appointment to give an undertaking to transfer to the Supplemental List on reaching the age of seventy-five. Statutory authority was given to these arrangements by the Supplemental List Act 1941, which also empowered the Lord Chancellor to place a justice on the list if it seemed desirable that he should cease to exercise judicial functions by reason of age or infirmity or other like cause. Since then most justices whose faculties have become impaired have transferred voluntarily and it has seldom been necessary for the Chancellor to use his statutory powers.

A defect in the 1941 Act was that any justice could transfer to the Supplemental List without the Lord Chancellor's authority merely by instructing the Clerk of the Peace or the town clerk, who had custody of the commission, to place his name on the list. A number of justices took this opportunity to avoid their magisterial obligations while retaining the social advantages of the office. This was remedied by the Justices of the Peace Act 1949 which provided that every justice must be placed on the Supplemental List on reaching the age of seventy-five but that otherwise none might transfer without the Lord Chancellor's approval. Approval was forthcoming only where a justice who had given good service became unable, through no fault of his own, to continue to attend court.

The age for retirement to the Supplemental List was fixed by the 1949 Act at seventy-five mainly because that was the limit recommended by the Royal Commission, but some members of the Government thought that it should be lower and it was agreed that the Bill should be amended to reduce the age to seventy. On the day of the Bill's second reading in the Commons, however, Winston Churchill reached his seventy-fifth birthday and thereafter no one on either side of the House was prepared to move the amendment. It was not until the Justices of the Peace Act 1968 that the age for compulsory retirement was finally reduced to seventy.

Lest benches should become denuded of experienced justices by the sudden application of the new age limits both the 1949 and 1968 Acts postponed the full effect of the new provisions for a period of five years after the Acts came into force. The 1949 Act did this by empowering the Lord Chancellor to retain an over-age justice on the Active List if he thought fit up to a period of five years from the commencement of the Act. Choosing those who were to be reprieved was a most invidious task and only served to exacerbate the feeling of grievance among those who were obliged to go immediately. I endeavoured to console them with the thought that there was nothing new in the idea of compulsory retirement from judicial office. As long ago as 1381, one of the demands made by Wat Tyler and his rebellious peasants was that 'old justices should be hung'. Clearly the elderly of 1949 had something to be thankful for.

Benefiting from the lesson learnt in 1949, Parliament provided in the 1968 Act for the age to be reduced from seventy-five to seventy by five annual instalments, thus relieving the Lord Chancellor of the distasteful job of choosing the fittest. In the five years following the 1949 Act some 4300 justices were placed on the Supplemental List on reaching the age limit. There were undoubtedly more who ought to have been transferred but whose ages were not known to the Lord Chancellor's Office. Some seemed a little forgetful; one justice who had stated in 1930 that he was seventy claimed in 1950 to be seventy-four. Between 1968 and 1973 the additional transfers resulting from the reduction of the age limit to seventy numbered only 460.

The most usual form of physical impediment rendering a justice unfit to perform his duties is deafness. Deafness and blindness are bars to appointment as a magistrate and are grounds for transfer to the Supplemental List if they occur subsequently. It is the duty of Advisory Committees to watch for these and other forms of physical deterioration and to report instances to the Lord Chancellor. Usually a deaf justice will readily accept transfer to the Supplemental List but, as the Royal Commission commented: 'It is notorious that those who are affected with this infirmity are apt to shrink from confessing it even to themselves'. During the Chancellorship of Lord Jowitt the chairman of the Stratford-upon-Avon bench was reported to have become too deaf to hear proceedings in court. Everyone shared this view except the chairman himself and, when Lord Jowitt asked him to retire, he demanded a personal interview with the Lord Chancellor. This duly took place and Lord Jowitt had no hesitation in deciding that the chairman was too hard of hearing to perform his duties. The chairman was transferred to the

Supplemental List, but he was not prepared to take the matter lying down. At the next AGM of the Magistrates' Association he moved a motion, which was heavily defeated, opposing the re-election of Lord Jowitt as president. Later Lord Chancellors were spared this occupational hazard by being created president *ex officio* under the Royal Charter which the Magistrates' Association was granted in 1962.

All reasonable allegations of inability or misbehaviour must be investigated, and such cases are normally referred initially to the local Advisory Committee for enquiry. If the committee concludes that the justice ought not to continue to act they submit the matter to the Lord Chancellor for appropriate action. In many of these cases the justice does not accept the committee's findings and there is then further enquiry by the Secretary of Commissions, usually involving a personal interview. It is rare for the Lord Chancellor to see a justice himself, though he would normally do so if the justice asked for an interview. This places a heavy responsibility on the Secretary of Commissions and his staff, for whom the procedure is sometimes highly unpleasant and even harrowing.

On one occasion I received a report that a woman justice had become emotionally disturbed. She had formed an attachment for her local doctor, and when this was not reciprocated her general behaviour became abnormal. Attempts by the chairman of her bench and by friends to persuade her to cease attending court were unsuccessful and arrangements were made for her to see me. I explained as kindly as I could that it was in her own interest as well as that of her court that she should not sit while she was in her present condition. She broke down in my office and there was a distressing scene. I pointed out that this in itself indicated that she was not in a fit state to sit in judgment on others but she retorted that the work of the bench meant everything to her and that if she were prevented from sitting she would take her own life. When I referred the matter to the Lord Chancellor he had no hesitation in deciding that the lady should cease to attend court. Before informing her of this decision I took the precaution of telephoning two other justices on her bench who were well known to her to explain the position. They later rang me back to say that they had seen her and were satisfied that she now accepted the need to stand down. I therefore wrote to her explaining that she would remain on the commission and was merely being barred from sitting until such time as she had recovered. The following morning the clerk to her court telephoned to tell me that she had been found dead with her head in a gas oven and my letter in her hand.

Justices, like other members of the community, are sometimes involved in matrimonial proceedings and these cases have more than doubled in the past thirty years. Opinions have differed widely as to whether a person should remain a magistrate in these circumstances, but successive Lord Chancellors have declined to remove justices solely because they had been through the divorce courts, even if they were the 'guilty party' under the old law which required proof of a matrimonial offence. The Lord Chancellor made it clear that he was not a *custos morum*. He was not concerned with the private lives of the justices unless these reflected on the reputation of the bench. If therefore a justice's matrimonial behaviour caused local scandal the justice might be removed, whether or not there had been divorce proceedings, but as the years passed Lord Chancellors, faced with an escalating divorce rate and a less critical view of matrimonial behaviour by the population in general, tended to adopt a more and more lenient approach. Until the 1960s, a justice who was cited as co-respondent was normally required to resign, but Lord Elwyn-Jones declined to take this course in a case where the justice subsequently married the respondent and where it appeared that the previous marriage had broken down irrevocably before the co-respondent's intervention.

Sometimes the Lord Chancellor received information indicating that a justice was engaged in activities which were illegal or morally improper. Occasionally these were of such a highly confidential nature as to preclude investigation by the Advisory Committee. In these circumstances delicate enquiries were made by the Lord Chancellor's Office through such channels as they thought fit. Fortunately these cases were extremely rare, but an example was where it was established that a justice was an active homosexual. This was regarded as a ground for immediate removal from the Commission when all homosexual behaviour was a criminal offence; but with the wider acceptance of such practices by the Sexual Offences Act 1967, it could be argued that a justice who indulged in abnormal sexual activity in private and without infringing the provisions of the Act should not be regarded as unfit to remain a magistrate. This contention had considerable strength where the justice's sexual inclinations were unknown beyond his own close circle. The prevailing view, however, was that in circumstances of this kind the majority of the population would consider it wrong for a magistrate to remain on the bench. Furthermore, it was pointed out that there was a twofold risk in that a justice who is addicted to homosexual practice may unwittingly cross the boundary between what is and what is not permitted by criminal law and that he can also lay himself open to blackmail. For these reasons the Lord Chancellor remained of the opinion that a justice who indulged in homosexual practice even without infringing the Act should not remain in office and in the few cases of this kind that were brought to his attention the justice resigned.

As society becomes more tolerant of sexual behaviour under conditions where it was formerly condemned, it is to be expected that there should also be a growing tolerance for sexual activities traditionally regarded as perverted, and the day may come when all forms of homosexual behaviour are accepted and are permitted by law. If that day arrives the present rule will no doubt be reviewed, and whether or not it is revoked will turn upon the state of public opinion. The criterion of public opinion is applied consistently and has led to the removal of justices whose behaviour could not amount to a criminal offence but was likely to be censured if it became public knowledge. Thus, a male transvestite who masqueraded in public in female clothing was required to resign, because public confidence in the courts was likely to be weakened if it were known that justices behaved in this way, although transvestism is not an offence and may be regarded as a harmless activity.

Criticism of a justice's conduct sometimes comes from colleagues on the bench and occasionally reaches a point where the other justices refuse to sit with the alleged offender. The outstanding example of this was the case of Mrs Esther Iwi. Mrs Iwi, the wife of a well-known solicitor, was appointed to the Hendon Bench in 1949. The Hendon justices had a custom, not encouraged by the Lord Chancellor, to break for coffee during their morning sitting. Soon after Mrs Iwi joined the bench, the chairman, Mr Montesole, remarked during one of these breaks that the total of fines so far imposed that morning had been below average and the bench would have to do better during the second half. Mrs Iwi took exception to this remark and reported the matter to the Lord Chancellor. Mr Montesole, while agreeing that his comment might not have been in the best taste, maintained that it was a lighthearted remark which no reasonable person could have taken seriously, and the other justices who had been present supported him. They in their turn took exception to Mrs Iwi's action and informed the Lord Chancellor that they were not prepared to sit with her again.

The Lord Chancellor, Lord Jowitt, saw all the parties in his room and came to the conclusion that Mrs Iwi had been in the wrong. At that stage it should have been possible to resolve the matter without further strife. Mrs Iwi was potentially a good magistrate and it is in the interest of the bench that justices should not always see eye to eye. Unfortunately, the two sides would not be reconciled and Lord Jowitt required Mrs Iwi to resign, largely because he thought he was faced with a probable breakdown of the administration of justice in Hendon if she remained on the bench. Mrs Iwi then brought an action for libel against the chairman in the High Court.

Mrs Iwi conducted her own case with great ability, and the hearing, before Mr Justice Donovan and a jury, was noteworthy, *inter alia*, for the intervention of the Attorney General, Sir Reginald Manningham-Buller (later Lord Chancellor Dilhorne) who appeared on behalf of the Lord Chancellor to claim Crown Privilege. The alleged libels were contained in documents received by the Lord Chancellor from various sources and the Attorney General submitted an affidavit by the Lord Chancellor claiming absolute privilege for all communications passing between the Lord Chancellor, the Secretary of Commissions, Advisory Committees and chairmen of benches. The affidavit asserted that, in the public interest and to ensure proper administration of justice in magistrates' courts, the contents of such documents ought not to be disclosed and that complete security and immunity should be assured for all persons who volunteer information, or who are asked to give information, to the Lord Chancellor or an Advisory Committee or to any person acting on his or their behalf. The court upheld this claim[5] and Mrs Iwi was therefore unable to obtain discovery of a number of documents which she considered material to her case. Nevertheless, the jury found that the publication to the Lord Chancellor and his staff of the material before the court was defamatory, but they also found that the defendant was not actuated by malice.

Mrs Iwi therefore lost the action but, inspired by her experience, she was subsequently called to the Bar and practised as a barrister.

All of the cases so far described related to the conduct of individual justices. As far as the general public is concerned allegations of misconduct are more often directed towards a whole bench or at least against all those who sat on a particular occasion when, it is alleged, some miscarriage of justice took place.

Complaints relating to decisions of magistrates' courts are treated by the Lord Chancellor with the greatest caution; those who come to him clamouring for the dismissal or public reprimand of a bench of justices are told that it is not open to him in his executive capacity to interfere in the proceedings of a court of law. The magistrates have an absolute discretion to reach whatever decisions they think fit within the limits set by Parliament. The Lord Chancellor is justified in interfering only where the magistrates' decision is so manifestly perverse as to raise doubts as to their fitness to adjudicate. No justice would be dismissed for an error of judgment, though persistent errors indicating incompetence would be regarded as proper grounds for removal. So too would a decision of the bench which showed that the justices had not acted impartially. During the past thirty years no Lord Chancellor has found it necessary to remove justices because of a decision taken in court, but previously such cases were not uncommon and three which did much to undermine public confidence in the courts occurred in 1945 and 1946. In each of these cases a public enquiry was held at the direction jointly of the Lord Chancellor and the Home Secretary.

In the first case a priest was charged before the Stoke magistrates with indecent assault on a boy. The clerk to the justices, who had been approached by a mutual friend on behalf of the accused, arranged for the case to be heard by two of his junior justices an hour before the normal sitting of the court. The prosecution were not informed of the arrangements and were not represented at the hearing. The accused elected summary trial and pleaded guilty, and the two justices bound him over for twelve months, although they had no power to hear the case at all without first taking account of any representation by the prosecution that it was fit for summary trial.

Lord Goddard, the Lord Chief Justice, was appointed to hold an enquiry. His report castigated the two justices, and above all the clerk, and all three were dismissed (the justices by the Lord Chancellor and the clerk by the Stoke magistrates). *The Times* commented:

> If they [the justices] have not the authority and strength of character to stand up to their Clerk when he oversteps his proper sphere, they may be acquitted of conscious transgression, but they certainly ought not to be on the bench.

The next case also occurred in 1945. The chairman of the Gillingham Bench in Yorkshire wished to evict his groom, whom he had dismissed, from one of his cottages and he took proceedings for recovery of possession in a specially convened court composed of two of his colleagues. They duly issued a warrant of ejectment. The chairman had perfectly good grounds for dismissing the groom, who knew nothing about horses and had obtained the post by false pretences, but the chairman could have sought an ejectment order in the County Court. He chose to proceed at a special sitting of his own court because he was in a hurry to get another groom to look after his hunters. It was a classic example of justice being done but not manifestly being seen to be done.

Lord Justice Tucker held an enquiry and commented in his Report:

> In my view a magistrate, so far from using his position to further his own private convenience, should be prepared to put up with a greater degree of inconvenience than an ordinary litigant if there is any danger of conflict between his rights as an ordinary citizen and his position as a Justice of the Peace.

The chairman was dismissed from the Commission.

The last of this unhappy trilogy was an episode which occurred in 1946, and became famous as the 'Pig Case'. It was the subject of a ballad often sung thereafter in the Wales and Chester Circuit mess. The clerk to the justices at Aberayron in Cardiganshire was prosecuted on behalf of the Minister of Food in that, without authority under the Defence Regulations, 'he did cause to be slaughtered livestock for human consumption, to wit one pig', and that he had made a false statement regarding the ownership of the said pig. He was tried by seven of his own justices, including the ageing chairman who had come to rely entirely upon his clerk to tell him what to do, and when he found his clerk in the dock instead of in his usual place he was totally unable to cope. The justices dismissed both charges against their clerk without calling upon the defence.

Lord Justice Tucker was again appointed to hold an enquiry. He found that the justices, in reaching what was clearly a bad decision, had not acted dishonestly or with conscious bias, but they had obviously acted wrongly and the chairman was removed.

The Aberayron case ought to have been tried by justices brought in from another area, and this practice has been followed since then in cases where a justice or court official has been charged with some offence (usually motoring) before his own bench.

These three cases were the worst miscarriages of justice in magistrates' courts after I joined the Lord Chancellor's Office. Measures taken since 1949 to improve the competence of the courts should ensure that such events do not occur again, and it has not been found necessary to hold any further public enquiries, though there was one occasion when Lord Chancellor Dilhorne decided to conduct an enquiry in person. A court had imposed what appeared to be a grossly lenient sentence on some youths convicted of assault causing actual bodily harm on a policeman. Lord Dilhorne sent for the chairman and his two colleagues. He sat in judgment in the Moses Room of the House of Lords, beneath the painting of Moses descending from Sinai with the tablets of the Law and not far from the site of the old Star Chamber where many earlier justices had been summoned to give an account of themselves. The three magistrates appeared before him to show cause why they should not be removed from the commission. It must have been a traumatic experience for them. In the event they were let off with a reprimand. This was the only occasion in recent times when such a procedure was adopted and it is not one that should be embarked upon lightly.

In the cases already mentioned the bench acted with undue leniency or in a manner favourable to a justice or a clerk. Complaints that magistrates have imposed too harsh a sentence have been extremely rare and are usually based on erroneous information. Soon after I became Secretary of Commissions a woman was convicted and fined for picking three tulips in a public park. She had three small children and some newspaper reports implied that she had picked the flowers to brighten a poor and dismal home for their benefit. Immediately there was a demand for the removal of the brutal magistrates. What was not revealed to the public was that the women made a practice of taking flowers from public places and selling them and that she had been charged with this offence on a previous occasion, when the court gave her a conditional discharge. She had completely ignored the warning that was then given to her and the court had no alternative on the second occasion to imposing a fine which they were satisfied she could pay without detriment to the children. The conclusion to this story was a happy one for the woman because numerous well-wishers sent her enough money to pay the fine many times over.[6]

Cases involving children are usually the most emotive. The one which aroused the greatest feeling in recent times was that of the Desramault family in 1970. Mrs Desramault was English, her husband French. They had one child, Caroline, born in 1970. In December 1970, Mrs Desramault brought proceedings against her husband before the Gosforth magistrates. They awarded custody to the father, who immediately returned with the child to France. The mother appealed to the Chancery Division of the High Court, which reversed the magistrates' decision two months later, but by then the child was outside the jurisdiction. During the ensuing three years the case was dragged through the courts of France and Switzerland (whither the father had fled with his daughter in defiance of an order of the French courts) until Caroline was finally restored to her mother in March 1973.

The obloquy which greeted the decision of the Gosforth magistrates exceeded all other outbursts in recent years. A mistake had been made and there would be no point in attempting to minimise the serious consequences which the justices' decision had on the unfortunate child, but had it been possible to make a calm analysis of this case it would have been seen that there was no justification for the savage abuse, some of it motivated by xenophobia, to which the two justices were subjected without any opportunity to defend themselves. Although the Lord Chancellor himself stated publicly that the decision could not be defended and the vice-chancellor, Sir John Pennycuick, who heard the appeal, stated that it was manifestly contrary to the welfare of the child, neither of them suggested that the magistrates conducted the hearing unfairly or gave their decision without proper attention. The magistrates were described by some of the media as ignorant and callous sadists who had conducted the proceedings with total disregard for the child's welfare. The true facts were that both justices (a man and a woman) had had considerable experience of children: one was a member of the Children's Committee of the County Council and the other was the headmaster of a school and had spent his whole life in teaching. They spent more than five hours hearing the case and then deliberated for half an hour before reaching their decision. They had before them in court not only the child's parents, but also the two grandmothers, either of whom was likely to play a prominent part in the care of the child if custody were granted to that side of the family. Weighing up the merits of all the parties the magistrates formed the opinion, rightly or wrongly, that it was in the best interest of the child to be placed in the care of her father. They ought not to have decided the issue without asking for the reports on both parties, but it would have taken some time to obtain these reports, especially from France, and both parents asked that the matter be decided immediately. The magistrates made a mistake in yielding to this but they assumed that the mother's solicitor would apply for a stay of execution pending appeal. For some reason, which never emerged, the solicitor took no action for two days and then adopted the surprising course of writing to the Member of Parliament for a neighbouring constituency.

The Lord Chancellor was called upon to dismiss the two justices, but refused. He decided that they had heard the case with care and that their principal concern had been the welfare of the child. They had made an error of judgement but the mistake was no greater than others that had been made by judges at all levels. The tragedy lay in the result of their error which, unlike most others that had been made by the courts, could not be rectified within a reasonable time by a higher tribunal.

The only satisfactory outcome of the Desramault case was that everyone was alerted to the problem. Since then the courts have been alive to the danger and the Domestic Proceedings and Magistrates' Courts Act 1978 provided that where a magistrates' court makes a child custody order it may direct that no person shall take that child out of England and Wales except with the leave of the court.

This chapter has shown how the Lord Chancellor and his staff deal with cases of inability or misbehaviour which are brought to their notice, and today there can be few, if any, significant deficiencies among magistrates which do not come to the Lord Chancellor's attention. The public, the press, legal practitioners, Members of Parliament and local councillors are quick to focus attention on any failings they may detect, and it is the duty of Advisory Committees and sub-committees to scrutinise the activities of the justices in their respective areas.

The cases mentioned in this chapter were very exceptional and involved barely one in 500 of the justices who have served since the war. The majority occurred more than twenty years ago. Considering that over 2 million criminal cases are disposed of by magistrates in the course of a year in addition to their substantial domestic and other civil work, the country may draw some satisfaction from the rarity of the occasions that lead to justifiable criticism.

There is the other side of the coin. The increasingly critical public scrutiny of judicial behaviour has coincided with an erosion of the traditional policy of protecting the independence of the judiciary at almost any cost. The effect of this, when it comes to the magistrates, is that they and their courts are constantly subjected to censure, mostly unmerited, against which they have little or no redress, and on the occasions when others attempt to intervene on their behalf their efforts receive no publicity. Statements made by the Lord Chancellor in Parliament or elsewhere in defence of magistrates who have been unjustly criticised go unreported. The attack was news, the defence is not. If some of our modern institutions and organisations were subject to half the unmerited criticism accorded to magistrates there would be a vociferous outcry throughout the land.

Freedom of speech is essential to a free society and magistrates' courts must be open to critical observation like everything else. In the oft-quoted words of Lord Atkin: 'Justice is not a cloistered virtue; she must be allowed to suffer the scrutiny and respectful, even though outspoken, comments of ordinary men.' But in the present climate the public gains a false impression of magistrates, whom they still picture in the image of years gone by. Confidence in the magistrates' courts remains far below what it ought to be and respect for the law is undermined. Coinciding with this is the risk that unjust ridicule and criticism may lead imperceptibly to resentment of criticism and reaction against it by the magistrates.

If the 'outspoken comments of ordinary men' are justified the Lord Chancellor and others have appropriate powers, which they do not hesitate to exercise, to deal with the matter. When, however, they are untruthful or distorted and unfair the public should be made aware of the true facts and not be allowed to remain indefinitely in a state of disapproving ignorance. There is a long way to go before this ideal is reached.

12 The Justices' Clerk

The linchpin of the administration of justice by part-time magistrates is the justices' clerk. He is chief executive and administrator of the court and also its legal adviser. (Where there are Stipendiary Magistrates the same clerk serves them and the justices, but until 1974 there were certain areas where separate clerks to the stipendiaries were appointed under local Acts.)

This unique office, like the whole system of Justices of the Peace, results from historical development depending in the earlier stages more on accident than on design. By Tudor times magistrates were discharging a number of duties from their private houses and individual justices found it convenient to appoint a personal clerk to assist them, and by the nineteenth century petty sessional benches were entrusting clerical matters to a single clerk whose status began to change from that of a personal servant to an official experienced in the law. In *Tom Jones* Squire Weston's clerk 'luckily . . . had a qualification that no clerk to the justices should be without . . . some understanding of the law of this realm'. The importance of the office advanced rapidly with the extension of summary jurisdiction under various Acts from 1847 onwards and as work at Petty Sessions exceeded that at Quarter Sessions the justices came to rely for advice upon the Petty Sessional Clerk rather than the Clerk of the Peace. The clerks themselves saw their office in a new light and in 1839 they formed a professional body, the Justices' Clerks' Society, which was incorporated in 1903. In 1842 Samuel Stone, clerk to the Leicester justices, published his *Justices' Manual*, which became the leading reference authority for all magistrates' courts and has always been edited by justices' clerks.

In 1947 the quality of many clerks still left much to be desired, but they were important public figures in their localities, and in many places they dominated the bench. They were underpaid but, as the Roche Committee observed:[1] 'The position of clerk is one of dignity and the holding of that position may itself be regarded as part of the reward'. During the following three decades the justices' greater proficiency induced them to be less ready to accept without question pronouncements by their clerk, and to this extent the influence of the clerk in court declined, but in other respects the importance of his office and of the functions he performed increased significantly. There was a change from a system based largely on part-time clerks to one comprising full-time officers with emphasis on professionalism and legal qualification. A marked expansion of their duties resulted in clerks devoting more time to administration and less to sitting in court, though there was as much need as ever for them to be available to give authoritative advice to their justices on points of law and procedure.

The new generation of whole-time clerks became status-conscious and their efforts throughout the period to gain further recognition were seen by some as emanating solely from a desire to elevate themselves into judicial office. This charge was justified in the case of a few individuals but the majority adopted a realistic and responsible approach to a revolutionary situation and the reforming policies advocated by the Justices' Clerks' Society were convincing.

As a body, the clerks acquired considerable influence in a wide field beyond the confines of their courts. Their representatives served on the 1948 Royal Commission and on every committee concerned with magistrates' courts appointed since then, and the evidence submitted to these enquiries by the Justices' Clerks' Society was usually among the most cogent received from any quarter. Some individuals attained positions of eminence; for example, Sir Sydney Littlewood, having been clerk to the Kingston-upon-Thames justices, was knighted for his work in establishing the legal aid system and later became President of the Law Society.

The clerks' most interesting achievement was their invasion of the Stipendiary Magistracy. Before 1949 the possibility of a justices' clerk becoming a stipendiary was considered quite out of the question. All of those then serving were ineligible in any event because they were solicitors and only barristers were qualified to serve as stipendiaries; but the 1949 Act extended the field to solicitors and in the early 1950s several clerks approached me and asked whether they might be considered. Lord Simonds, who was then Lord Chancellor, was not prepared to accept any candidate unless he was in active practice, but as time passed I became more doubtful about the validity of this policy, especially as the number of applicants from practising members of the profession began to dwindle while the need for additional appointments increased, and some clerks appeared to be potentially good material. There was an unacceptable risk in appointing as a stipendiary a person who had never shown his paces other than as a court clerk, and it was impracticable to make a clerk a justice so that he had a trial run; but the Lord Chancellor had power to appoint a deputy stipendiary on a temporary basis during the unavoidable absence of a stipendiary. In 1954 I suggested to the new Lord Chancellor, Lord Kilmuir, that the most promising applicants among the clerks be tried out in this way and, if found satisfactory, should be considered with the other candidates when vacancies occurred. He agreed, and in 1956 L. M. Pugh, clerk to the Sheffield justices, was appointed stipendiary for Huddersfield, at the end of his year as President of the Justices' Clerks' Society. He was also the first solicitor to become a stipendiary. Eleven years later the first justices' clerk was appointed to the Metropolitan Bench. He was E. L. Bradley, a barrister, clerk to the Poole justices and formerly a member of the Home Office. On appointment to the bench Bradley became a zealous member of the Magistrates' Association, serving with distinction as chairman of their Legal Committee. (When the Magistrates' Association was founded in 1920 it was given a cool reception by the Justices' Clerks' Society, but in the 1930s both organisations began to see the advantage of working together, and in 1966 a joint committee of the two bodies was established and three justices' clerks were co-opted to the Association's council. In 1977 Geoffrey Norman, clerk to the North Hertfordshire and Stevenage justices, was appointed secretary of the Magistrates' Association.) From 1970 onwards there were frequent appointments of clerks to the stipendiary bench and by the end of 1983 twelve had been so appointed – five barristers and seven solicitors, eight in London and four in the provinces. By the late 1960s more than 50 per cent of those clerks who had served for ten years or more were applicants, and a greater number would have been appointed had not the Lord Chancellor felt obliged to impose a limit lest it should seem that the stipendiary bench had become the perquisite of the clerks.

When the Crown Court was established in 1972 the clerks hoped that they might serve as deputy Circuit Judges and

Recorders but Lord Hailsham was opposed to this largely on the ground that, even if they sat only in places outside their own commission areas, the fact that they presided in a higher court could disturb their relationship with their own justices. This was a considerable disappointment to the clerks but an avenue to the Circuit bench was open to them through appointment as stipendiaries. Several former clerks who had become stipendiaries sat regularly as deputy Circuit Judges or Recorders, and in 1980 one of them (Kennth Cooke) was appointed a Circuit Judge. He was soon followed by two others.

A few clerks were appointed Justices of the Peace while still serving as clerks but the numbers were small due to the rule that a clerk may not serve as a justice within the commission area of his court.

The first lady to be appointed a part-time clerk was Miss L. M. Hollowell of Stowmarket in 1944. Three years later Miss Joan Adair was appointed in Kingston-upon-Thames as the first whole-time lady clerk.

The Roche Committee found in 1944 that the 1037 divisions in England and Wales (excluding the Metropolitan area where there had been full-time clerks from the start) were staffed by 822 clerks of whom 90 were whole-time and 732 part-time. Having regard to the increase in the amount of business and of the number and complexity of the Statutes applying to the courts, the committee concluded that the proportion of whole-time clerks should be increased, though they recognised that this would involve clerks serving wider areas and therefore becoming less accessible to their justices and to the police and the public. During the following twenty years a policy of extending the whole-time system was pursued, involving the elimination of many part-time offices and a large-scale combining of divisions under a single clerk, and by 1977 there were 374 clerks in England and Wales outside the Metropolitan area, composed of 312 whole-timers and 62 part-timers.

The appointment of clerks has always rested with the justices, though the Home Secretary's confirmation has been required since the Criminal Justice Act 1914 (a Statute largely inspired by the then Home Secretary, Winston Churchill). Until the Justices of the Peace Act 1949 each division appointed its own clerk (except in Middlesex, where the Standing Joint Committee made the appointment), but the retention of this system would have made it difficult to increase whole-time appointments and the smaller divisions lacked the experience necessary for making good selections. The Roche Committee considered whether clerks should be appointed by local authorities or by the Home Secretary or the Lord Chancellor (who was already responsible for the appointment of county court staff), but concluded that 'a satisfactory relationship between justices and clerk is more likely to come about if the justices have some responsibility for selecting and controlling him'. Accordingly, the Justices of the Peace Act 1949 provided that justices should continue to appoint their clerks but that this power should be vested in the new Magistrates' Courts Committees. The committees could also dismiss a clerk, both appointment and removal being subject to the Home Secretary's approval.

Before 1851 clerks were remunerated by being allowed to take certain fees to which their justices were entitled, but under an Act of that year it became permissible to pay them salaries. The remuneration was still low in 1947 and the following years saw a drive by the Justices' Clerks' Society for the adoption of an adequate national scale. After a long struggle this was achieved in 1953 under an agreement reached by a Joint Negotiating Committee which had been set up. The clerks' salaries did not, however, keep up with the increasing scope of their duties, quite apart from inflation, and inadequate remuneration remained a cause of dissatisfaction and was one of the factors responsible for poor recruitment to the service.

Awakening consciousness of the importance of the clerks' role focused attention on the qualifications required for the office. Until 1877 there were no statutory qualifications but the Justices' Clerks Act of that year required clerks to be barristers or solicitors or to have worked as an assistant to a clerk for a specified period. By 1947 about 90 per cent of clerks were legally qualified (all of them solicitors) but this was largely because part-time clerks were usually local solicitors who also engaged in private practice; only 35 per cent of the whole-timers were lawyers, the rest being qualified by virtue of service as assistants. The Roche Committee had concluded that 'Nothing but a professional qualification will fully meet the circumstances', and the Justices of the Peace Act 1949 required that a clerk should be a barrister or solicitor of five years' standing, an existing or former justices' clerk or, in special circumstances, a person qualified by at least ten years' experience prior to 1960 as a justices' clerk's assistant.[2] From then onwards the number of barristers attracted to the office increased and by 1977 the clerks included 65 barristers and 220 solicitors, out of a total of 345 in office. One of these was Brian Harris who was also the editor of *Justice of the Peace*. In 1982, while President of the Justices' Clerks' Society, he achieved the unique distinction of becoming the first clerk to be made a QC.

From 1949 there was a continuing expansion of the clerk's duties, embracing not only the increased volume and complexity of court work but also a number of entirely novel commitments, chief of which were the training of justices, the clerkship of Magistrates' Courts Committees and the administration of legal aid.

As already explained, the clerks played a leading role in the training of justices from the inception of schemes under the 1949 Act. Many became training officers for their respective areas, for which they were entitled to small increments in salary not commensurate with the work involved. There was some criticism of a system in which judicial officers were trained by the clerks to their courts but, although this could be open to objection in principle, it generally worked well in practice, and in the absence of a nationwide training service it would have been impossible to find enough other suitable people to undertake these duties.

The position of the clerks in regard to Magistrates' Courts Committees changed dramatically after 1974. When the committees were first established in 1953, clerks to borough justices became clerks to the borough committees *ex officio*, but in the counties the committees were required to elect their clerks. This difference was dictated by the fact that the Act could not stipulate which of the many clerks in a county should become the committee clerk; but although the Act gave committees an unrestricted choice the government assumed that as a general rule one of the justices' clerks in each county would be chosen as clerk to the committee. What in fact happened was that the Lord Lieutenant, who as *Custos Rotulorum* was *ex officio* a member of his county committee, was required to convene the first meeting and it was hardly surprising that he should bring with him his clerk of lieutenancy who, in almost every county, was also clerk to the county council and Clerk of the Peace. When the meeting reached the question of electing a clerk, there was the clerk of the county council, who was also the Lord Lieutenant's right-hand man and whom the members of the committee already knew as Clerk of the Peace, quietly taking notes of the proceedings. It would have been more than surprising if this individual had not been appointed clerk to the committee in almost every county, which indeed he was. In many areas the result was better than most justices' clerks would admit. A good Clerk of the Peace, who was usually also secretary of the county Advisory Committee and had the interests of the courts at heart, could do much to bridge the financial gap between the magistracy and the county council and could ensure that the magistrates received the funds they needed. On the other hand, there was a tendency for the Magistrates' Courts Committee to be regarded as a committee of the county council, and in many places necessary spending by the committee was inhibited. Clerks of the Peace were abolished by the Courts Act 1971 while the Local Government Act 1972 altered the areas of all Magistrates' Courts Committees and combined the former borough committees with those of the new counties or metropolitan districts. Reorganisation of the committees and the appointment of new clerks followed when the 1972 Act came into force in 1974, with the result that in all 36 of the metropolitan districts and in 27 of the 47 non-metropolitan counties a justices' clerk was appointed clerk to the Magistrates' Courts Committee. In all, 65 of the new magistrates' courts were served by justices' clerks.

The whole administration of the magistrates' courts therefore came to rest largely upon the justices' clerks. They received an additional salary as clerk to the Magistrates' Courts Committee but the work made it difficult for them to maintain a close relationship with the justices in their own divisions. Erosion of the traditional personal relationship between clerk and justices had been in evidence for some time and was due in part to the proliferation of courts in the busier divisions, where the clerk could be present in one court only, leaving a subordinate to staff the others. With increasing administrative duties clerks frequently found themselves unable to attend court at all. In 1947 the justices' clerk himself was present in about 9 courts in 10; by 1977 the average was not more than 1 in 10. This continuing trend has led to a new problem in that many clerks have now become managers of large and complex offices and, whereas as lawyers they are well qualified to advise their justices and to conduct their courts, they have had comparatively little training in administration.

A peculiar feature of the system is that although the clerk is legal adviser to his justices, their decision on points of law is theirs and theirs alone, and they and not the clerk are held responsible. Advocates address their legal arguments to the justices even though the justices probably do not understand them, and the Court of Appeal refers to justices 'misdirecting themselves' when, in fact, they have probably been misdirected by the clerk. For such an extraordinary system to work efficiently the clerk must not only be well versed in law and procedure but must be in a position to tender advice whenever his justices require it. During the thirty years following the war nothing had a more disturbing effect on the magistrates' courts, and especially on the clerks, than the words of Lord Goddard, LCJ, in the Court of Appeal in R. v. East Kerrier JJ. ex parte Mundy,[3] when he ventured to observe, *obiter dicta*, that a clerk ought not to accompany his justices as a matter of course when they retired to consider a case. Until then many clerks retired with their justices whenever they thought their advice might be required, and Lord Goddard's observations were seen as a serious threat to the clerk's position as legal adviser. In discussions I had with Lord Goddard at the time it was clear that he was surprised and somewhat dismayed by the furore his remarks had caused and he endeavoured in several subsequent cases to water down to some extent what he had said. In R. v. Welshpool JJ. ex parte Holley[4] he explained that in East Kerrier he had not meant that 'if a point of law had been raised during the hearing the justices should not ask their clerk to come into the room with them so that they could at once consult him'; and in R. v. Barry (Glamorgan) JJ. ex parte Kashim,[5] he said 'We did not mean, of course, in the East Kerrier case, that if a question of law were raised the clerk ought to stay in court till the justices said: "Come out with us." ' Lord Goddard also issued a Practice Direction[6] in which he stated that justices might consult their clerk: (1) on questions of law or of mixed law and fact; (2) on questions regarding the practice and procedure of the court; (3) for information as to sentences imposed by their bench or by neighbouring benches; and (4) so as to refresh their memory as to any matter of evidence which had been given. Unfortunately, Lord Goddard had also stated on another occasion that disregard by justices of his instructions would be ground for complaint against them to the Lord Chancellor. Thereafter justices were inhibited by this threat from asking their clerk to retire with them in all but the most clear-cut cases.

Lord Goddard's dicta were quoted with apparent approval by his successors and by the President of the Probate, Divorce and Admiralty Division, but Lord Parker, LCJ, told me that he had reservations about the doctrine and Lord Widgery, in the course of a *tour d'horizon* in 1973 said:[7]

It must be stressed that in these days, when legislation becomes more and more complicated, and when problems of law and practice become more and more oppressive, that justices should not be discouraged from seeking the assistance of their clerk within the legitimate field in which he can advise them.

An important step was taken in 1968 when, at the instigation of the clerks, the Justices of the Peace Act declared that the clerk's function included: (1) giving advice on law, practice and procedure, at the request of the justices, on questions arising in connection with the discharge of their duties; (2) giving such advice on request when not personally attending on the justices; and (3) bringing to the attention of the justices any point of law, practice or procedure that is or may be involved in any question arising in connection with the discharge of their functions.

The ghost of East Kerrier however, continued to haunt the scene and there would seem to be sound reasons why the rule should be abrogated. It was based on the famous dictum of Lord Hewart, LCJ, in R. v. E. Sussex JJ. in 1935 that 'justice should not only be done but should manifestly and undoubtedly be seen to be done', but as Lord Parker, LCJ, later observed, the continued citation of this principle 'may lead to the erroneous impression that it is more important that justice should appear to be done than that it should in fact be done'.

The rationale of the earlier decisions was that a clerk should not retire as a matter of course because this would induce people to conclude that he might influence the justices. The initiative must rest with them. In the case law and the 1968 Act the emphasis is on justices requesting advice before the clerk can give it. The 1968 Act confirmed the clerk's right to draw his justices' attention to the fact that a point of law might arise, but it is not always possible to foresee that it is going to arise in the course of the justices' deliberations. Too much fuss seems to have been made of the impression conveyed by the clerk's retirement. Although the East Kerrier doctrine is useful to practitioners seeking grounds for appeal, most defendants attach no special importance to the disappearance of the clerk through the same door as the justices. They see him conferring with the chairman at various stages of the proceedings (in many courts there is far too much whispered comment between chairman and clerk) and when he does retire at the justices' request it is unlikely that most defendants appreciate that he will deal only with points of law. Once he is out of sight he is clearly in a position to express opinions on any aspect of the case. Likewise he has every opportunity to impart information to his justices when the court adjourns. On the other hand, although points of law do not arise frequently in magistrates' courts there are often questions of mixed law and fact, and justice is more likely to be done if the clerk is in a position to tender immediate advice to his justices whether they are in court or in the retiring room.

The impression that the clerk is interfering unduly in the judicial process is created not so much by his retiring with the justices, as by the justices, through laziness or lack of self-confidence, leaving too much of the conduct of proceedings to the clerk. He is then obliged to assume a prominent, positive role which suggests that he is arrogating the magistrates' functions. This was the pattern in many courts in the 1940s and 1950s, but by the 1960s a more acceptable situation developed and it became rare for a court to be dominated by its clerk (though regrettably a few instances remained).

At the AGM of the Justices' Clerks' Society in 1966 Lord Parker suggested that justices' clerks should be placed on the Commissions of the Peace so that they could exercise minor judicial functions. This was echoed by other authorities and ten years later the Society of Conservative Lawyers recommended that clerks should sit as deputy magistrates and that their clerical and administrative duties should be transferred to other officials. Others suggested that the clerk should sum up in public and should have authority to rule on points of law.[7]

The prospect of the clerk performing quasi-judicial functions was recognised by the Justices of the Peace Act 1968, under which the Justices' Clerks' Rules 1970 enabled clerks to perform a number of functions otherwise exercisable by a single justice. Some clerks welcomed the proposals to give them judicial status. They would have liked to assume the role of a County Court registrar, particularly when, after the Courts Act 1971, the registrars were relieved of their administrative duties. A few clerks saw themselves as virtually legally qualified chairmen of the bench. Not all however, wanted to lose their administrative control, and the Justices' Clerks' Society was divided on the issue. Happily, the wiser counsel seemed to prevail. The most promising future for justices' clerks lies in the direction in which they are already headed. To put the legally qualified clerk on the bench would sow the seed of destruction of the lay magistracy and with it the office of justices' clerk itself; and it is difficult to see that anything would be achieved thereby. Some clerks still feel that it would be to their advantage to follow the County Court registrars and become virtually whole-time judicial officers, but there is no scope for another judicial post below that of magistrate as there is in the County Court, where the registrar does work which would otherwise fall on the judge. Moreover, the justices' clerk occupies a unique position which is of far greater importance to the machinery of justice in general than that of a minor judicial officer.

A more rational policy lies in the development of the office of justices' clerk along existing lines. This would involve revision of the East Kerrier doctrine to establish the clerk's position as legal adviser and to enable, indeed require, him to proffer advice on his own initiative whether invited to do so or not. As far as practicable the advice should be given in open court so that it may be challenged, and the clerk should be personally responsible for the advice he gives. At the same time, there should be clear recognition of the clerk's position and status.

It is submitted that this can be achieved only within the framework of a national court service, as indicated in Chapter 14, which would provide a worthwhile career structure, a more effective system of recruitment and training and would also relieve the clerk of his more routine duties. This would not mean that he would become purely a court official. Courts functioning in the context of a part-time lay magistracy must inevitably have at their centre an officer in the peculiar position of the justices' clerk who provides legal expertise while maintaining a special personal relationship with his justices.

13 Stipendiary Magistrates

Stipendiary Magistrates were first appointed in the eighteenth century in what is now Inner London but was then part of Middlesex.

As Professor R. M. Jackson points out,[1] 'The system of paid magistrates had its origin in two great defects of the administration of justice in the metropolis, namely, the poor quality of the justices and the absence of any adequate police force.' The Justices of the Peace in this area had become so corrupt that the government felt obliged to replace them. In fact, as explained in the next chapter, some duties continued to be performed by the justices, though until 1964 most of the work was disposed of by the metropolitan Stipendiary Magistrates[2] (metropolitan police magistrates, as they were called until 1949). The stipendiaries were also in charge of the constables until 1829, when all police duties were removed from the magistrates and placed under a Commissioner.

In the rest of England and Wales magistrates' courts were always staffed by lay justices, though in some urban centres which grew with the industrial revolution stipendiaries were also appointed conjointly with the justices to deal with the increasing work.

It was to be expected that with the improved proficiency of the lay magistrates after 1950 there would be a relative decline in the importance of stipendiaries, and this was the pattern for nearly three decades. Outside London the number of stipendiaries dropped from 18 in 1949 to 11 in 1977 while the lay justices increased by nearly 50 per cent. In London, although the metropolitans rose from 26 to 41 they were required from 1964 to share the work on virtually equal terms with the justices. Since 1977, however, the increased burden of work, and in some places a backlog of cases, has induced the Lord Chancellor to look more to the stipendiaries, not with a view to replacing the justices, but as a means of disposing of the arrears and relieving pressure which they can accomplish more effectively than their lay colleagues (as explained on page 194). The number of metropolitan magistrates rose to 46 by 1983, while outside London the number was raised to 12 in 1982 and further increases are likely.

Until 1949 stipendiaries were appointed by the Crown on the recommendation of the Home Secretary, but the Justices of the Peace Act transferred this responsibility to the Lord Chancellor. In London the Chancellor (and formerly the Home Secretary) could recommend a maximum of forty appointments on his own initiative.[3] Outside London there were a few places where local Acts provided for a single stipendiary to be appointed on the recommendation of the Minister wherever a vacancy occurred, but in other parts of England and Wales no appointment could be made unless the local authority first submitted an application to Her Majesty in Council and was prepared to pay the salary from local funds. The result was that provincial stipendiaries were not necessarily appointed where they were most needed but only where the local authority wished to have one; usually for reasons of prestige or because the council were on bad terms with their justices. From the outset I was anxious to remedy this illogical situation but local authorities cherished their right to a stipendiary even though most of them did not exercise it, and it was not until 1973, when all local government areas other than counties lost their Commissions of the Peace, that we obtained authority to include a provision in the Administration of Justice Bill empowering the Lord Chancellor to appoint stipendiaries where, and only where, he thought they were required. More than one stipendiary could be appointed in each commission area subject to an overall maximum of 60 in London and 40 in the rest of England and Wales. This limitation on numbers seemed pointless, but the Magistrates' Association and some of the Lord Chancellor's colleagues (including the Home Secretary, who had not previously shown any preference for lay justices), while expressing complete confidence in the present Lord Chancellor, feared that his successors might flood the country with professional magistrates. There were no signs of such an invasion after the Act came into force and by the end of 1977 the number of stipendiaries had been increased by only two: one in London and one in Sheffield.

When the 1973 Act was passed I circulated every Magistrates' Courts Committee and Advisory Committee, asking them to report on the desirability of appointing a stipendiary in their area.

The replies revealed an interesting pattern based not upon the real requirements of the area, but upon whether or not it had previously had a stipendiary. Most places with no previous experience of professional magistrates were resolutely opposed. This was understandable because the committees were composed exclusively of justices, who felt that they were already doing the job satisfactorily and saw no reason why they should be over-shadowed by a professional. Many also emphasised that they were endowed with excellent clerks who were well able to deal with any legal problem that might arise. What was most striking about the replies, however, was that, with the exception of Swansea (where the relationship between the justices and a former stipendiary had been an unhappy one) all justices in places already having a stipendiary were prepared to fight to the last ditch to retain the appointment. In some cases members of the Commons, stirred to action by their constituents, hastened to the Lord Chancellor's room to lobby him on behalf of their local stipendiary.

These demonstrations, impressive though they were, were not taken at their face value and members of my office spent some time visiting provincial areas to satisfy themselves of the true requirements. It transpired that some areas which already had stipendiaries were too small and the court work insufficient to justify a whole-time appointment, but in each of these cases arrangements were made to extend the area of jurisdiction, usually on a peripatetic basis, which enabled the post to be retained. As already mentioned, the only additional provincial appointment up to 1977 was in Sheffield. Work there was in arrears and greater use could not be made of the justices because of lack of accommodation. The need for a stipendiary was appreciated by the justices, who welcomed the appointment, and it proved highly satisfactory.

Greater use was made of another provision of the 1973 Act which enabled the Lord Chancellor to appoint temporary deputy stipendiaries at his discretion. As the number of lengthy old-style committals began to increase, deputy stipendiaries were ap-pointed to take them if the justices were unable to sit for the length of time required. This also added to the opportunities for candidates for full-time appointment to be given trial runs; but by 1977 the number of requests for such appointments had become so numerous that there was difficulty in satisfying them. Barristers in particular were not always able to take two or three weeks on end away from their practices.

As I have said, until 1949 the post of stipendiary was confined to practising members of the Bar. The Justices of the Peace Act extended the qualification to both barristers and solicitors of seven years' standing and, as already noted, the first solicitor, L. M. Pugh, was appointed in Huddersfield in 1957. The first metropolitan appointment was of L. E. Barker in 1960. By 1983 twenty solicitors had been appointed, fifteen in London and five elsewhere.

During the 1950s the Lord Chancellor tried to maintain the previous policy of appointing only those in active legal practice, but applicants from the practising Bar began to drop as the need for additional appointments increased. There were several reasons for this. Practice became more lucrative with increasing work, the development of legal aid and a shortage of counsel, and at the same time the salaries of stipendiaries began to drop behind those of other comparable posts, as explained later. Although a number of solicitors applied, none had had any appreciable court experience or were of the standard required. A solicitor differs from a barrister in that as his career proceeds he usually spends less time in court. The successful solicitor has had little recent court experience, and if he is a senior partner his firm suffers if he leaves it. A solicitor who likes court work and advocacy usually transfers to the Bar. Towards the end of the 1950s, therefore, the Lord Chancellor began to open the door to persons engaged in other forms of legal work. Chief among these were justices' clerks, followed by members of the Director of Public Prosecutions' Office. Between 1957 and 1977, 67 metropolitan and provincial stipendiaries were appointed, composed of 9 former justices' clerks, 4 former members of the DPP's Office, 1 former member of the staff of the Criminal Injuries Compensation Board and 1 former colonial Chief Justice, while those from active practice numbered 45 barristers and 7 solicitors. The appointment of magistrates direct from posts in which they were involved in the prosecution process is open to criticism and, although there were several strong applicants from departments such as that of the Solicitor to the Metropolitan Police, the Lord Chancellor would not consider them unless they resigned their office and had a spell of at least twelve months in practice or in some other field before they applied. Miss Pamela Long did just that. Having resigned from the police solicitor's department she was appointed a London stipendiary a year later in 1978. She also achieved another unique distinction in that her husband, K. J. H. Nichols, was already a London stipendiary (they do not, of course, sit in the same division). Members of the DPP's staff are treated somewhat differently, being regarded as eligible for direct appointment provided that they have not recently been engaged personally in conducting prosecutions in court. It was in this way that D. A. Hopkin (son of a former Metropolitan Magistrate) was appointed in 1970; he became Chief Metropolitan Magistrate in 1982.

A reversal of the recruitment situation began in 1980 when practising barristers reappeared in significant numbers among the applicants, and from then on an increasing proportion of appointments went to the practising Bar. The reason for the revival of interest in stipendiary posts was twofold; the number of magistrates being appointed Circuit Judges suggested that this was a convenient stepping-stone to the Circuit bench and, secondly, the economic recession pervading the rest of the world had at last hit the Bar. Between 1977 and 1983 new appointments comprised 13 barristers and four solicitors, all in practice, and three justices' clerks.

In 1947 there was no *cursus honorum* in the whole-time judicial hierarchy. Although County Court judges were appointed to the High Court bench from time to time the proposition that judges should be promoted rung by rung up the judicial ladder, as in most other countries, was not accepted in Britain; and if a man applied for appointments as a stipendiary it was on the understanding that, if accepted, he would remain in that office throughout his career and should not look for advancement.[4] The climate began to change when, shortly before the Courts Act 1971 was passed, three metropolitan stipendiaries were appointed whole-time deputy chairmen of Quarter Sessions (T. K. Edie to Middlesex sessions in 1970 and Miss Jean Graham Hall and R. G. Rees to Inner London in 1971). Since 1972, although most of those holding judicial office must still expect to remain at the same level, the upward path has not been barred and there has been a certain amount of movement along it: 18 stipendiaries (13 metropolitans and 5 provincials) had been appointed Circuit judges by 1983.

The first woman stipendiary, and the first woman to join the professional judiciary, was Miss Sybil Campbell, who was appointed a metropolitan magistrate in 1945. She was also one of the first women barristers, being called by the Inner Temple in 1922. She gained a reputation for imposing stiffer penalties than her male colleagues and within a year of her appointment 5000 factory workers protested against her sentence of six weeks' imprisonment on a station porter who stole three tablets of soap. Lambeth Trades Council demanded her removal but the Home Secretary, Mr Chuter Ede, refused. By the time Miss Campbell retired in 1961 her public image was one of toughness but fairness. After 1961 there were no women stipendiaries until 1965, when Miss Graham Hall was appointed to the metropolitan bench. She was a barrister and formerly a probation officer and, as already mentioned, she became a deputy chairman of Inner London Sessions and in 1972 was among the first people to be appointed a Circuit judge. In 1967 Miss Nina Collins was appointed to the metropolitan bench, followed by Mrs Audrey Frisby in 1972. Miss Collins joined Miss Hall on the Circuit bench in 1976, and a year later she had the unique experience of being joined there by her husband, R. J. Lowry, QC, who became a Circuit judge in 1977. Since then three more ladies have been appointed stipendiaries, all in London.

From 1972 a number of stipendiaries also served as deputy Circuit Judges and Recorders. A shortage of judicial officers for the Crown Court and County Court enhanced the attraction of using stipendiaries in this capacity to augment judge-power on a temporary basis. They were usually more readily available than a busy practitioner (their place in the magistrates' courts could be filled by justices or by deputy stipendiaries during their absence) and there was some advantage to both the Crown Court and the magistrates' courts in the exchange of expertise between the two. When sitting in the Crown Court, however, the stipendiary received no extra remuneration and he was not allowed to take the daily fee of £45 (raised to £49 in 1978) payable to a barrister or solicitor who sat in the same capacity. As shown later, a stipendiary's salary was less than that of a Circuit judge and the authorities could therefore have been tempted to take unfair advantage of this situation whereby the state virtually got the services of a Circuit judge at a debased rate of pay.

The removal of stipendiaries from office has been referred to in Chapter 11. Complaints were proportionately more numerous in regard to the metropolitan stipendiary courts than other magistrates' courts. This was partly due to the fact that public attention was focused more upon the metropolitan courts than upon those of justices or provincial stipendiaries (many research workers have based their findings on field work conducted exclusively in London and mostly in the stipendiary courts, which gives a totally unrealistic picture so far as the rest of the country is concerned), but whereas the great majority of metropolitan magistrates conducted their work without arousing adverse comment one or two were prone to making unguarded remarks. A legal practitioner who has spent much of his working life addressing courts finds it more difficult than a lay justice to maintain silence when he sits on the bench. It has been remarked that a lawyer always finds plenty to say and his difficulty lies in refraining from saying it. He would do well to heed the old advice of the mother whale to her baby whale: 'Always remember, dear, that you can only be harpooned if you are spouting.'

The Lord Chancellor's constitutional role when dealing with complaints against magistrates was considered in Chapter 11. His task is equally difficult whether the criticism is directed at a stipendiary or a lay justice. He is expected by Members of Parliament and the press to act whenever a stipendiary appears to have overstepped the line of propriety, but it would be improper for him to intervene where the magistrate has acted within his discretion, even though he may think that the decision was wrong. He may point out that a certain remark was unwise, but he can take no further action unless satisfied that the magistrate's conduct indicates unfitness to hold judicial office. In an extreme case he may remove a stipendiary for inability or misbehaviour. No stipendiary has been dismissed in this century but a few have been reprimanded.

In 1952 the Chief Magistrate, Sir Laurence Dunne, drew the Lord Chancellor's attention to a controversial article on homosexual crime by Frank Powell, a metropolitan magistrate, which had been published in the *Star*. The Lord Chancellor informed Powell that it was wrong for anyone in a permanent judicial capacity to write to newspapers or otherwise enter the public lists on controversial issues and that this applied just as much to stipendiaries as to the Supreme Court, but it was also made clear that the Chancellor could not remove Powell if he persisted in publishing controversial articles. In the event Powell cancelled the publication of further articles and undertook not to write any more. The view was subsequently taken that if a stipendiary were to continue to publish literature against the wishes of the Lord Chancellor he might be removed, not because he disregarded the Lord Chancellor's instructions, but because the articles brought the administration of justice into disrepute (if such were the case).

In 1947 the salaries of metropolitan magistrates were the same as those of County Court judges (£2000: the Chief Magistrate received £2300) but the judges were given an increment when they began to take undefended divorce actions and the metropolitans dropped behind. By 1977 the Chief Magistrate had been reduced to the same level as a Circuit judge (£13,000) while the other metropolitans received £11,750. These were raised to £27,750 and £24,000 in 1982. The salaries of provincial stipendiaries were originally fixed by the local authority and as in the case of Recorders thé rate depended more upon the authority's generosity than any other consideration. Under the 1949 Act the amount of salary was fixed by the Home Secretary after consultation with the authority and in 1956 the Criminal Justice Administration Act transferred the Home Secretary's responsibility to the Lord Chancellor. The Chancellor fixed a scale based on the population of the stipendiary's area, but this had to be amended from time to time to keep pace with inflation and with other comparable salaries and not all authorities responded sympathetically to the Lord Chancellor's proposed increases. There were some invidious scenes at council meetings where the performance of the stipendiary was compared unfavourably with that of council officials. If a council refused to accept the Chancellor's figure he usually proceeded to fix the salary at what he thought was the proper national figure. The result was highly unsatisfactory. The council, as paying authority, were dissatisfied, while the stipendiary, although he got his rise, had his reputation besmirched without any means of defending himself. It was not until the Administration of Justice Act 1973, which made the Lord Chancellor the sole authority responsible for all stipendiary appointments, that salaries were transferred from the rates to the Consolidated Fund and were fixed by the Chancellor with the approval of the Minister for the Civil Service.

Since 1973 stipendiaries have been appointed for the whole of a commission area (usually much wider than the previous stipendiary areas) and must be prepared to sit anywhere within the region. In view of the extended commitment the opportunity was taken to assimilate all stipendiary salaries and to bring the provincial rates up to the London level.

Stipendiaries were also at a disadvantage compared with County Court judges, and later Circuit judges, in regard to superannuation. Provincial stipendiaries became eligible for the first time to receive pensions under the Justices of the Peace Act 1949, but both they and the metropolitans had to serve for twenty years before qualifying for the full rate (half their finishing salary) whereas County Court judges did so after fifteen years. The Lord Chancellor and his staff endeavoured, without success, to bring the stipendiaries into line with the judges. The Treasury, and later the Civil Service Department, agreed that a differential was wrong but insisted that parity meant raising the judges' qualifying period to twenty years and not reducing the stipendiaries' to fifteen.

Another source of grievance was the lowering, by the Justices of the Peace Act 1968, of the compulsory retiring age for stipendiaries from seventy-two to seventy. This Act was largely inspired by Lord Gardiner, who was always on the look-out for measures to encourage young blood, and in it he reduced the retiring age for justices of the peace from seventy-five to seventy. In his view all judicial appointments including those of the professional judiciary, at least below Supreme Court level, should be terminated at seventy, and he therefore took the opportunity to apply this limit to stipendiaries. The 1968 Act was confined to magistrates so it could not affect the judges, but it was Lord Gardiner's intention to apply the same retiring age to them at the first opportunity. In 1970 there was a change of Government before anything could be done and Lord Gardiner's successors did not share his views on the age of retirement; Lord Hailsham commented that 'judicial quality sometimes improves with keeping'. Stipendiaries appointed after 1968 were therefore in the invidious position of having to retire before other members of the lower professional judiciary. When it became clear that the retiring age for the others would not be reduced steps were taken in the Administration of Justice Act 1973 to enable stipendiaries to continue in office with the Lord Chancellor's approval up to the age of seventy-two (which was the statutory retiring age for Circuit judges though this could be extended to seventy-five).

The average age for first appointment as a stipendiary remained fairly constant at forty-nine until 1983 but there were considerable individual fluctuations. In 1976 Sir Ivo Rigby (formerly Chief Justice of Hong Kong) was appointed at sixty-five, but more recently younger stipendiaries have been appointed, four of them aged under 40 and the youngest aged 37.

Although the impact of stipendiaries on the administration of justice is less today than it was thirty years ago the quality of their work is generally higher, particularly in the provinces, and successive Lord Chancellors in recent years have been impressed by the manner in which they have discharged their duties. It was not part of the Lord Chancellor's policy to allow the status of stipendiaries to diminish as it tended to do. In 1971 some of the metropolitan magistrates advanced a tentative proposal that stipendiaries should be accorded the title 'His Honour Judge', and, to this extent at least, be equated with Circuit Judges. The Lord Chancellor, Lord Hailsham, was sympathetic and was prepared to accede to the request, but the Lord Chief Justice did not regard it with favour and it was finally abandoned on the ground that it would create an undesirable distinction between the stipendiaries and the lay justices.

Some authorities have urged the extension of the system of stipendiaries so that ultimately they would replace the lay justices. In most other countries the lower criminal courts are manned exclusively by whole-time salaried professionals and Lord Merthyr, as a member of the 1948 Royal Commission, recommended in a minority report that a similar system should be introduced in Britain. The rest of the Royal Commission, however, were convinced of the value of the lay magistracy and were firmly of the opinion that it should be retained. In the course of time Lord Merthyr himself was converted and was elected chairman of the Council of the Magistrates' Association, where he became one of the strongest supporters of the office of Justice of the Peace.

A number of suggestions have also been made for extending the stipendiary system to augment that of the justices. In 1967 the Law Society published a memorandum proposing that cases likely to give rise to difficult questions of law or complicated issues of fact should be dealt with by a bench of two lay magistrates sitting with a legally qualified chairman;[5] but this suggestion received little support. The Bar Council, in evidence to the Royal

Commission on Assizes and Quarter Sessions, recommended that stipendiaries should be appointed on a Circuit basis and should travel from bench to bench taking the chair in turn. It is said that stipendiaries are better able to handle cases involving complicated points of law than a lay bench even when assisted by an experienced clerk. This may be true, but the occasions upon which such cases arise are few and far between and when they do occur they often happen unexpectedly and one could not ensure that a stipendiary would always be available to take them.

Stipendiaries can undoubtedly play a useful part in assisting justices with help and advice in many aspects of their work and they can make a valuable contribution to training, though much tact is needed on the part of all concerned to avoid friction between the roles of the stipendiary and the justices' clerk. Where a stipendiary has a clear advantage over a lay bench is in the speed with which he can dispose of the work and this is the principal consideration taken into account by the Lord Chancellor when deciding on the need for additional appointments. The rapid disposal of court business is not necessarily in the public interest as it may lead to hurried and unjust decisions, but provided that each case is considered with proper care it is to the advantage of the accused that it should be tried without undue delay. In 1972, with the help of Sir Frank Milton, the Chief Metropolitan Magistrate, I carried out some research into the relative disposal rates of metropolitan magistrates and lay justices in Inner London. We took a number of offences which were tried in both types of court and we found that on average the stipendiary disposed of about 60 per cent more work in a two-hour session than a bench of three justices. As was to be expected, the difference increased with the complexity of the case. A plea of guilty to a minor motoring offence took virtually the same time in both courts, but a defended charge of careless driving might last three times as long before the justices if they had to adjourn to discuss both conviction and sentence, and longer still if they needed legal advice from their clerk. This same exercise was also directed towards estimating the number of justices needed to replace one stipendiary. At that time the metropolitan magistrates averaged 186 days sitting a year and the lay justices forty-two half-day sittings (morning and afternoon attendances counting separately for the justices), so the annual total for each justice was twenty-one full days compared with 186 for a stipendiary. Assuming that each lay bench was composed of three justices, one stipendiary sat for the same length of time as 27 of his lay colleagues in the course of the year. Adding this to the greater speed of disposal by stipendiaries we came to the conclusion that about 42 justices would be needed to dispose of the work done by one metropolitan magistrate. The number would of course have been much greater if every justice completed only the minimum obligatory number of twenty-six half-day attendances a year but the average was considerably higher as many justices sat far more frequently than the minimum.

So long as the lay justices do their work competently it cannot be claimed that stipendiaries are essential, and in most parts of the country, urban as well as rural, justice appears to be administered to the general satisfaction of the population and of the Supreme Court without the presence of a stipendiary. On the other hand there is some indefinable factor which seems to result in justice being administered even better in places where there is a stipendiary working in conjunction with the lay justices and augmenting their work. This appears to be the majority view of members of the legal profession and of others directly concerned in the courts. There are certainly some types of case which can be tried better by a stipendiary than by a lay bench; these include not only those involving complex points of law but ones which raise emotive issues (justices tend to be moved by emotional events in and out of court to a greater extent than stipendiaries) or where local political issues are involved. Some types of case, notably matrimonial ones, are best tried by a stipendiary sitting with justices. Apart from this, where a harmonious relationship is established between the stipendiary and the justices the overall impression of observers is that, although logically indefensible, judicial machinery operates more efficaciously with the dual system than where there are either stipendiaries or justices alone.

14 Administration and Organisation

In England the administration of criminal justice was always regarded as a local responsibility, on the principle that crime is a local matter and that the duty of apprehending and trying offenders should fall on those living in each area. The jury system developed from the same origins. Administering and financing the criminal courts rested therefore with the local community. This remained the position in all criminal courts until 1972 when the Crown Court, with its national court service financed by the state, replaced Assizes and Quarter Sessions; but the new system did not include the magistrates' courts. They had not been within the terms of reference of the Beeching Commission because they did not suffer from delays to the same extent as the higher courts and to include them might have delayed the commission in making its recommendations, which were required urgently. Also, reforms in the administration of magistrates' courts had been introduced within the previous twenty years under the Justices of the Peace Act 1949.[1]

Before 1949 the cost of magistrates' courts was met entirely by the local authorities (except in what is now Inner London). Fines and fees collected by the courts were paid to the local authority unless a statute directed otherwise, but by 1944 these exceptions, which included road-traffic fines, were so substantial that there was a deficit which fell on the rates. The Roche Committee, in their 1944 Report, recommended that magistrates' courts, which were then virtually independent of one another, should be grouped for administrative purposes under committees to be called Magistrates' Courts Committees. (Although the Report did not say so, the idea was taken from the old General Purposes Committee in some boroughs.) This was implemented in the 1949 Act under which a separate committee was set up in each county and county borough and in eight large non-county boroughs.[2]

Committees are composed of magistrates elected by their colleagues in each division and are responsible for the provision of buildings, staff, furniture and other matters necessary to carry on the court business.

The cost is borne initially by the local authority which is obliged to pay such sum as the committee determines (after consultation with the authority). If the authority thinks the magistrates' proposed expenditure is unjustifiable or excessive, it may appeal to the Home Secretary, whose decision is final. Fees were abolished in 1967 and all fines are now paid to the Home Office, who return to the authority an amount representing the proceeds of certain fines, plus two-thirds of the difference between these and the actual expenditure. In practice the amount of the grant has usually represented about 80 per cent of the total cost. In 1976 expenditure, including loan charges, on magistrates' courts amounted to £43 million and fines collected in these courts to £36 million.

Overall responsibility for expenditure on magistrates' courts rests therefore with the Home Office, but the auditing of the courts' accounts is carried out on behalf of the Home Office by the Internal Credit Service of the Lord Chancellor's Department which, in recent years, has come to concern itself with a far wider range of issues than the accounts themselves, such as office layout and the physical security of premises and staff. Since 1977 it has also advised on the acquisition by courts of computers. These have been installed in many courts not only to improve accounting procedures but for a wide range of tasks including listing of cases and production of documents.

Committees were also empowered to submit proposals to the Home Secretary for the amalgamation of petty sessional divisions or the alteration of their boundaries and, during the first twenty years after Magistrates' Courts Committees were established the number of divisions was reduced from 938 to 842. Further reductions were strongly resisted by the divisions who would have lost their separate status but by 1978 there were only 640 places in England and Wales where magistrates' courts sat and this has remained the figure since then. There are still nearly 100 courts which deal each week with less than one defendant accused of an indictable offence.

The influence of local authorities on magistrates' courts has tended to be restrictive. Many authorities were not interested in the administration of justice, over which they had no effective control, and preferred to spend their funds elsewhere. It is true that the initiative rested with the Magistrates' Courts Committees but, as was pointed out earlier in relation to training, many committees tended to accept the line taken by their councils on which numbers of local justices served, and even when this was not the case the council's influence could impede the fulfilment of a committee's policy.

The system also failed to ensure that magistrates' courts were built when and where they were needed and only where they were needed and were properly maintained. In some places court buildings were totally inadequate, while in others they were of a much higher standard than was required, depending upon the policy of the local authority.

Staffing arrangements were equally deficient. There was no career structure and no regular channel of promotion to enable a clerk in one area to obtain a higher post in another. This led to poor recruitment. There were no effective means of interchange of professional staff between courts. A magistrates' court could not even borrow staff on a temporary basis from a neighbouring court when its own people were away ill. In many places staff were insufficient in number to be able to discharge all the duties which should have been performed. This resulted, for example, in ineffective fine enforcement and in there being no accurate statistics of the cases dealt with in magistrates' courts (published figures were based solely on returns supplied by the police which covered only a part of the picture).

Centralised control would have ensured that magistrates' courts sat whenever and wherever they were required (and only when and where required) and would have led to greater efficiency of staff by providing a nationwide career structure, effective training, common standards and the replacement of large numbers of part-time staff with fewer and more efficient whole-time officers. It would also have ensured more rapid disposal of work and the elimination of arrears and, although there would have been substantial setting-up costs, considerable long-term saving would have been gained from the greater efficiency of the staff and the more economic use of accommodation. Economies would also have been achieved by the use of joint services. This applies not only to services provided in respect of court buildings, but also to other matters, such as printing: the vast numbers of forms and documents required for the magistrates' courts were printed by some 200 different local printers whose work varied considerably in cost and quality.

In 1966 the Justices' Clerks' Society urged the government to centralise administration under the Lord Chancellor. Neither the Lord Chancellor nor the Home Secretary viewed this proposal with enthusiasm, the Lord Chancellor because it would have meant a vast expansion of his office and a further widening of his already over-extended field of responsibility, the Home Secretary because of the repercussions it would have had on his existing jurisdiction, particularly on the probation and after-care service. The subject was therefore shelved for a few years, but when the Lord Chancellor became responsible for administering all other courts under the Beeching scheme he was pressed from many quarters to include the magistrates' courts as well. The Lord Chancellor's Office would have been willing to accept this responsibility, albeit reluctantly, but in spite of the obvious advantages of this course there were some who opposed it, and in 1970 it was decided to test opinion by issuing a consultative document to those principally concerned. The great majority of those consulted were in favour of centralisation under the Lord Chancellor. The principal protagonists of the *status quo* were the county councils and their clerks. The counties were reluctant to lose something they had possessed for centuries, even though what they stood to lose was a financial obligation over which they had no control. The clerks of county councils, who were an influential body, objected to a development which would affect their own authority within their counties and might deprive many of them of their appointments as clerks to Magistrates' Courts Committees. Against them were ranged a formidable array of organisations, including the Bar Council, the Law Society, the Magistrates' Association, the Stipendiary Magistrates' Society, the Justices' Clerks' Society and the Greater London Council, all of whom supported a country-wide structure on the grounds of efficiency and economy.

Those who opposed centralisation argued that transfer to central government of responsibility for the magistrates' courts which had their roots deep in history would be a move against the general trend for greater devolution. Much store was laid on the need to preserve the involvement of the local community in the administration of justice, but in fact this did not depend upon the association of local authorities with the magistrates' courts. Local involvement does not require local authority involvement. If responsibility were taken over by the central government the citizen would continue to be involved in his local magistrates' court through the Justices of the Peace, all of whom would continue to be appointed on a local basis and would sit only in the local courts. Moreover, although the responsibility of the Magistrates' Courts Committees for administration would have had to be curtailed in some respects, there was no reason why these bodies should not have been preserved in an advisory capacity and allowed to retain some of their functions. The committees themselves were concerned about the prospect of losing the right to appoint justices' clerks, which would necessarily follow if the Government were to become responsible for the payment of salaries; but it would not have been impossible to devise a system whereby each committee, or even bench, chose the clerk from a short list approved by the Lord Chancellor.

While these divergent issues were being considered, the Justices' Clerks' Society began to modify their views. They were somewhat disillusioned by the terms of service offered to previous court officers who joined the Crown Court staff, and at the same time one of their main sources of dissatisfaction with the existing system was removed when, as already mentioned, local government reorganisation resulted in the majority of the new Magistrates' Courts Committees having a justices' clerk as their clerk. The Government, in the throes of local government reform, did not think the time propitious to embark upon further measures affecting the local authorities. Furthermore, centralisation would have meant turning the justices' clerks and their staffs, numbering some 3500, into civil servants (if the probation and after-care service had also been taken over another 5000 staff would have been included) and all recent governments have recoiled in horror from anything that looked like swelling the ranks of the Civil Service if it could be avoided. Moreover, the Home Office were still saddled with their peculiar problems and were especially concerned about the impact that a change would make on the position of the probation and after-care service. It would have been difficult to leave the existing organisation of the service, which was on similar lines to that of the magistrates' courts, as it was. A choice would have had to be made between incorporating the service in the new local authority social work departments set up in accordance with the recommendations of the Seebohm Committee,[3] a course to which the service itself would have been strongly opposed, or converting it into a national courts and prison service provided by the Home Office. In any event, it seemed out of the question to contemplate a fundamental structural reorganisation of the probation and after-care service at that time, when what was needed was a rapid expansion of the service to enable it to cope with a widening range of tasks.

It was therefore decided to preserve the essentials of the existing system and to try to regularise and improve it. Some progress was made in this direction, such as by improving staff training and amalgamating petty sessional divisions. This involved some closing of court houses, which not everyone regarded as progress. Where the case loads were light, courts were closed on economic grounds to save the cost of buildings and staff, which sometimes caused hardship to the local population if they had already been deprived of their public transport; but they were few in number with no effective voice in national affairs so they lost their railway line, their bus service and their court house. There were, however, many well-informed people who were convinced that it was only a matter of time before mounting arrears, shortage of experienced staff and the need to increase efficiency would force the government into assuming overall control through an integrated system for all the courts. There is reason to think that they were right.[4]

Happily the organisation of the magistrates themselves in their respective courts presents a tidier and more sensible picture than the fragmented administrative structure within which they have to operate. Until 1949 there was no statutory limit on the number of justices who might sit at one time. Attempts had been made in 1925 to limit the numbers of justices in each area, but these met with scant success and the Royal Commission observed in 1948 that there were far too many justices on the commissions and that often far too many sat together on the bench: fifteen or more were not uncommon. In 1944 the Roche Committee had recommended that a bench should not normally consist of more than five justices but that a maximum of seven should be permitted lest a lower limit should deprive some justices of the opportunity to attend. This view was endorsed by the Royal Commission, and the Justices of the Peace Act 1949 empowered the Lord Chancellor to make rules governing the number of justices who might sit at one time. In 1950 he followed the Roche Committee's recommendation by fixing the maximum at seven (the rules also limited Quarter Sessions to nine including the chairman).[5] At the same time, the Lord Chancellor issued a directive to benches indicating that three was the best number for a court and that, save in exceptional circumstances, not more than five should sit.

Having prescribed the size of the court the Lord Chancellor, Lord Jowitt, went on to lay down the numbers of justices he would allow to serve in each division. Until then it had been assumed that, in assessing the required number of justices, account should be taken of the need for them to be resident in every area to provide out of court services, particularly to sign documents. The Royal Commission had questioned this hypothesis on the ground that there were plenty of persons besides justices who were qualified to sign most kinds of form, and Lord Jowitt decreed that the sole criterion in fixing the number of justices should be the amount of work done in court. Peripheral duties were to be ignored unless there was evidence that the public were suffering hardship through the non-availability of a justice in a particular area. Meanwhile my office set about persuading other departments to extend the lists of those authorised to countersign forms.

Lord Jowitt's bench establishment was based on the supposition that every justice should average not less than one sitting every two weeks (except where this was impossible because the bench sat less frequently than once a fortnight). It followed that if not more than seven justices could sit at one time a fortnightly bench must not have more than seven justices otherwise they would not be able to comply with the minimum annual requirement. A maximum of seven was therefore fixed for a fortnightly bench and fourteen for a weekly bench; above that each case was considered on its merits. At that time there were still many rural benches which met only once a month, and even less, and Lord Jowitt limited these to five justices; until we learnt a lesson from the Scilly Isles. Justices in the law-abiding Scilly Isles were in the happy position of having very little work and they met only a few times a year. Five justices had seemed ample until the day a message arrived in my office that someone had been charged with an offence and there was only one justice available to try him. We enquired what had happened to the other four. It transpired that one was ill and the other three comprised the captain and two other members of the crew of the steamer which plied between the islands and the mainland, and at this crucial moment the steamer was fogbound in Penzance harbour. Thereafter benches sitting less than once a fortnight were allowed a maximum of seven justices, and care was taken to see that not too many were 'in the same boat'.

In the course of time it became convenient to lay down guidelines for all sizes of bench and in 1963 a directive was issued fixing the maximum at twenty for a bench sitting once a week, twenty-five for twice a week and thereafter an additional four (raised to five in 1968) were allowed for each weekly court. The figures could be exceeded in exceptional circumstances, for example where there was a shortage of women or of justices qualified to sit in the juvenile court.

Urban benches have always tended to become understaffed and rural benches overstaffed. Some urban benches do their best to keep their numbers to a minimum even though this means that each individual has to sit far more frequently than the obligatory twenty-six attendances a year, and some justices average well over 100 annual sittings. This does not meet with the Lord Chancellor's approval because it results in the bench being confined to those who have ample time to spare, but whereas every Lord Chancellor since 1949 has been careful to prevent benches from becoming too large, it was not until 1965 that a serious effort was made to raise the numbers in undermanned areas. Since then some benches have been obliged to accept additional appointments against their wishes.

The rules made in 1950 limiting the number of justices who might sit at one time also provided for the annual election of a chairman and one or more deputy chairmen in each division. As the Royal Commission pointed out, the efficiency of a court and the reputation in which it is held depends more upon the personal qualities of the chairman than upon any other factor, but until 1949 chairmen had usually been chosen because they were senior in length of service, even though their faculties might have been impaired. The 1949 Act required the Lord Chancellor to make rules governing the method of electing the chairman and deputies. When drafting the rules our principal concern was to ensure that the justice best qualified for the post was elected, irrespective of seniority or of his political or social background. Secret ballot and the prohibition of nominations in advance went a long way towards achieving this object, but there are still exceptions where, contrary to the spirit of the rules, the most senior justice is elected solely because his colleagues do not wish to hurt his feelings, or where the justices from one political party agree in advance among themselves to vote for a justice designated from among their own number.

Two further defects emerged with the passage of time. The first was the potential influence of local government *ex officio* justices, many of whom showed no interest in the magistracy except once a year when they turned up to vote at the election of the chairman. They were not in a position to compare the merits of the candidates and their sole intention was to vote for a member of their own political party. In some places there were several *ex officios* in the same division and their votes could be decisive. This danger was removed by the Administration of Justice Act 1964 which disqualified *ex officios* from voting for the chairman or deputy chairmen of their benches and from being elected to these offices themselves. The second problem arose in divisions which were so large that it was a long time before a justice could get to know all his colleagues and therefore, like the absentee *ex officio*, he was not in a position to know who was most suitable for the chairmanship. This difficulty could not be entirely eliminated but we endeavoured to meet it by providing, in the Justices of the Peace Act 1968 and the rules made thereunder, that a justice might not vote at an election of officers within twelve months of appointment to the bench. By introducing this qualification, which was generally regarded as desirable, I unwittingly laid the Lord Chancellor open to attack from a number of persons who, ignoring the precedents provided by the Supplemental List and *ex officio* justices, accused him of apartheid in creating a class of justice without a franchise. It has been suggested that if the prohibition on nomination of candidates in advance were lifted this would enable all members to focus attention on the nominees and thereby gain some knowledge of them, but this proposal has been opposed on the ground that it would lead to lobbying.

It has been suggested that chairmen should serve for a limited term and then make way for new blood. The Royal Commission of 1948 was of the opinion that a chairman should remain in office for as long as possible provided that his faculties remained unimpaired, and for this reason the rules placed no limit on length of service but merely provided a check by requiring the chairman to stand for re-election each year. By the late 1960s a fairly vociferous group was pressing for a limit of three years and I decided to ask every Advisory Committee and Magistrates' Courts Committee for their views. The replies were about three to one against imposing any limit, and the rules therefore remained unaltered.

The 1949 Act made it obligatory for the chairman or a deputy chairman to preside if present, and it was rare for a court to sit with any other justice in the chair. As the work increased and courts sat more frequently the pattern changed. It was not possible for the chairman or one of the deputy chairmen to preside in every court and in these circumstances the justices decided among themselves who should take the chair. There was no harm in this if the presiding justice was reasonably experienced, but in places where a number of courts sat at the same time it was not uncommon for the chairman and deputy chairman to sit with the senior court clerks in those courts which were expected to have the more important cases, leaving other courts to be presided over by justices of limited experience assisted by comparatively inexperienced clerks. The rule that the chairmen or deputy chairmen must preside if present was modified in 1977 by the Administration of Justice Act which provided that another justice might take the chair if invited to do so by the chairman or deputy. This was introduced as a training expedient to enable a justice to gain experience of chairmanship under supervision.

A notable change of attitude towards presiding in court emerged in the late 1960s. Until then newly appointed justices were content figuratively to take a back seat, and indeed seldom opened their mouths unless consulted, but by 1975 a large proportion, especially of the younger justices, were striving to take the chair at the earliest opportunity.

Separate regulations apply to the composition of specialist tribunals (juvenile, domestic and licensing). Domestic courts are composed of at least two and not more than three justices (a stipendiary may sit alone) and the public are excluded. Where the court is constituted of lay justices it includes, so far as practicable, both a man and a woman (there is not a mandatory requirement as in the case of the juvenile courts). Before 1935 domestic proceedings in London had been within the exclusive jurisdiction of the stipendiaries but from then onwards lay justices took an increasing part and a pattern developed whereby two justices sat with a stipendiary as chairman. This proved to be a particularly effective tribunal because the stipendiary could handle complicated points of law which tend to arise more often in domestic cases than in others coming before magistrates' courts, while the justices were better able to assess all the facts which needed to be taken into account when calculating what a husband, or wife, might reasonably be expected to pay.

Before 1978 there was a further difference between juvenile and domestic courts in that any justice might participate in domestic proceedings and it was not until the Domestic Proceedings and Magistrates' Courts Act 1978 that domestic panels were established under rules made by the Lord Chancellor. As explained earlier, the Finer Committee's proposals to abolish the matrimonial jurisdiction of magistrates and to set up a separate system of family courts was abandoned, and the 1978 Act was based on the Law Commission's recommendations but the future of the family court concept is uncertain.

In 1947 all justices in a division could take part in licensing sessions unless they were directly involved in the liquor trade, and since the Licensing Act 1953 every division has had to elect annually a licensing committee of not less than five and not more than fifteen justices, and from 1963 this committee has also heard applications for betting and gaming licenses.

A few words need to be added about the administration of courts in London which, like many other things in the capital, have always been peculiar. Before the creation of the County of London in 1888 the area, apart from the City, was administered by justices of Middlesex and Surrey who, by the eighteenth century, did a brisk trade in pocketing fines and fees and became so corrupt that in 1792 metropolitan magistrates' courts with whole-time Stipendiary Magistrates were established by the Middlesex and Surrey Justices Act,[6] which provided that all fees should be paid over to a Receiver and that none should be taken by the lay justices except for licensing and certain other work. It was assumed that this would soon throw the justices out of business and therefore they were not expressly deprived of the right to hold courts. Some of them, however, resolutely continued to do so, with the result that up to 1964 London had a hybrid system wherein the metropolitan Stipendiary Magistrates did the lion's share of the work (except in Hampstead, where there were no metropolitans) largely because the police did not bring cases before the justices, but most local authority prosecutions were taken to the justices, who also did the whole of the licensing work.

In addition, the justices sat in the domestic and juvenile courts. There were therefore two entirely separate systems with separate staff and with different magistrates sitting in different buildings. Among other disadvantages this gave the prosecution a choice of tribunal.

In 1937 the Maxwell Committee[7] recommended that the courts of the stipendiaries and the lay justices should be amalgamated, but this was not immediately pursued because of the war. The proposal was revived in the 1950s when pressure on the stipendiaries began to build up and when the standard of the London justices had improved to a point where it was thought right to entrust them with full jurisdiction. In 1962 the Aarvold Committee[8] was appointed to consider what measures were required to implement the recommendations of the earlier committee. Their proposals for integration entailed the justices exercising the same jurisdiction as justices elsewhere and sharing this with the stipendiaries (only a few subjects such as fugitive offenders being reserved exclusively to the stipendiaries). Administration of the combined system was to be in the hands of a committee of magistrates, similar to a Magistrates' Courts Committee elsewhere but composed equally of stipendiaries and justices. The chairman of this committee was at first the chairman of Inner London sessions but under the Courts Act 1971 he was replaced by the Chief Metropolitan Magistrate. Apart from this function the Chief Magistrate has no authority over the lay justices, who have their own bench chairmen, while among his professional colleagues he is only *primus inter pares* with certain powers to allocate work.

Before 1964 the justices sat mostly in town halls (not the best of places from the citizen's point of view, as much of their work involved the enforcement of payments to the local authorities) while the stipendiaries had their own buildings. The Aarvold plan envisaged joint buildings, each with court rooms for stipendiaries and justices and with a common staff.

All these proposals were embodied in the Administration of Justice Act 1964, but financial restraint retarded the construction of custom-built court houses and it will be many years before the building programme is completed.

When the 1964 Act came into force the County of London had been transformed into the much larger area of Greater London by the London Government Act 1963. The 1964 Act therefore divided Greater London into five areas, each with its own commission and Quarter Sessions, and it limited the appointment of stipendiaries to the central area, to be known as Inner London, leaving the four outer areas to be administered by justices alone.

Reference has already been made to the unique position of the Lord Mayor and Aldermen of the City of London. The City owned and administered the courts at the Guildhall and Mansion House (the only court in a private house left in the United Kingdom). In 1964 the City sailed serenely on, unperturbed by the turbulence in the surrounding areas of London, but in 1968 Lord Gardiner's Justices of the Peace Act placed the administration of the City courts in the hands of a Magistrates' Courts Committee which included justices appointed to the City commission by the Lord Chancellor.

15 Scotland, Northern Ireland and the Isle of Man

Justices of the Peace are to be found in all parts of the United Kingdom, the system having been extended on the English pattern at various stages in our history, but it was only in England and Wales that they flourished continuously to the present day; elsewhere much of their court work was transferred to professional magistrates.

The Lord Chancellor's functions in respect of magistrates have been directed mainly towards England and Wales, but a feature of the years under review in this book was that they saw the end of his involvement in the appointment of justices in Scotland, which had lasted for two and a half centuries, and they also witnessed his assumption, for the first time, of responsibility for all magistrates in Northern Ireland.

SCOTLAND

Justices of the Peace were introduced into Scotland by James VI, who later became James I when the Scottish and English crowns were united. He was faced with a lawless society not altogether dissimilar to that of the Plantagenets two centuries earlier and he hoped to strengthen the royal authority by appointing magistrates directly responsible to the Crown. They were also intended to be a counterpoise to the sheriffs who, although royal officers, had become hereditary. In fact, there was a good deal more lawlessness in James's Scotland than there had been in Edward III's England – the north of the country was disrupted by rebellious highlanders and the south by rampaging Border Rievers – and it was partly for this reason that his first attempt to

209

introduce justices, in 1587, failed. He was more successful twenty years later, and justices first began to function in Scotland under an Act of 1609.

In the course of time they came to perform duties similar to those of justices in England (including local government work until the establishment of Scottish county councils in 1889) but they never flourished to the same extent as their colleagues south of the Border. This was probably because Scotland had no powerful middle class or squirearchy. The Plantagenets had been able to rely upon the knights of the shires and in later centuries the backbone of the English and Welsh system was the landed gentry. In the highlands there was no one between the clans and their chiefs, while in the lowlands law was dominated by the nobility, as often as not at loggerheads with the Crown. It is significant that there was never a property qualification for Scottish justices as there was in England and Wales until 1906. Apart from a brief period of conspicuous success under the Protectorate, when Cromwellian ordinances empowered Scottish justices for the first time to try noblemen, they remained somewhat ineffective until the 1745 rebellion, after which their jurisdiction was encroached upon by the Sheriff courts which began from 1747 to develop on modern lines.

The Justice of the Peace courts exercised jurisdiction mainly over country areas. In the Scottish cities, or burghs, responsibility had rested since the Middle Ages with the provosts and civic dignitaries and in the course of time the burgh courts came to be manned by bailies, who were members of the town council elected by their fellow councillors.

By 1947 most Scottish justices did little more than sign papers. They handled virtually no court work except in a few places (principally the city of Aberdeen and the counties of Ayr, Renfrew and Fife, where they provided the juvenile courts under the Children and Young Persons (Scotland) Act 1937). Most of the court duties were discharged by the Sheriff Substitute and by the bailies in the burghs. The Justices of the Peace accounted for only about 10 per cent of all persons, including juveniles, tried in the Scottish criminal courts, whereas at that time English justices were dealing with 98 per cent of the total. In spite of this, Scottish justices in 1947 numbered approximately 6200 and were relatively more numerous per head of population than in England and Wales. In urban areas, particularly Glasgow, the number of justices was excessive and steps were taken after 1949 to reduce it, but in country districts appointments continued to be influenced by the Scottish predilection for justices' signatures on documents, which necessitated the presence of justices in even the smallest places. A recent manifestation of this appeared in 1983 with the introduction of a 'do-it-yourself' divorce procedure. The necessary affidavits require signature before a notary public, commissioner for oaths or a justice, and as the latter provide a free service they have proved to be overwhelmingly the most popular signatories. By 1977 the figures were a closer reflection of the work done. There were then about 5000 justices in Scotland compared with 23,000 on the Active List in England and Wales. By 1981 Scottish justices had dropped in number still further to 4100 (including 275 *ex officios*) while south of the Border the number had increased to 25,500.

During the thirty years following the war the relative importance of the lay summary courts in Scotland declined while the Sheriff court became overloaded, largely because legislation did not take account of the role that the lay courts could have played. In 1946 the number of persons proceeded against in the Sheriff courts was 31,656 compared with 48,855 in the burgh courts and 7797 in the Justice of the Peace courts. In 1970 the figures were 116, 714, 84, 855 and 8616 respectively.

Before 1707 Scottish justices were appointed by the King and Privy Council but under the Act of Union responsibility for placing names on the Scottish commissions was given to the Lord Chancellor, and so it remained until 1954. The 1948 Royal Commission considered whether these duties should be transferred to a Scottish Minister or judicial officer such as the Lord Justice General. They decided against judicial officers on the grounds that they were not answerable to Parliament, that their judicial duties were heavy and that they had no staff. The most likely Minister was the Secretary of State for Scotland, who already recommended most Scottish judicial appointments, acting on the advice of the Lord Advocate, but the commission found against him because he was 'less removed from political influence than the Lord Chancellor'. In the absence of a suitable Scottish authority the commission recommended that the Lord Chancellor should remain responsible for justices in Scotland, but they thought that control from Westminster was too remote and they therefore proposed that a Scottish official should be appointed

Secretary of Commissions for Scotland with his office in Edinburgh. This recommendation was accepted to the extent that a sub-department of the Lord Chancellor's Office was established in St Andrew's House, but Lord Jowitt insisted upon retaining a single Secretary of Commissions. I therefore remained Secretary of Commisions for the whole of Great Britain but routine matters were delegated to an Assistant Secretary of Commisions for Scotland.[1] Lord Jowitt also appointed a committee under the chairmanship of the Lord Justice Clerk to advise him generally on matters concerning justices in Scotland.

The recommendations of the 1948 Royal Commission were soon forgotten in so far as they concerned Scotland. In 1954, the Royal Commission on Scottish Affairs, while recognising that the system operated satisfactorily under the Lord Chancellor, were anxious to find duties which could be transferred from Westminster to Edinburgh and accordingly recommended that the appointment of Scottish justices should be placed under the Secretary of State for Scotland. The only reason they gave was that this seemed right in principle.

The transfer was duly effected on 1st April 1955 by Statutory Instrument under the Ministers of the Crown (Transfer of Functions) Act 1946. J. E. de Watteville, who was then Assistant Secretary of Commissions in Edinburgh, became the first Secretary of Commissions for Scotland. Thereafter the Lord Chancellor retained no connection with Scottish justices save that, as appointments continued to be made under the Great Seal of Great Britain, all Scottish fiats and commissions were sent to the Crown Office in Westminster for names to be added or removed (and for peculiar reasons that I need not enlarge upon I continued to provide Scottish Lords Lieutenant with expense allowances and notepaper).

The appointment of Justices in Scotland had always been regarded as a civic honour and a reward for political services to a greater degree than in England and the 1948 Royal Commission had feared that the history of Scottish justices would be dominated even more by political considerations after the transfer to the Secretary of State. The practical consequences might not be appreciable in view of the minimal amount of court work done by most Scottish justices, but they were nevertheless magistrates and the Lord Chancellor himself had resisted the change on the ground that it was wrong in principle to take any step tending to increase the possibility of political bias in judicial appointments. In fact the Scottish Advisory Committees have made great efforts, especially during the last ten years, to observe principles similar to those applied in England and party politics have influenced appointments far less than was expected. A totally different picture, however, is presented by the *ex officio* justices nominated by local councils, usually on a political basis, to which I now turn.

In the early 1970s a review of the magisterial system in Scotland was carried out in the context of Scottish local government reform, and burgh courts were abolished and with them the office of bailie. A working party on the lay summary courts was appointed under the chairmanship of Sir Ronald Johnson, Secretary of Commissions for Scotland, and their report, issued in 1972, was largely endorsed in a Government White Paper the following year.[2] It was proposed that all lay courts should be composed of justices appointed on the Queen's behalf by the Secretary of State and that their conditions of service should resemble closely those in England. There were also to be Stipendiary Magistrates in Glasgow and in such other districts as the state of business required. These were to be appointed by the Secretary of State and not by the local authority as previously.

These proposals ran into opposition from the legal profession, who questioned the propriety of setting up courts in which neither the judges nor the clerks were lawyers (whereas previously clerks to justices were all lawyers – most in private practice – it was now proposed that the justices' court should be manned by the sheriff clerk service whose personnel is not legally qualified). The Government accordingly abandoned its proposals and decided to substitute a stipendiary system. This commended itself to the lawyers but aroused the ire of the local authorities, whose councillors would no longer have been able to serve as magistrates. At that point there was a general election. The Conservatives were replaced by Labour and the new Government, with a slender majority and with support lying mainly in the local councils, adopted a new scheme, the brain child of Bruce Millan the Secretary of State, whereby all existing courts of summary jurisdiction were merged in a new District Court whose judges were drawn from four groups: Justices of the Peace (appointed by the Secretary of State), *ex officio* justices (appointed by the local authorities), stipendiaries (also appointed by local authorities) and in addition to these, anyone holding office as a burgh magistrate or police judge before 14 May 1975 automatically became a justice for the burgh area. All the *ex officios* were to be councillors, each authority electing up to a quarter of its number for this purpose. When composed of justices the court was to have the same jurisdiction as the previous inferior courts, except the Small Debts Court, and when constituted by a stipendiary (who had to be either an advocate or a solicitor of not less than five years' standing) it was also to have the powers of a Sheriff Court. Justices could sit singly.

The Lord Chancellor urged the rejection of the proposed system of *ex officio* justices and local government-appointed stipendiaries as being retrograde, but his colleagues were determined to satisfy the local authorities. It was agreed, however, that all justices, including *ex officios*, should undergo courses of instruction (until then there had been no general system of training in Scotland) and that the Secretary of State should have power to transfer a justice who declined to attend a course to a Supplemental List. He was also given power to suspend an *ex officio* justice if he considered him unfit to adjudicate (the Lord Chancellor had had this power in respect of English and Welsh *ex officios* since 1906).

With these modifications the proposals were implemented in the District Courts (Scotland) Act 1975 and the opportunity was lost to remove local authority involvement from the administration of justice in Scotland. Scotland was left with a system more outdated than the one that Parliament had rejected seven years earlier as being no longer suitable for England and Wales.

NORTHERN IRELAND

Justices of the Peace were abolished in Southern Ireland after the creation of the Irish Free State, but under the District Justices (Temporary Provisions) Act 1923 'peace commissioners' could be appointed in each county with the same powers as those previously possessed by justices, which were relatively minor in character. In Northern Ireland the Justices of the Peace were retained, but in 1935 most of their judicial functions were transferred to legally qualified Resident Magistrates under the Summary Jurisdiction and Criminal Justice (Northern Ireland) Act.

The Lord Chancellor's involvement in the administration of justice in Northern Ireland was occasioned by the outbreak of violence which began in 1969 and led to direct rule from Westminster. By an Order made under the Northern Ireland Constitution Act 1973 the Lord Chancellor replaced the Governor as the appointing authority for Justices of the Peace and Resident Magistrates on 1st January 1974. Until then justices were appointed in each county on the nomination of the Lord Lieutenant. When the Lord Chancellor assumed responsibility one of the first tasks was to establish an Advisory Committee, with the Lord Lieutenant as its chairman, for each of the eight commission areas (six counties plus Belfast and Londonderry). Most of the Lords Lieutenant resented this intrusion but were good enough not to make their feelings too apparent. The committees and the policies they were required to apply were basically the same as in England and Wales, except that care was taken to play down party politics and no mention was made of the political allegiance of candidates. Instead, a record was kept of their religious persuasion with a view to establishing a reasonable balance between Protestants and Roman Catholics. As in England and Wales efforts were made to secure an occupational cross section. Steps were also taken to reduce the number of justices. There were 1655 at the beginning of 1974, 1478 at the end of 1977 and 1297 by 1983. As Northern Ireland justices do not attend court it is not easy to keep track of them and during a review in 1982, when the Commission areas were revised, it was found that more than 300 were dead or had moved to other areas. By September 1983 all of these spurious justices had been removed from the Commissions leaving only about 950 serving throughout the province.

The most difficult task was to find sufficient numbers of persons willing to serve as justices, particularly among the Roman Catholics. The office was not sought after as it was elsewhere and appointment could constitute a real danger to the justice and his family. This applied especially to Catholics, whose acceptance of office could be regarded by extremists as support for the regime. For this reason even less court work was done by Justices of the Peace after 1969 than before, and the whole burden, except in the juvenile courts, fell upon the Resident Magistrates.

There were, and still are, seventeen whole-time Resident Magistrates. In 1977 there were also two part-time Deputy

Resident Magistrates but, with increasing work, the number had been raised to eight by 1983. All are qualified barristers or solicitors and, before making an appointment, the Lord Chancellor consults the Lord Chief Justice of Northern Ireland. There are usually more solicitor than barrister applicants and in 1977 whole-time RMs comprised five barristers to twelve solicitors. By April, 1983 solicitors numbered fourteen to three barristers. In 1977 these included nine Protestants, seven Roman Catholics and one Jew; in 1983 there were nine Protestants and eight Roman Catholics.

It is an understatement to say that it took considerable courage to serve as a Resident Magistrate. It was dangerous enough to hold any public office in Northern Ireland during these troublous times, but the Resident Magistrates were among the most likely targets for attack, as was proved by the occasions on which their courts were bombed and the fact that, within a period of five years, two were killed and the others, with their families, were subjected to harassment and intimidation. For their dedicated work they, like others in public service in Northern Ireland, received no special recognition, and their salaries were the same as those of stipendiaries in England. They did not complain about this, but they and others responsible for maintaining the law were resentful of what they saw as the failure of those outside the province to understand their problems and of the lack of support they received, especially from some sections of the media. On one occasion the Lord Chief Justice of Northern Ireland commented: 'If Satan had been thrown out of Heaven last night the BBC would have been there to see that he got equal coverage.'

Juvenile courts in Northern Ireland are composed of a Resident Magistrate as chairman sitting with persons drawn from a lay panel of men and women appointed for the purpose. These people are not justices but resemble those who serve as justices in other parts of the United Kingdom. From 1974 they were appointed by the Lord Chancellor on the advice of a selection committee whose chairman, Charles Mullen, was the Resident Magistrate chairman of the Belfast juvenile courts. Training for panel members was introduced in 1974 and administered by the Lord Chancellor's Department.

The powers of the Northern Ireland juvenile courts were considerable and included orders for Borstal training, which in England could be made only by the Crown Court (Borstal was abolished in 1981 and replaced by a Juvenile Offenders' Centre). It could be said that their work was of greater importance than that of any other court in the United Kingdom, for so much of the violence in Northern Ireland was perpetrated by youngsters. Whatever may have been their initial motives they were soon headed along the path of the hardened, violent criminal, and the future of law and order in the province depended to a considerable extent upon the way in which these children and young people were handled.

A study of offences committed in Northern Ireland after 1969 seems to confirm that crime in general increases proportionately to a weakening of law and order. In such circumstances people tend to have less respect for all branches of the law and less inclination to obey it. At the same time the police and others engaged in law enforcement are preoccupied with the more serious offences involving public disorder and are precluded from attending to less serious matters. This was illustrated by the steep rise after 1969 in all road traffic offences in Northern Ireland compared with the rest of the country.[3]

Much of the work involved in establishing and maintaining the new arrangements in Northern Ireland devolved upon officials of the Northern Ireland Office, some of whom also served the Lord Chancellor, notably Brian Hall and Frank Edgar. Edgar was appointed Assistant Secretary of Commissions for Northern Ireland with an office in Dundonald House at Stormont and upon him fell the burden of operating the new system. Resident Magistrates, juvenile courts and Justices of the Peace were all his concern, as well as many other matters, and the successful outcome of these operations under difficult and often disturbing conditions was due in no small measure to the able, dedicated and scrupulously fair manner in which he conducted his duties.

The administration of the courts was the responsibility of the Northern Ireland Office and the Secretary of State, but by the end of 1977 it had been decided that the whole of the courts administration should be brought under the Lord Chancellor and conducted on lines similar to those operating in circuits in England and Wales; but it was also decided to go still further and to include all magistrates and juvenile courts in the new system. This policy was implemented by the Judicature (Northern Ireland) Act 1978. On 18 April 1979 a unified and distinct Civil Service of the Crown, called the Northern Ireland Courts Service, came into being. Its function is to facilitate the conduct of business of the Supreme Court, the County Court, Magistrates' Courts and Coroners' Courts. The officers and staff of the Courts Service, numbering about 6000, are appointed by and are responsible to the Lord Chancellor.

THE ISLE OF MAN

The administration of justice in the Isle of Man differs considerably from that in the United Kingdom. This is largely due to the island's peculiar history. Originally Celt and closely linked with Ireland, it was invaded by the Vikings and became part of the Scandinavian kingdom before coming under Scottish and then English suzerainty. The Tynwald, or Manx Parliament, and the Deemsters, who are the judges, date from the Scandinavian period.

Justices of the Peace were not introduced into the island until 1835. Since the war they have operated under a single commission in four petty sessional divisions, and there is also a juvenile court panel. There is one stipendiary, called High Bailiff, whose office dates from 1777.

Until 1983 justices were appointed on the recommendation of the Lieutenant Governor acting on the advice of an Advisory Committee. There is reason to think that in making these appointments the Lord Chancellor acted in a purely executive capacity and could not refuse to accept the Lieutenant Governor's submission. There is no record of his having ever done so. There were a few occasions while I was Secretary of Commissions when a Manx list did not meet with the Lord Chancellor's entire approval, but the matter was resolved either by the Advisory Committee gracefully altering their recommendations or by the Chancellor deciding not to press his point. In 1983 a Manx Act removed all doubt by making the Governor solely responsible for appointing justices.

The island justices have been based largely on the English pattern and during the past thirty years Manx legislation has closely followed that of Westminster in this sphere. The Justices of the Peace Act 1949 was adopted almost in its entirety. When one turns to the justices' powers and duties, however, the differences are greater. Manx magistrates have wider jurisdiction than those in England but the most striking contrast is in their sentencing powers. Corporal punishment was retained in the island after it was abolished in England. Whipping continued to be ordered for certain offences in the case of males over eight and under twenty-one years of age, the cane being used on boys under fourteen and the birch on older offenders. By 1977 these powers were being challenged as inconsistent with the International Convention on Human Rights, but the Manx courts were reluctant to lose them. It was claimed that they were an effective deterrent to the gangs of young hooligans who sometimes visited the island from the mainland, where they were liable to no such treatment. In 1978 the matter was taken before the European Court of Human Rights which found against the Isle of Man.

16 The Commonwealth

When I was at Oxford I surprised myself and my friends by winning a University prize for an essay on 'The Statute of Westminster 1931'. That Act was the final piece of legislation by the British Imperial Parliament confirming the independent status of the self-governing Dominions and I took for my theme Maine's dictum that the movement of progressive societies is from status to contract. Maine's basic philosophy has been largely borne out by the history of the Commonwealth during the last half-century, but in 1931 there were few who foresaw the events that would occur during the last forty years, when one of the greatest empires in history disintegrated and the constituent parts reappeared as some forty independent countries on the map of the world.

By the 1970s, obsession with the European Economic Community on the one hand and mounting criticism of British policy by former colonial territories on the other began to arouse scepticism among British politicians, who questioned the future validity of the Commonwealth concept. Commonwealth relations reached a low ebb at the Prime Ministers' meeting in Singapore in 1971 yet, in spite of the abrasive atmosphere, there emerged from that conference the Declaration of Commonwealth Principles which, *inter alia*, emphasised the importance of the Commonwealth's common heritage and the necessity for the Rule of Law. The next meeting of Heads of Government, in Ottawa in 1973, under the leadership of Mr Trudeau, began a new phase in Commonwealth relations and the meeting two years later in Jamaica confirmed the continued validity and political unity of the Commonwealth bond.

To the question 'why do we have a Commonwealth?' cynics would answer 'because no one has thought of a good reason for abolishing it'. But there is far more in it than that. The Commonwealth is potentially a stabilising force in shaping the world of tomorrow. Apart from the United Nations, there is no other group of countries which brings together the aligned and the non-aligned, the industrialised and the developing economies, and which bridges the threatening abyss of racial conflict. Commonwealth countries have the advantage of common traditions, a common background, a shared common language in addition to national languages and an understanding of one another which enables them to work together with ease and frankness. The Commonwealth offers a framework for co-operation between its members and an opportunity for mutual help and constructive debate on an international scale which is not enjoyed by any other group of countries.

The Commonwealth, however, is not merely an association of governments. The governments are able to act together in the way they do largely because their relations with one another are given an extra dimension through the unofficial links which join their peoples. One of the cohesive forces among Commonwealth countries lies in their having laws and legal institutions of the same type and lawyers brought up in the same tradition. Although a few Commonwealth countries have legal systems based on the Civil Law, the great majority share the heritage of the English Common Law, which affects the lives of nearly one-third of the population of the world.[1] An English barrister or solicitor can go into almost any Commonwealth court and feel at home, not only because in most cases he will find judges and counsel wearing wigs and robes in the British tradition (even in the hottest climates), but because the law and procedure are basically the same.

The network of contracts between Commonwealth countries in legal matters is particularly strong in consequence of a number of links which have been established during the past thirty years. At government level there are regular meetings of Commonwealth Law Ministers. Commonwealth Law Conferences, which provide a forum for consultation and co-operation between legal practitioners, have been held at intervals since 1955. In the 1960s and 1970s further legal links were formed by the establishment of a number of full-time organisations – the Commonwealth Legal Advisory Service (1962), the Legal Division of the Commonwealth Secretariat (1969), the Commonwealth Legal Bureau (1969), the Commonwealth Magistrates' Association (1970) and the Commonwealth Legal Education Association (1971).

The new Commonwealth countries were faced with a serious

shortage of qualified lawyers in every sector – legislative drafts-men, judges, court staff and practitioners. The chief objective of the organisations mentioned above was to remedy this situation as quickly as possible through the provision of legal training and education, much of the cost being borne by the Commonwealth Foundation and the Commonwealth Fund for Technical Co-operation. Dissemination of legal information was also achieved through various regular publications such as the *Commonwealth Law Bulletin*, issued by the Commonwealth Secretariat, and the *Commonwealth Judicial Journal* of the Commonwealth Magistrates' Association. Legal education was at first hampered by a shortage of law schools in the developing territories while places available for overseas students at the Inns of Court School of Law were reduced, but soon the need was being met by the establishment of law faculties at the new Commonwealth universities – of the West Indies, Malaysia, Nairobi and the South Pacific, to mention a few.

The Commonwealth magistracy is a heterogeneous body. Professional magistrates predominate in all countries other than England and Wales, but often the judiciary includes large numbers of laymen, many of whom, as explained later, are not Justices of the Peace. Justices of the Peace spread from Britain in the wake of colonisation and are still to be found in many countries of the Commonwealth and in some states of America. The American Justices of the Peace first appeared when it was still customary for their English colleagues to take fees and this practice continued after the War of Independence, whereas it was dying out in England by the time justices were introduced into other colonial territories. (The authority which was vested in some American justices to perform the marriage ceremony seems to have been derived from the time of Cromwell, which was the only period when this function could be performed by justices in England.)

In Australia, Canada and New Zealand the office of Justice of the Peace followed the English pattern, though with fewer powers, and in all three of these countries the bulk of the work is now performed by professional magistrates. There may be consider-able variation within the same country; thus in New South Wales justices hold a purely honorific office whereas in the adjoining Australian state of South Australia they have important court duties.[2]

Elsewhere the pattern has varied according to the type of

colonial administration which operated in the country. In most parts of Africa judicial functions were performed by colonial officials and on their departure their work was taken over by whole-time magistrates. In the islands of the Caribbean, on the other hand, the Justices of the Peace flourished and, although the bulk of court work is now performed by stipendiaries, the justices still occupy an honourable position in some West Indian countries, where they are appointed on the recommendation of a Custos Rotulorum as formerly in England.

In some countries justices are known by a different name. In India the British-orientated system of Honorary Magistrates was introduced in 1861. It is gratifying to find that after the severance of constitutional ties between India and Britain the *Manual of the Honorary Presidency Magistrates of Madras* opened with the words 'The system of administration of justice that now prevails in this country is one of the most valued legacies of the British rule and the institution of the Honorary Presidency Magistrates is a part of that legacy'. Although Honorary Magistrates continued to operate in independent India, new rural tribunals have been set up to deal with petty cases, both criminal and civil. These are called Naya Panchayats and are similar to benches of lay justices. They are composed of local people and their object is to ensure that the villagers can get justice from their fellow men on the spot, expeditiously and without expense. The law they administer is based on the English Common Law.

Justices of the Peace have never been the only system of lay judiciary in many Commonwealth countries. Customary law has always exercised an important influence over the lives of the ordinary people in African, Asian and Pacific territories, and this has usually been administered not by professional judges, but by a chief aided by councillors or by councils of elders, frequently with a degree of popular participation. These customary courts still dispose of the bulk of cases in which the ordinary citizen in many new Commonwealth countries is involved. There are some areas where the customary courts have been replaced by modern English-style courts constituted by career magistrates but many of these persons are not professionally qualified. The fact is that, in one way or another, a vast amount of judicial work in the Commonwealth was, and still is, performed by non-legally qualified people. In most African and Pacific countries 90 per cent of cases are dealt with in this way.

In most Commonwealth countries there is no judicial tier between the High Court bench and the magistracy, and in developing countries the former is regularly recruited from the ranks of the career magistrates, who in turn may be promoted through various grades. The powers of a chief or senior magistrate may be very great indeed: in countries retaining capital punishment he may impose the death penalty, and when exercising this authority he sits alone without a jury (most of the newer countries have dispensed with juries in both civil and criminal trials).

In spite of the impressive powers they could exercise and the fact that many worked under heavy pressure, the security and independence of Commonwealth magistrates left much to be desired and in some places the conditions under which they had to operate were appalling. In the circumstances it was surprising that most magistrates maintained a high degree of efficiency, though inevitably there were some places where the standard was intolerably low. In one African country the Chief Justice was obliged in 1971 to admonish a number of magistrates who regularly came to their courts two or three hours late and often arrived drunk. Some governments showed too little consideration for the magistrates, and during the years following independence when the new regime felt insecure all ranks of the judiciary suffered from encroachment by the executive.

It was in this context that my thoughts turned in 1969 to the formation of a Commonwealth organisation which would cater for the needs of all types of magistrate, particularly in the field of training and legal education. There was no permanent judicial organisation serving the Commonwealth. Chief Justices met informally from time to time but these conferences, which had been inspired initially by Sir Garfield Barwick of Australia, tended to lapse after 1965 and in any case they had no permanent secretarial back-up nor were they concerned with the lower levels of the judiciary. No thought had been given to the potential value of magistrates' views. Magistrates are closer to the ground than Chief Justices; they see what is going on at grass-roots level among all sections of the population; they are in a better position than anyone to show that a piece of legislation may be good in theory but cannot operate under certain conditions. Magistrates can make a valuable contribution in the field of law reform, as they do in England, but in developing countries they are seldom given the chance.

The idea of a Commonwealth Magistrates' Association emanated from Mrs Clare Spurgin, a Vice-President of the Magistrates' Association of England and Wales who had played a leading part in the establishment of several international judicial organisations. In the 1950s she had arranged meetings between Indian and British magistrates, which led, in 1964, to Britain being invited to send delegates to an Honorary Magistrates' Congress in New Delhi at which the formation of a Commonwealth body was discussed. The proposal had a favourable reception but there was not sufficient support in India or elsewhere to establish an organisation on this scale. Clare Spurgin then approached me and I agreed to get the project off the ground. At the summer conference of the Magistrates' Association of England and Wales in York in 1969 I convened a meeting of those interested in the formation of a Commonwealth association. Only seven justices attended; among them was Mrs Dorothy Winton, soon to become chairman of the Middlesex Branch of the English Association, who offered her services. I readily accepted and for ten years Dorothy Winton played a leading and invaluable role in every phase of the establishment and development of the Commonwealth Association. She was succeeded in 1980 by O. K. Williams, an English justice with considerable business experience, who carried forward the work of consolidation and placed the Association on a sound economic footing at a time when it was obliged to rely largely upon its own financial resources.

We began by trying to establish contact with magistrates in each Commonwealth country but the result was disappointing. With the exception of Australia, where there was an enthusiastic response from the Australian Council of Justices' Association, replies were hesitant and many countries did not answer at all. We learnt later that in many developing countries magistrates felt inhibited from responding to approaches of this kind and were obliged to refer them to higher authority, where they were put aside and forgotten. It soon became apparent that if we were to make any progress we needed to aim at the top and to secure substantial financial backing. The British Government was not disposed to spend public money on fostering relations between Commonwealth magistrates and our own Magistrates' Association lacked sufficient funds. The prospect was distinctly gloomy until I approached the Commonwealth Foundation, through its Director, John Chadwick. They agreed to make a generous grant, and it is true to say that had it not been for the Foundation's support, both at the outset and in subsequent years, the Commonwealth Magistrates' Association could never have become an effective international body nor achieved its major objectives. Later the Association became indebted to many other bodies, especially the British Council and the Canadian International Development agency. We also received moral support from the Legal Division of the Commonwealth Secretariat whose two successive directors, Tom Kellock and K. T. Fuad, became prominent in the Association's activities. Having been assured of the Foundation's financial backing I then sought the help of the Lord Chancellor, Lord Gardiner, who immediately agreed to write to the Minister of Justice or Chief Justice in each Commonwealth country inviting him to send a representative to a conference in London to discuss the formation of a Commonwealth magistrates' organisation. After our previous disappointment the response was electrifying. In less than two months an acceptance had been received from every country.

The first Commonwealth Magistrates' Conference was held in London in July 1970. There had been a change of Government in Britain a month earlier and Lord Gardiner had been succeeded by Lord Hailsham who, unlike his predecessor, was sceptical of the Commonwealth's future. When I asked him to open the conference he commented encouragingly, 'Starry-eyed nonsense, my dear, you are wasting your time.' (He frequently addressed his staff as 'my dear', especially when he disapproved of what they were doing.) However, he came to the opening ceremony and gave us his blessing.

The delegates were more enthusiastic than the Lord Chancellor. They resolved unanimously that a Commonwealth Magistrates' Association (CMA) should be established and they drafted a constitution. As I had chaired the conference they evidently assumed that they had found a willing horse and they elected me President and Chairman of the Council. Dorothy Winton was appointed Secretary. Headquarters were established initially in London though it was stressed that they might move to another country at a later date. Membership was open only to national associations of magistrates and not to individuals, and the first to join was the Association of England and Wales, closely followed by the Australian Council of Justices' Association; but the next two years were disappointing to those who had witnessed the enthusiasm of the 1970 conference. The ardour tended to wane when the conference dispersed and the returning delegates were obliged to convince their national associations or governments not only of the merits of a Commonwealth organisation, but that the advantages to be derived from membership justified the expenditure involved.

We also encountered an unanticipated obstacle in the inimical relations which existed between professional magistrates and Justices of the Peace in some countries, particularly New Zealand and parts of Australia. The professionals resented the justices and feared that their own status would be degraded if they were seen to be associated with them. These sentiments were strongest in areas where the office of justice was purely a sinecure and the CMA endeavoured to meet this by disqualifying from membership any group of justices who did not adjudicate in court. In later years much was done by the Association to heal these differences between the two classes of magistrate but initially, as the stipendiaries usually carried more weight, their opposition deterred several countries from joining.

By 1972 only five countries had joined and it was clear that if we were to make any progress during the formative stage we needed the backing of governments and heads of judiciary. I therefore adopted a five-year inaugural plan designed to sell the Association to Commonwealth governments. Part of the strategy was to mount a series of first rate pan-Commonwealth conferences which would attract leading figures in the legal and political world and would impress them with the importance of the work we were trying to do. This policy proved highly successful. Three major conferences were held, with increasing impact: Bermuda in 1972, Nairobi in 1973 and a final triumph in Kuala Lumpur in 1975, where the conference was opened in great splendour by the Prime Minister of Malaysia, Tun Razak, before a vast audience drawn from every country of the Commonwealth, most of them represented by Chief Justices or Law Ministers as well as by judges and magistrates.

A unique experiment was conducted at the Nairobi conference where representatives from almost all Commonwealth countries took part in a sentencing exercise – the first such event to be held on an international scale. Among the interesting points which emerged was the wide disparity between the maximum penalties which could be imposed in different countries for the same offence. This was partly because a number of countries still retained corporal punishment and the death penalty but above all because matters which were regarded as of minor importance in one country raised major issues of policy in another. What was more interesting, however, was that high maximum penalties did not usually lead to more severe penalties being imposed by the judges and there was a remarkable consensus of opinion among participants in the exercise as to the proper level of treatment.[3]

The success of these conferences was due in large measure to the generous support given by the host countries, particularly Malaysia where the hospitality of the federal and state governments was on a lavish scale and the planning and administration was brilliantly conducted by a committee headed by the Lord President of the Federal Court, Tun Mohamed Suffian. Tun Suffian was a staunch friend of the Association and was elected Vice-President in 1975, becoming President five years later. He was generally regarded as the outstanding judicial figure in South East Asia and he did much to enhance the CMA's prestige throughout the world. We were also fortunate in having the personal backing of several other leading personalities who were pre-eminent not only in their countries but in the world at large. The Bermuda conference was dominated by Sir Hugh Wooding, Chief Justice of Trinidad and Tobago and the first West Indian to sit as a member of the Judicial Committee of the Privy Council. In Nairobi and Kuala Lumpur we had Lord Denning. Lord Denning was more revered overseas than in his own land and in most Commonwealth countries he was regarded as the greatest legal luminary of the century. The news that Lord Denning was to attend a conference was sufficient to draw leading lawyers and judges from far and wide. From 1973 onwards he was tireless in his support of the CMA and took a leading part in all its activities. The Association owes him much and it showed its appreciation in 1975 by electing him its first life Vice-President. The Kuala Lumpur conference was enhanced by the presence of the Lord Chancellor himself, Lord Elwyn-Jones. He was a great ambassador who did much for the British image in the many countries he visited. His witty speeches, enlivened by an unlimited fund of anecdotes, his deep sincerity and understanding of the problems of others and above all his engaging personality and Welsh charm created a most favourable impression on all who met him, many of whom had expected the Lord High Chancellor of Great Britain to be aloof and forbidding with little genuine concern for their affairs. The Malaysian conference was followed by further pan-Commonwealth meetings – in Oxford in 1979 (opened by Lord Chancellor Hailsham nine years after he had opened the inaugural conference in London) and in Trinidad and Tobago in 1982, where the dominant figure was Lord Diplock who, like Lord Denning, was elected a life Vice-President.

By the end of the Malaysian conference the CMA was so well established that we could concentrate on our main objective of improving and furthering the interests of the magistrates and at the same time contributing to the development of legal training and administration in areas where professional skills were in desperately short supply.

This was particularly true of the Pacific which, although it had enjoyed civilisation for more than 3000 years, was only just emerging as an entity; like Africa a little earlier it was a giant slowly awakening in the dawn of a new era. Common interests and a growing demand for unity were developing among its scattered countries in the wake of colonial independence. As in many other parts of the former Empire the Pacific courts reflected a blend of the British system with local customary jurisdiction. Nowhere in the world was there a better example of the inconsistencies created by such a mixture: unwritten custom conflicting with written Statute, or the incompatibility of the British insistence upon isolating the point at issue with the traditional practice of dealing with the dispute or crime in its total content. The work of magistrates was inhibited by powerful social customs such as the cult of gift-giving (to judges as well as to everyone else) and the obligation to defer to members of one's family. Magistrates were lay adjudicators, though trained in court procedure, and most practitioners were not legally qualified.

In 1976 a seminar to study these problems in depth was organised jointly by the CMA and the University of the South Pacific with financial backing from the Commonwealth Fund for Technical Co-operation. It was opened by the King of Tonga in Nuku Alofa and was attended by magistrates and government officials from all seventeen Commonwealth Pacific countries and from American Samoa. The principal subject for investigation was training. How does one operate a training system in the absence of adequate facilities and of qualified teachers? I brought out with me from England a quantity of training devices, including sound tapes and video film equipment. These had considerable potential but the most promising experiment in the mechanical field was the use of two-way television through space satellite, which enabled small classes in distant islands to be conducted by a tutor in the University Law School in Fiji, or elsewhere, almost as if they were in the same room – an intriguing contrast between the traditional Pacific way of life and space communication through Telstar. This historic seminar, at which many valuable conclusions were reached, was the most worthwhile operation undertaken by the CMA up to that time. Although I chaired it, the credit must go the principal organisers, Guy Powles of the New Zealand Bar and Ron Crocombe of the University of the South Pacific. The seminar revealed a clear need for co-ordinated effort and plans were laid for a permanent organisation to achieve this.[4]

The Association's policy from 1976 was based on regionalisation, with emphasis on local rather than world-wide meetings. The big conferences would still be used at intervals for discussion of issues of universal interest, such as the independence of the judiciary, which was under serious threat in many countries, but more practical benefit could often be derived from having limited objectives and pursuing these in depth. The world suffered from a spate of large international gatherings, which were mainly social events from which little real benefit was derived. We therefore aimed at giving magistrates on a regional basis a clear insight into their own role and an opportunity to consider ways in which the system of which they were such an important part could be improved. The CMA also endeavoured to serve all levels of the judiciary by providing a forum for discussion and exchange of views, by arranging for the temporary transfer of judges between different countries and by disseminating ideas and information through the *Commonwealth Judicial Journal* and other literature.

Shortly after the Pacific seminar an East African conference was held in Nairobi on the initiative of the Kenya Magistrates' Association. In 1977 the Resident Magistrates' Association of Jamaica, with the support of the CMA, enlarged their annual conference to include delegates from the whole of the Commonwealth Caribbean. The West Indies are generally regarded as more homogeneous than the Pacific with its diverse ethnic groups, yet there is considerable variety in the Caribbean too and although the population of most of the islands springs from Africa there are exceptions: the people of Belize, for example, being of mixed Maya and Spanish blood. In 1977 the judicial system in the Commonwealth countries of the Caribbean was closely aligned to that in England. Although most of the senior judges were West Indian (whereas those in the Pacific were still expatriates from Australia, Britain and New Zealand) they had been brought up in the British tradition and had been called to the English Bar.

The Jamaican seminar was the first occasion on which magistrates and officials from different Caribbean countries had met to debate local legal matters of mutual interest, of which the principal were family law, extradition and the social control of land by law.

During the first ten years the Council always met in London, except on occasions when meetings were made to coincide with the major conferences, but efforts are now made to vary the venue and to hold meetings outside the United Kingdom. The first of these was in Canada in 1981 followed by Sri Lanka in 1983.

The experience of the CMA in the 1970s was that, although on the surface there was occasional 'Brit-bashing', as Mr Heath described it after Singapore, there was in all countries a warm admiration for British institutions particularly in the legal field and, as Commonwealth leaders moved beyond the condemnation-of-colonialism stage, there was a universal desire to preserve the links provided by the Commonwealth framework.

The idiosyncratic English system of administering justice is not necessarily ideal for every climate, but it has taken root throughout most of the Commonwealth and has been successfully adapted to local conditions. Individual countries had their own peculiar problems in keeping up with the rapidly changing world of the 1960s and 1970s, but this did not mean that there was not a vast field of common interest. In 1977 there was abundant evidence that all Commonwealth countries recognised, and had come to cherish, their common legal heritage.

17 The Future

The preceding chapters have sketched the changing face of the magistracy, both lay and professional, during the past forty years. I have endeavoured to show that the administration of justice develops as a continuing process. The future is likely to be a projection of the past and the present, and I have indicated certain changes which are predictable, and some which I think desirable, in the foreseeable future. Among these are unified court administration, advanced training for justices within the limitations inherent in a part-time system, clarification of the position of the justices' clerk, better information to assist the sentencer, improved procedure and work distribution to avoid delays and increase efficiency, and the continuing need, in spite of recent changes in the arrangements for selecting lay justices, for still better methods of ensuring that all those appointed to the bench are entirely suitable for the work and are drawn from all the principal sectors of the population.

It is to be hoped that attention will not be paid to those who wish to resort to an elective method of appointing magistrates and that the time will come when the present emphasis on political considerations will be diluted. Most benches already mirror the communities they serve; if the public wish them to be appointed on a purely 'representative' basis they must be prepared to accept a lower standard of justice than that administered by magistrates selected by an impartial body from persons who are best fitted for the work – which is the essence of the present system, both lay and professional.

Progress in reforming and modernising the criminal justice system in Britain since the Second World War has been inhibited by the need for those responsible to be constantly looking for ways and means of retrenchment instead of expansion. This has resulted in failure to exploit to the full promising new developments such as attendance centres and detention centres and latterly the provision of the Children and Young Persons Act

1969. Fine new ideas were implemented in an atmosphere of euphoria and then failed to come up to expectation through insufficient financial support. Financial considerations are likely to continue to be restrictive and therefore those involved in new projects should first decide what is needed and then see how available resources can be made to meet it.

Future progress must depend to a large extent on research. Although there has been a spate of research activity in the past ten years, this has not been nearly enough, and there is a very real need for more evaluative research into sentencing and court procedure. There is scope for approaching this from new angles, particularly that of the 'consumer' – the man in the dock and the general public.

The tendency for the work of magistrates to increase is bound to continue unless some of their present duties are transferred elsewhere or there is an appreciable drop in crime. There is no sign of the latter in the foreseeable future. Society gets the criminals it deserves, and there would seem to be little prospect of improvement in the present level of delinquency so long as it is treated with the complacency evident during the last two decades when there has been an ostrich-like attitude, which the public are only just beginning to overcome, towards the upsurge in criminal activity.

As to shifting the burden from the magistrates to other tribunals, I have shown that the trend has been in the opposite direction, with the principal object of relieving the higher courts. This is likely to continue but there is a limit to the number of additional duties that the part-time lay courts can absorb. Although Stipendiary Magistrates could undertake more complex work, the Justices of the Peace should be kept within their traditional role as administrators of local justice and their functions ought not to extend to a point where they are seen to be out of their depth. The most promising option is decriminalisation, described on pages 101–3.

It has been suggested that justices might be given wider jurisdiction if they sat with a legally qualified chairman. There might be some merit in this if it enabled magistrates' courts to dispose of cases which would otherwise have to be tried in the Crown Court (the justices would continue to sit with lay chairmen when trying cases within their present jurisdiction). There should be no question of establishing a new tier of court between the

Crown Court and the magistrates. This would be a retrograde step, reverting to the position of Quarter Sessions condemned by the Beeching Commission. When trying intermediate cases the court would still be a court of summary jurisdiction in every sense but would be empowered to deal with a wider range of offences because of the presence of the lawyer chairman, as Quarter Sessions were able to do after 1938. There is no logical reason why on these occasions the court should not have extended sentencing powers to enable it to deal with a wider range of offences. Justices already have such powers in the Crown Court and it could be argued that they could now be given wider discretion even when they do not have a legally qualified chairman. If justices were considered fit to impose six months' imprisonment in 1948 they should be capable of exercising greater powers of custodial sentence today.

A system of summary courts with legal chairmen is not a novel idea. It was proposed in 1945 in a pamphlet issued by the Conservative Party and later another version was suggested by the Law Society, but it was rejected because it seemed unnecessary and because it raised difficult practical questions: such as who were to be the chairmen, whether they should be whole-time appointments and, if they were to be remunerated, how should the rate be fixed so as to attract the right person without jeopardising other comparable posts. If, however, pressures continued to build up and if the cost of the courts continues to escalate, some form of intermediate jurisdiction by specially constituted summary courts will have to be reconsidered. There would be advantage in exploring the idea in conjunction with an expansion of the system of Stipendiary Magistrates, who might provide the chairmen of the extended jurisdiction courts.

One of the principal arguments against the universal replacement of justices by stipendiaries has always been that there would not be enough lawyers available to man all the stipendiary courts. This was stressed by Lord Jowitt in his evidence to the 1948 Royal Commission and it is true in the short-term, but it cannot be maintained that if reasonable rewards were offered it would not be possible over a period of time to create a body of qualified stipendiaries, drawn from both branches of the legal profession, who would be sufficient in numbers and ability to operate all magistrates' courts. It is unlikely that this would ever be done because there would be no need for it if the lay justices continue to give satisfaction; but it should not be too difficult, given a little time, to find enough stipendiaries to chair magistrates' courts when exercising wider jurisdiction.

Proposals to bring indictable offences within the exclusive jurisdiction of magistrates' courts are invariably met with vehement opposition from the press and the legal profession, who have an uncritical admiration for the jury system. Heated arguments were aroused in Parliament when the government sought, in the Criminal Law Bill 1977, to implement the James Committee's recommendations that minor theft should be triable only summarily. The public was led to assume erroneously that an Englishman had an inalienable right since time immemorial to be tried by a jury, whereas in fact it has been purely a matter of chance whether some of the offences created by statutes during the past 100 years were or were not made triable on indictment. The jury has been abolished entirely in many other countries and in some of these, Holland in particular, the criminal justice system has been applauded by penologists. In some countries where there are no juries laymen sit with the judges as assessors. This is the case in Scandinavia, and in West Germany two lay *Schöffengerichte* sit with the judge. On the other hand it must be recognised that criminal jury trial has retained its popularity in the United States, where it has an even greater stronghold than in Britain and where the system has been more thoroughly researched than anywhere else. The fact is, however, that the public confidence which juries enjoy is based on almost no evidence. In this country there has been no empirical investigation of the jury room to enable us to know how juries reach their verdicts, but an enquiry into the jury system by Baldwin and McConville in 1979 threw considerable doubt upon the validity of juries' decisions. The enquiry was begun in the expectation that it would prove favourable to trial by jury, but it revealed that there are more questionable acquittals than was generally supposed and, more important, that over 5 per cent of those found guilty by juries are convicted in doubtful circumstances and are left, for all practical purposes, without effective remedy on appeal. The confidence of Baldwin and McConville in the system was shaken and they concluded that 'trial by jury is an arbitrary and unpredictable business'.

In 1933 the right to a jury in civil cases was removed except for a limited class of case by the Administration of Justice Act. There are many who think that this should be extended to some criminal trials, especially in cases of commercial fraud. It is claimed that the financial facts in these cases are so complicated that it is not reasonable for the guilt or innocence of the accused to depend upon the understanding of jurors selected at random from the electoral roll (which includes virtually every citizen over the age of 18, more than 1 per cent of whom are illiterate). Mr Justice Gibson, the chairman of the Law Commission, has proposed that in fraud cases the jury should be replaced by a judge sitting with skilled assessors. Lord Hailsham, while Lord Chancellor, was sympathetic to this idea and seemed willing to consider the possibility of magistrates sitting with the judge for this purpose.

Whether or not the jury should be abolished is largely a constitutional and political question, and in any event the jury has too great a hold on public imagination in Britain to be uprooted in the foreseeable future. If, however, the disposal of business by the courts is to be expedited this could be achieved effectively, without any danger to the accused and at considerably less cost than the present system, if a number of offences now triable on indictment were brought within the exclusive jurisdiction of summary courts, possibly presided over by legally qualified chairmen. In 1976 the James Committee found that the average cost of a number of selected cases was £431·39 when tried on indictment while the estimated cost of trying them summarily would have been £136·44. In the House of Lords in 1981 Lord Roskill, in R. v. Lawrence[2] which had taken four days to try in the Crown Court, commented: 'It is difficult to believe that any magistrates' court would not have dealt with this case, if not in a morning, at least within one full day and reached the correct answer'. If there is concern that people should be tried by their peers, as guaranteed by Magna Carta, I would submit that today this is achieved by a bench of justices quite as well as by a jury and with more likelihood of justice being done. Contrary to general belief, magistrates are not more prone to convict than juries. The Home Secretary pointed out in the House of Commons on 27th January 1977 that the acquittal rate for a number of offences was greater in the magistrates' courts than in the Crown Court. For thefts, the rates varied according to the type, but in those under £5 the magistrates acquitted in 64 per cent of contested cases while juries acquitted in 61 per cent. For offences in the public order group, magistrates acquitted 57 per cent as against 28 per cent acquitted by juries. For assaults on the police, magistrates acquitted in 27 per cent of cases and juries in 20 per cent. It has been said that these figures, and others given by the Lord Chancellor in the House of Lords, do not give the true picture, but however one interprets them they bear out the contention that the accused will have no less fair trial before magistrates than before a jury; and if one accepts that it is as great a miscarriage of justice for guilty persons to be acquitted as for the innocent to be convicted it is significant that when a jury is retained for several days and required to try a number of consecutive cases they are markedly less naïve when they reach the last case than they were at the first.

Most of these questions are academic unless summary jurisdiction continues to be based on its present foundations. It is becoming increasingly difficult to reconcile a system of part-time, unpaid lay justices with the demands of modern life, which make it difficult for them to give sufficient time to attending courts and undergoing courses of instruction and sentencing exercises. As yet there is no lack of volunteers, who include a sufficient number of men and women capable of performing the work satisfactorily, but the picture could change if further large-scale demands were made on their time. From the point of view of the public and the government there has been a remarkable vindication of the conclusions of the 1948 Royal Commission that the system of lay justices should be continued, and so long as justices command respect as the adjudicators of the man in the street it seems likely that the system will survive. Although not everyone charged with an offence wishes to be tried by a lay bench, the office of Justice of the Peace has become too deeply ingrained in the culture and way of life of the people to be uprooted without good cause. The most likely pattern for the future seems to be an increase in the number of stipendiaries in the busiest areas but a continuation of lay justice courts elsewhere on much the same lines as they operate now.

It might be assumed that my faith in the future of the lay magistracy is the natural prejudice of one who has been responsible for the system during much of his working life, but throughout most of that period I was equally responsible for legal appointments and, as a member of the legal profession myself, my prejudice would have been more likely to be directed against the lay element, as indeed it was when I first joined the Lord Chancellor's Office. Like the Lord Chancellors under whom I served, however, I was converted by realisation of the intrinsic merits of the system, to which I referred in the first chapter, where I also drew attention to various attributes, particularly in regard to cost-effectiveness and elasticity of manpower, which tended to endear the lay magistracy to successive Governments. The broader social and political composition of the lay magistracy has also appealed to the politically minded, who see it as an opportunity to democratise the courts.

Nevertheless, the strong position which the Justices of the Peace occupy today could quickly be eroded if they were unable to continue to move with the times, as they have done since the 1948 Royal Commission. Although potentially the system of lay justices can be very good, in practice it can be very bad, as has happened in the past. Constant effort is needed to see that it does not slip backwards; but that is no longer enough in a rapidly changing world where it is for the magistrates themselves and for the Ministers and others responsible for the summary courts to see that they adapt to evolutionary social and economic movement. This applies more forcefully to the lay magistrates than to other judicial officers because they are more susceptible to public disapprobation, but in some degree it applies also to the stipendiaries and indeed to the whole judiciary. There is increasing recognition that the courts exist for the benefit of the community to which the interests of the judges, administrators and legal practitioners are subordinate. The emphasis has been increasingly on the consumer. In my speech at the opening of the Fourth Commonwealth Magistrates Conference in Malaysia in 1975, I pointed out that in the atmosphere of diminishing respect for the rule of law the administration of justice had to meet and come to terms with the phenomenon of a changing society, and I went on:

> The courts must adapt and adjust themselves to meet the present situation . . . Law is based on acceptance by the population. This involves a rethinking of the role of the judiciary in the modern world. We must be orientated towards social as much as purely judicial problems, for today we are dealing with situations rather than being preoccupied with the application of strict points of law. We do not live in a stable society where judicial decisions are universally accepted. We are being constantly reminded that the law was made for man and not man for the law.

Notes

CHAPTER 1   THE OFFICE OF MAGISTRATE

1 A property qualification was imposed by a Statute of 1439 whereby every justice was required to have property in the county of at least £20 a year. This was because 'some of the Justices are of small behaviour by whom the people will not be governed'. The qualification was increased to £100 in 1737 but abolished in 1905.
2 F. W. Maitland, 'The Shallows and Silences of Real Life', *Collected Papers* (Cambridge University Press, 1911) p. 472.

CHAPTER 2   THE MAGISTRACY SINCE THE SECOND WORLD WAR

1 These figures are only a small fraction of the number of offences actually committed. It is generally agreed that only between 10 and 15 per cent of crimes come to the notice of the system, and even this is a gross underestimation if minor offences such as motoring are included.
2 See below, p. 121.
3 Now re-enacted in the Justices of the Peace Act 1979.
4 See below, p. 159.
5 There are now 57 branches covering every area of England and Wales.

CHAPTER 3   THE LORD CHANCELLOR AND HIS OFFICE

1 The Lord Chancellor was responsible for civil legal aid from its inception in 1949, but criminal legal aid was within the province of the Home Secretary until 1980 when, on the recommendation of the Royal Commission on Legal Services, this too, together with responsibility for costs, was transferred to the Lord Chancellor.
2 In 1945 the office comprised the Secretary of Commissions himself, one clerical officer and one typist. In 1969 it had increased to six senior officers (Secretary of Commissions, Deputy Secretary and four Assistant Secretaries) with full supporting staff. Of the senior staff, two were barristers and two solicitors. All had their offices in London except the Assistant Secretary of Commissions for Northern Ireland whose office was in Belfast.
3 Cmnd 218 (HMSO, 1957).

CHAPTER 4   THE SELECTION AND APPOINTMENT OF JUSTICES

1 Within the County Palatine of Lancaster the Chancellor of the Duchy and not the Lord Chancellor has always been responsible for the appointment and removal of justices, but this did not apply to training or to the composition and procedure of the magistrates' courts which, as elsewhere, were the responsibility of the Lord Chancellor. The Lord Chancellor also recommended the appointment of Recorders, chairmen of Quarter Sessions and Stipendiary Magistrates within the Duchy. Changes in local government boundaries necessitated the redefining of the Duchy's area of responsibility and the Administration of Justice Act 1973 provided that this should be the counties of Lancashire, Greater Manchester and Merseyside. The Duchy Office worked closely with the Lord Chancellor's Office on matters concerning justices and the policy applied by the two Ministers was almost invariably identical.

2 This was because when Sir Robert Peel, the Prime Minister, formed the first police force in 1829, control was vested in two newly appointed justices who were given no judicial duties. These later became Commissioners of Police but continued to derive their authority from their appointment as justices.

3 The first lady Alderman was Lady Donaldson who was elected in 1975. She had been appointed a JP in 1960 and served on the London juvenile court panel until 1965. She was the wife of Mr Justice Donaldson who, in 1982, succeeded Lord Denning as Master of the Rolls.

4 Before 1973 the office of Keeper of the Rolls was known by its Latin name of Custos Rotulorum, which dated from the fourteenth century when one of the justices in each county was required to keep the rolls of the sessions (later the duty was performed on behalf of the Custos by the Clerk of the Peace). For the origin of the office see Harcourt v. Fox 4 Modern Reports 173.

5 In 1983 the undertakings required of a candidate before appointment were:
    (1) to complete a course of basic instruction within one year of appointment;
    (2) if appointed to a juvenile or domestic court panel, to complete a course of instruction in the special work of juvenile courts within one year of appointment;
    (3) to carry out a fair share of the duties at both Petty Sessions and Crown Court;
    (4) to resign if unable to comply with any of these conditions;
    (5) to inform the Lord Chancellor of any conviction or court order made against the candidate, either before or after appointment.

6 In recent times the offices of Custos Rotulorum and Lord Lieutenant have usually been held by the same individual and strictly speaking it was as Custos that a Lord Lieutenant was appointed chairman of his county Advisory Committee. The Lieutenant, who was a personal appointment by the Sovereign, was selected on the advice of the Prime Minister and the Custos on the advice of the Lord Chancellor. Appointments were made under the Royal Sign Manual but a change was effected by the Administration of Justice Act 1973 whereby in future the Lord Chancellor was to designate one of the justices in each county to be Keeper of the Rolls.

CHAPTER 5   THE POLITICAL AND SOCIAL COMPOSITION OF THE MAGISTRACY

1 *Sentencing the Motoring Offender* (London: Heinemann, 1972). Published on behalf of the Institute of Criminology, Cambridge.
2 These figures are approximate. They are derived from records kept in the Lord Chancellor's Office and from a projection of detailed analyses of certain urban and rural benches.
3 The first coloured woman justice was Mrs Pauline Crabbe, a social worker from Jamaica, who was appointed to the Hampstead bench in 1968.

CHAPTER 6   TRAINING

1 *Report of the Working Party on Judicial Studies and Information* (HMSO, 1978).
2 The grant for the year 1970 was £2000. In 1977 it was £10,500, which was slightly under one-third of the Association's estimate of the cost of the training services which it provided. In 1982 the grant was £47,860 which was about half the estimated training cost.
3 The studies by Dr Lemon and Dr Bond are described in two articles in *The Magistrate* (the journal of the Magistrates' Association) of February 1980, p. 20 and January 1982, p. 2.

CHAPTER 7   WORK AND PROCEDURE

1 *Report of the Committee on the Distribution of Criminal Business between the Crown Court and Magistrates' Courts*, Cmnd 6323 (HMSO, 1975).
2 Increase in legal aid in magistrates' courts after it became available in October 1968 is shown by the number of applications and grants:

	Applications	*Grants*
1st October–31st December 1968	20706	17812
1969	102684	88193
1972	164553	147181
1975	257691	234744
1977	333756	296615

From 1981 the numbers dropped following a circular from the Lord Chancellor to justices' clerks urging them to save as much as they could on legal aid.
3 Samples of a few urban and rural benches taken in 1951 and 1974 suggested that the percentage of magistrates who could drive had risen from 78 to 93 between the two dates. These samples were not wholly reliable but the latter figure is supported by a study conducted by Roger Hood between 1965 and 1967 which showed that in his sample nearly 90 per cent of magistrates could drive (Roger Hood, *Sentencing the Motoring Offender* (London: Heinemann, 1972) p. 61).
4 Road Traffic Act 1960 and Road Improvement Act, 1960.

5 County Courts were first established in 1846 and now number some 300 in England and Wales. They have a purely civil jurisdiction determined by financial limits on the claims which may be brought before them. Throughout most of the period covered by this book the limit was £500, but it is an indication of the expansion of civil work in the High Court and the fall in the value of money that the amount was raised to £750 in 1970, to £1000 in 1974, to £2000 in 1977 and to £5000 in October 1981.

6 For example: Housing Act 1961, Public Health Act 1961, Town and Country Planning Act 1971.

7 Cmnd 5629 (HMSO, 1974).

8 Now Section 144 of the Magistrates' Courts Act 1980.

9 The existence of a rule committee does not wholly exclude the need to incorporate procedural law in Statutes. In 1952 all enactments relating to the jurisdiction, practice and procedure of magistrates' courts were consolidated in a Magistrates' Courts Act. This was re-enacted with amendments by the Justices of the Peace Act 1979 and the Magistrates' Courts Act 1980.

10 The first reference to the 'Great Unpaid' appeared in the *Edinburgh Review* in 1826.

11 Now contained in Part V of the Justices of the Peace Act 1979.

12 During the twenty years 1962–1982 the number of policemen rose from 78,000 to 121,000 while recorded crime increased by 200 per cent and the clear-up rate dropped from 44 per cent to 37 per cent.

CHAPTER 8   THE JUVENILE COURTS

1 Until 1964 the chairmen and members of London juvenile courts were appointed by the Home Secretary. Lord Dilhorne took the view that as the Lord Chancellor was by then responsible for virtually all judicial appointments these functions should also be transferred to him. The Home Secretary, Mr Henry Brooke, reluctantly agreed and the transfer was effected by the Administration of Justice Act 1964, Section 12.

2 In London the juvenile courts were composed solely of stipendiaries from 1908, when they were established, until 1933 when the stipendiaries began sitting with lay justices, but by 1945 the stipendiaries had given up this work. A few began sitting again in the 1950s and in 1983 there were seven on the juvenile panel.

3 The Juvenile Courts (Constitution) Rules 1954 provided that a juvenile court should comprise both a man and a woman, but that if at any time no man or no woman was available the court might proceed with only men or only women present.

4 *Report of the Committee on Children and Young Persons*, Cmnd 1191 (HMSO, 1960).

5 *Children and Young Persons: Scotland*, Cmnd 2306 (HMSO, 1964). Implemented by the Social Work (Scotland) Act 1968.

6 See below, pp. 134, 137, 138.

7 Eleventh Report, Cmnd 6494 (HMSO, 1976).

8 *The Times*, 21st October 1976.

9 Percentage increase in offending over the period 1955–75 was:

aged 14–16:   311 per cent
aged 17–20:   415 per cent

Percentage increase over the period 1969–75 was:

aged 14–16:   44 per cent
aged 17–20:   32 per cent

CHAPTER 9   QUARTER SESSIONS AND THE CROWN COURT

1 Justices of the Peace (Size and Chairmanship of Bench) Rules 1950.
2 Administration of Justice (Miscellaneous Provisions) Act 1938.
3 Many judges, including members of the High Court and even Law Lords, were elected chairmen or deputy chairmen in their own counties. The first recorded instance of a Lord Chief Justice sitting with justices was in 1964 when Lord Parker sat as chairman of Staffordshire sessions. (In 1974 Lord Widgery was the first Lord Chief Justice to sit with justices in the Crown Court.) Lord Dilhorne sat with justices at Northamptonshire Quarter Sessions after being Lord Chancellor.
4 Brecon, Denbigh and Huntingdon.
5 Warrant under the Royal Sign Manual, dated 31st July 1969 and published in the *London Gazette* on 1st August. On the same date the title was also conferred on the additional judges of the Central Criminal Court.
6 In 1945 London sessions sat on 168 days, Lancashire 55 days and Middlesex 62 days.
7 A few boroughs which had no court of Quarter Sessions enjoyed the privilege of appointing a Recorder, who had no judicial functions. An example was Kingston-upon-Thames which traditionally appointed the Attorney-General of the day as its Recorder. His remuneration was two sugar loaves. The Courts Act 1971, which abolished the old-style Recorderships, preserved these ancient customs by enabling any borough to appoint an 'Honorary Recorder' (Section 54).
8 [1926] A.C. 1; 10 T.C. 118, H.L. (E).
9 *Final Report of the Royal Commission on Taxation of Profits and Income*, Cmnd 9473 (HMSO, 1955) paragraphs 238–40; and *Report of the Interdepartmental Committee on the Business of the Criminal Courts*, Cmnd 1289 (HMSO, 1961) paragraph 208.
10 Boroughs with populations under 20,000 which lost their Recorderships were:

Berwick-upon-Tweed	Maldon
Bideford	Oswestry
Bridgnorth	Richmond (Yorks)
Carmarthen	Rye
Chichester	Saffron Walden
Faversham	Sandwich
Hythe	South Molton
Ludlow	Stamford

Sudbury	Tiverton
Tenterden	Warwick
Tewkesbury	Wenlock
Thetford	

Those which were retained were:

Abingdon	Bury St Edmunds
Andover	Devizes
Banbury	Lichfield
Barnstaple	Newbury

11 *Report of the Committee on the Business of the Criminal Courts*, Cmnd 1289 (HMSO, 1961).

12 Cmnd 4153 (**HMSO**, 1969).

13 New-style Recorders differed from their predecessors in that they were not affiliated to any borough, or to any other local government area, but might be required to sit in any part of the Circuit. They were also required before appointment to undertake to sit on not less than twenty days a year.

14 The Report was published in September 1969, accepted immediately by the Government of the day as the basis for planning, and accepted again by the new Government in August 1970. Legislation was introduced in the autumn of that year and became the Courts Act 1971, which was brought into operation on 1st January 1972. At the same time administrative action had been under way since the autumn of 1969 to implement those recommendations which did not require legislation, and these multifarious activities led to the dramatic changes in the Lord Chancellor's Office referred to in Chapter 3.

15 Printed as Appendix II on pp. 35–7 of the Association's *Annual Report, 1969/70*.

16 The Courts Act 1971 was superseded by the Supreme Court Act 1981. Under the Crown Court Rules four justices are legally required in licensing appeals and two for appeals and committals from juvenile courts. Otherwise appeals may be heard with one justice present.

17 See pp. 84 and 101 above.

18 This was the almost unanimous view of chairmen and deputy chairmen of Quarter Sessions but opinion was divided among judges sitting in the Crown Court, some finding justices helpful in dealing with sentences while others regarded their presence simply as a nuisance. In the Crown Court there have always been wide differences in the extent to which the judge dominates decisions on sentence. Many justices complain that the judge tries, and usually succeeds in ignoring their views, while others seem satisfied that on the occasions when there is a difference, which are rare, the opinion of the majority of the justices prevails.

19 Secretary of Commissions' circular, November 1971.

20 Although appeals and committals for sentence represented around 40 per cent of the numerical case load they accounted for only some 10 per cent of the court's time, 90 per cent of which was occupied in trials.

CHAPTER 10 SENTENCING

1 A significant portion of the increased cost arose from the proportionately larger prison staff. Between 1950 and 1977 the number of prisoners doubled but the prison staff trebled to 25,000.

2 I could not understand why this point was not taken earlier. Anyone who spoke to prisoners must have been impressed by the number of recidivists who claimed that if their first sentence had ended before they became attuned to prison life the shock of their early experience would have deterred them from risking a repetition. It seemed that the reasons why the authorities would not accept this view were not only their obsession with the reformative value of custodial training, but also the resistance of the prison staff, upon whom frequent turnover of inmates imposes a far greater burden than a fairly static population.

3 An Advisory Council on the Treatment of Offenders was set up by the Home Secretary in 1944 as a standing body to consider matters he referred to it. The council was dissolved when a Royal Commission on Crime and Punishment was appointed in 1964, but the commission was disbanded in 1966 without having completed its task and the Home Secretary then appointed the Advisory Council on the Penal System.

4 The use of suspended sentences after they became available on 1st January 1968 is shown in the following tables:

I   Persons proceeded against at magistrates' courts

Year	Total proceeded against	Found guilty	Imprisonment	Suspended sentence
1967	1663877	1554068	25529	–
1977	2161947	1944857	18466	22975

II   Persons tried at the higher courts

Year	Total tried	Found guilty	Imprisonment	Suspended sentence
1967	30265	25585	10450	–
1977	68721	57225	19505	10864

III   Persons sentenced at higher courts after conviction at magistrates' courts

Year	Total sentenced	Imprisonment	Suspended sentence
1967	10640	3893	–
1977	15727	4121	1230

5 These fines had been imposed by the Crown Court as well as by magistrates. Those collected during the previous twelve months in the same area totalled £50,241,686.

6 *Report of the Committee on the Enforcement of Judgment Debts*, Cmnd 3909 (HMSO, 1969).

7 A national study of compensation orders in magistrates' courts, which was undertaken by Julie Vennard of the Home Office Research Unit in 1974, showed that in cases of damage to property 90 per cent of defendants were ordered to pay compensation compared with only 9 per cent of persons convicted of assault occasioning actual bodily harm or wounding. In 1976 the number of persons ordered to pay compensation in summary proceedings in cases of violence against the person was again only 9 per cent.

8 This followed a previous experiment by four South Yorkshire benches in 1976. A Home Office study revealed that the South Yorkshire guidelines had resulted in a pronounced increase in the number of awards made for wounding and assault: from 2 per cent in the last quarter of 1975, before guidelines were implemented, to 24 per cent during the last quarter of 1976, some months after they came into use, and 28 per cent in the period July–October 1977.

9 Careless driving, failing to stop after an accident or to report or give particulars of an accident and driving while uninsured.

10 *Sentencing the Motoring Offender* (London: Heinemann, 1972).

11 *Report of the Committee on the Business of Criminal Courts*, Cmnd 1289 (HMSO, 1961).

12 See R. M. Jackson, *The Machinery of Justice in England*, 7th ed. (Cambridge University Press, 1977) p. 389.

CHAPTER 11   CONDUCT AND REMOVAL

1 *The Door Wherein I went* (London: Collins, 1976) p. 261.

2 Temporary illness is accepted as a reasonable excuse; chronic ill-health entails transfer to the Supplemental List.

3 Occasionally a justice whose general behaviour is impeccable exhibits a peculiar quirk. It was reported to me that the chairman of a certain bench made a practice of entering court with a pipe in his mouth. He was surprised when I asked him to desist and remarked peevishly, 'But I never light it'.

4 The law relating to privilege has been modified since the Iwi case but it is assumed that all communications between the Lord Chancellor and his Advisory Committees are still protected. This was accepted by the parties in several cases in the 1960s. The last occasion on which a court was required to rule on the point was in Doubleday v. Graham in 1958. This action, between the clerk to the justices and the town clerk of Hull, was tried at Leeds Assizes and the judge, Mr Justice Paull, upheld the Lord Chancellor's claim for privilege.

5 Other instances have occurred since the tulip case, some of which were reported in *The Magistrate*. See, for example, 'The Cutlery Case' (vol. XXII, no. 6, pp. 84–6) and 'Hard Case' (vol. XXIII, no. 4, pp. 54–5).

CHAPTER 12   THE JUSTICES' CLERK

1 *Report of the Departmental Committee on Justices' Clerks*, Cmnd 6507 (HMSO, 1944).
2 The 1949 Act was replaced by the Justices of the Peace Act 1979 which required a clerk to be a barrister or solicitor of not less than five years standing.
3 1952.   2 Q.B. 719.
4 1953.   2 All E.R. 807.
5 1953.   2 All E.R. 1005.
6 1953.   2 All E.R. 1306.
7 R. v. Southampton JJ. ex parte Atherton, 137. J.P. 571.
8 Professor Glanville Williams, *The Proof of Guilt*, 3rd ed. (1963) pp. 359–63; See also the article by Keith Clarke in *Criminal Law Review*, (1964) p. 620.

CHAPTER 13   STIPENDIARY MAGISTRATES

1 *The Machinery of Justice in England*, 7th ed. (Cambridge University Press, 1977) p. 311.
2 There was a transitional figure, called a Court Justice, between the JPs and the Stipendiary Magistrates. The first of these to occupy an office in Bow Street was Sir Thomas de Veil who was succeeded by Henry Fielding who is usually recognised as the first Chief Metropolitan Magistrate. An Act of 1792 set up seven offices with 24 paid magistrates in addition to the office at Bow Street. This was extended by the Metropolitan Police Courts Act 1839 which confirmed the office of Chief Magistrate and consolidated the courts under the title of Police Courts which they retained until 1949.
3 Administration of Justice Act 1964, Section 10.
4 It was also understood that when a stipendiary retired he would not return to practice. This was in accordance with the accepted principle that once a person accepted any judicial office he could not relinquish it to take up some other employment, whether in legal practice or elsewhere. This principle was applied in 1952 when a High Court judge wished to resign in order to accept a non-judicial post. In the 1960s, however, the rule was broken in the case of the higher judiciary, and when in 1974 J. H. Robbins, who had been appointed a metropolitan magistrate a year earlier, wished to return to practice at the Bar no obstacle was placed in his way. His was the only case of this kind that had occurred by 1978.
5 A similar suggestion had been made in a Conservative Party pamphlet in 1945. The proposals were not pursued because they seemed unnecessary.

CHAPTER 14   ADMINISTRATION AND ORGANISATION

1 The current Act governing the administration and financing of magistrates courts is the Justices of the Peace Act 1979 which is closely based on the 1949 Act.
2 Since the Local Government Act 1972, which altered the local government structure, there has been a separate committee for each non-metropolitan

county, for each district in a metropolitan county, for each of the four Outer London areas and for the City of London, but for no other area. Inner London, with its separate system, has a 'Committee of Magistrates'.

3 *Report of the Committee on Local Authority and Allied Social Services*, Cmnd 3703 (HMSO, 1968).

4 In 1974 the Layfield Committee recommended that financial responsibility for magistrates' courts should be transferred from local authorities to central government (*Report of the Committee on Local Government Finance*, Cmnd 6453, HMSO, 1974, paragraphs 38–9).

5 Justices of the Peace (Size and Chairmanship of Bench) Rules 1950.

6 This Act and others were repealed and consolidated by the Metropolitan Police Courts Acts 1839 and 1840, which were the principal Acts governing the organisation of the metropolitan magistrates' courts until 1964.

7 Departmental Committee on Courts of Summary Jurisdiction in the Metropolitan Area.

8 *Report of the Interdepartmental Committee on Magistrates' Courts in London*, Cmnd 1606 (HMSO, 1962). The author was a member of this committee.

CHAPTER 15 SCOTLAND, NORTHERN IRELAND AND THE ISLE OF MAN

1 The first was P. J. Rose, formerly Assistant Under-Secretary of State for Scotland, who was appointed in 1950.

2 White Paper on *Justices of the Peace and Justices' Courts*, (Scottish Office, 1973) Cmnd 5254 (HMSO, 1973).

3 Against a background of lower traffic density (27 vehicles per mile of road in Northern Ireland as against 83 in Great Britain) the following facts emerged:

(1) between 1969 and 1977 total accidents did not fall significantly in Northern Ireland although they fell by 11 per cent in Great Britain;

(2) over the same period road accident deaths rose by 21 per cent but fell by 18 per cent in Great Britain;

(3) in 1976 Northern Ireland had 7·7 deaths per 10,000 vehicles, as against 3·7 for Great Britain, and 61 deaths per 1000 injury accidents, as against 25;

(4) driver responsibility for accidents in Northern Ireland rose from 46 per cent in 1968 to 58 per cent in 1976;

(5) accidents caused by drunken driving increased by 55 per cent between 1970 and 1977; and

(6) between 1969 and 1977, 2573 deaths in Northern Ireland were caused by road accidents as against 1760 arising out of terrorism and inter-communal violence.

CHAPTER 16 THE COMMONWEALTH

1 The population of the Commonwealth in 1977 was estimated to be just over a thousand million, of whom more than half were under the age of twenty-five.

2 In South and West Australia and Tasmania JPs may sit in court though some never do so. Those who do adjudicate may, in certain circumstances (usually

bail applications), sit alone, otherwise they sit in pairs with the senior presiding. In Victoria their duties are almost entirely confined to document witnessing but they sit occasionally with the consent of the prosecution and counsel for the defence. There are training courses for those who sit in court. In New South Wales, Queensland and the Northern Territory those justices who perform any duties at all have purely administrative functions.

3 A detailed account of the sentencing exercise, which was conducted by Professor A. N. Allott of the School of Oriental and African studies, University of London, is given in the *Report of the Third Commonwealth Magistrates' Conference*, published by the Commonwealth Magistrates' Association in 1973.

4 The Report of the seminar, entitled 'Pacific Courts and Justice', contains a detailed account of judicial administration in the Pacific. It was published jointly by the CMA and the University of the South Pacific.

CHAPTER 17   THE FUTURE

1 John Baldwin and David McConville, *Jury Trial* (Oxford: Clarendon Press, 1979).

2 1981 All England Reports, 974 at p. 983.

Table of Statutes Cited

Index